# THE PROPHETIC SUPERNATURAL EXPERIENCE

Second Edition

Matthew Robert Payne
&
Laurie N. Hicks

*The Prophetic Supernatural Experience*
Copyright © 2014 by Matthew Robert Payne and Laurie Hicks.
All rights reserved.

No part of this publication may be reproduced, stored in a retrieval system or transmitted in any way by any means, electronic, mechanical, photocopy, recording or otherwise without the prior permission of the author except as provided by USA copyright law.

The opinions expressed by the author are not necessarily those of Publisher.

All scripture quotations unless otherwise indicated, are taken from the New King James Version Copyright 1982 by Thomas Nelson, Inc. Used by permission. All rights reserved

Cover Design by Bjarki Clausen
www.merkiverk.is
Email: merkiverk@merkiverk.is

Published by Revival Waves of Glory Books & Publishing
PO Box 596 | Litchfield, IL 62056 USA
www.revivalwavesofgloryministries.com

Revival Waves of Glory Books & Publishing is committed to excellence in the publishing industry.

Published in the United States of America

eBook: 978-1-312-50547-6
Paperback: 978-1-312-50670-1
Hardcover: 978-1-312-50542-1


Matthew's email survivors.sanctuary@gmail.com
Matthew's website http://www.matthewrobertpayneministries.net
You can find Matthew on his Facebook group called "Open Heavens and Intimacy with Jesus."

Laurie's email: shoelacebooks@yahoo.com
Laurie's website http://lauriehicksministries.com

# Dedications

**Dedication of Matthew Robert Payne**

I would like to dedicate this book to Sarah Moulds, who knew me as a legalist and who loved and encouraged me into a believer in the grace message. I am forever grateful for her friendship and her ability to communicate things with me that impact me. She is a great friend.

**Dedication of Laurie N. Hicks**

I would like to dedicate this book to my husband Mark Hicks, and to our two youngest children, Kenan McIntosh Hicks and Zachary Spalding Hicks, who have supported me throughout the writing and editing of this book.

## About Matthew Robert Payne

**Matthew Robert Payne** was saved in a Baptist church when he was eight years of age. He enjoyed the teaching and a rich relationship with Jesus. At twenty-seven he was water baptized and was also miraculously baptized in the Holy Spirit. He is the author of two other books, *The Musings of a Mad Prophet* and *The Parables of Jesus Made Simple* which are both available on Amazon. As a legalist most of his life, he was happy to be freed by the message of grace and the finished works of the cross in his later years. He resides in Sydney Australia and is the father of one son called Brandyn.

## About Laurie N. Hicks

**Laurie N. Hicks** has been married to Mark Hicks for eighteen years. Together they have five children and three grandchildren.

Laurie has been a waitress, data entry clerk, secretary, automobile claims adjuster, nursing assistant, bookkeeper, first grade teacher, administrative assistant, auto insurance underwriter, personal care assistant, and a published editor and writer.

She has been and done an array of things, but the one thing that inspires her the most is learning about the Word of God and then encouraging others by sharing what she has learned.

Master Prophet Bishop E. Bernard Jordan is her spiritual father. He has provided her with major prophetic direction concerning her marriage, children, and life in general. She has studied Bishop Jordan's prophetic teachings extensively since 2007.

# Table of Contents

**PART 1 : All about Prophecy** ..................................................................1

1 Introduction to the Prophetic Supernatural Experience ..........2
2 Some Definitions used in the Prophetic ..................................6
3 Choosing the Prophetic Experience ......................................12
4 Can all Christians be Prophetic? ............................................15
5 If all Christians can be Prophetic, why not you? ...................23
6 The Gift of Prophecy - What is it? .........................................30
7 Using Prophecy ......................................................................35
8 The Gift of the Word of Knowledge - What is it? .................39
9 Using the Word of Knowledge - A risky Gift. ......................44
10 The Gift of the Word of Wisdom - What is it? ....................48
11 Using Words of Wisdom ......................................................53
12 Can Prophecies Contain the Flesh? .....................................58
13 Are there Reasons Prophecies Do Not Come True? ............61
14 Why Some Prophecies You Think Are False Are Not..........
15 The Gift of Encouragement ..................................................73

**PART 2 : The Prophetic Person** .............................................................78

16 My First Experiences with Prophecy ..................................80
17 My Call to be Prophetic. ......................................................86
18 Being a Strange Fish and a Fool for Christ .........................93
19 Learning Obedience. ............................................................98
20 Developing a Deep Relationship with Jesus .....................101
21 Getting to Know the Father ...............................................109
22 Getting to Know the Holy Spirit .......................................115
23 Getting to Know the Bible ................................................120
24 Being a Prophet in Training ..............................................127
25 Learning to Deal with Revelation .....................................133
26 Conquering Pride ...............................................................138
27 Dealing with Rejection ......................................................139
28 Knowing What You Are Called To Do .............................148
29 Dealing with the Book of Revelation ................................151

30 Walking with the Presence and the Peace of God ............................. 154
**PART 3 : Ministering in the Prophetic .................................................. 161**
31 Prophetic Etiquette in Churches ......................................................... 162
32 Ministering the Prophetic to Christians ............................................. 169
33 Prophetic Evangelism .......................................................................... 173
34 Ministering in the Prophetic by E-mail ............................................. 178
35 Ministering in the Prophetic over Facebook ..................................... 182
36 Doing what the Father does ............................................................... 186
37 Prophetic Prayer .................................................................................. 190
38 Getting into the Anointing to Prophesy ............................................. 193
39 Handling a False Word ....................................................................... 198
40 Handling Satan's Attacks .................................................................... 203
**PART 4 : The Supernatural Experience ............................................... 208**
41 Hearing Jesus Speak ........................................................................... 209
42 Hearing the Father Speak ................................................................... 212
43 Hearing the Holy Spirit Speak. .......................................................... 216
44 Making the Bible come Alive ............................................................ 220
45 My Visions of Heaven ........................................................................ 225
46 My Visions of Heaven, Part Two ...................................................... 170
47 Meeting Jesus on earth in Visions ..................................................... 173
48 Meeting Angels on earth in Visions .................................................. 176
49 Having Visions and Talking to Jesus in your Sleep ......................... 180
50 Dreams and Interpretations ................................................................ 183
**PART 5: The Well-Known Secrets to the Anointing ......................... 187**
51 Being a Friend of God ........................................................................ 188
52 Developing Intimacy with God .......................................................... 191
53 Humility ............................................................................................... 195
54 Obedience to God ............................................................................... 200
55 Impartations of Mantles and Gifts ..................................................... 204
**APPENDIX**
Answers to Questions ............................................................................... 206

# Acknowledgments

I would like first and foremost to thank God the Holy Spirit for conceiving of this book and for showing me what to produce. I want to thank God and Jesus for ministering to me and showing me the way out of legalism and what it is to be a true New Covenant Prophet.

I wish to thank Laurie Hicks my co-author for all of her help. Not only did she co-write the book, but she sustained me with positive thoughts and encouragement during the process of it being self published.

I wish to thank all the people who have invested in my life up till this point for all the love they have shown me as well as the patience.

I wish to thank my mother June Payne for doing a major edit of this work of mine.

I wish to thank my readers for purchasing this book. I hope to hear from you as you prophesy over me to test your gift of prophecy.

I wish to thank Bjarki Clausen for the cover design who can be contacted at www.merkiverk.is if you want some artwork done or by email at merkiverk@merkiverk.is

# PART 1: All about Prophecy

## 1. Introduction to the Prophetic Supernatural Experience

*"And it shall come to pass in the last days, says God, that I will pour out of My Spirit on all flesh; Your sons and your daughters shall prophesy, Your young men shall see visions, Your old men shall dream dreams." Acts 2:17*

Why would I record fifty-five individual videos and then proceed to write a book on them called: *The Prophetic Supernatural Experience*? This is a natural question, and I will give an equally natural answer – it is all about God! You see, a few months ago I had a prophetic dream and then, a little later, I had a similar dream. I knew then that God was saying something important to me!

I decided to contact a friend who is gifted in dream interpretation. She explained that the Lord wanted me to write a second book. Like the book on *The Parables of Jesus Made Simple*, this new book was also meant to involve my own life experiences. God knew that my lack of inspiration for this second book was caused by the fact that I did not know, at that stage, how to even begin to write it!

A few days later, I received another prophetic word saying:

> "Matthew, I feel that the Lord is saying to you that you will be blessed in many ways soon and only you, or maybe a few others, will understand. The Lord says that He is going to bless you by opening up the airwaves. I see you possibly as a guest on a show or travelling and telling people about the prophetic."

Interestingly, she mentions the prophetic.

> "I see a book, in which even the secular world will be reached for Jesus. There will be a specific group of people whom you can reach and it will be God who opens the doors for you. There are people everywhere searching for answers; they are going through trials in their lives, as never before. People today are in search of the supernatural! Have you ever heard "It's supernatural" with Sid Roth? I believe that you can be blessed by watching his show."

The words 'prophetic' and 'supernatural' were both involved in that prophecy! Therefore, I personally cannot claim either credit or criticism for devising the title of the book you are now reading. The dream interpreter was in fact responsible for its title. In hindsight, I am not really convinced that she fully understood that both these words were involved in the prophecy over my life.

It was basically these two dreams that inspired me to make the videos and to write the book. In addition, when I first entered the prophetic, I searched for information on the subject, but I could not find exactly what I needed to know. I am still unable to find what I was looking for in Christian bookshops! I sincerely hope that my work on this subject will be comprehensive enough for the beginner. Also, I hope that people who have moved in the prophetic for years may like some of the stories and illustrations that I have used.

This book has not been written for mature Christians, who have been moving in the prophetic for years. Instead, it has been written for beginners – people who desire to know about, or who want to move in the prophetic.

For years, I have approached strangers in the street and given them a message that God has placed on my heart to share with them. Often, I do not consider this as being supernatural, even when I am doing it ten or even twenty times a week. I am used to walking up to a complete stranger and telling them about a problem in their life, and a solution that God has for them. It has gone beyond being thoroughly surprising to me, because it is part of my natural experience.

I guess it is similar to Heidi Baker in Mozambique, when God uses her to open blind eyes and deaf ears. For Heidi Baker it is still a supernatural work of God, but *she knows that He will do it!* However, the typical Christian is not used to operating in the supernatural. Many believers fail to be aware of the voice of Jesus, or the voice of the Holy Spirit, or that of the Father.

My desire is that, through this book, I can help to open the supernatural for you. You see, I want you to understand that the prophetic experience is a *supernatural* experience. But, most

# 1. INTRODUCTION TO THE PROPHETIC SUPERNATURAL EXPERIENCE

importantly, it is also something I believe that every Christian can do! It is something that God can gift you in and something that you can follow and practice. I am not saying that I, myself, will give you every tool to operate in the prophetic experience, but in the last chapter of the video series there is an impartation – a prayer for you to receive the gift of prophecy, together with enough information in the book to carry on with the gift once you have received it.

Over the years, I estimate that I must have prayed for about three-hundred people to receive the gift of prophecy. I also estimate that ninety-five percent of them received the gift. Actually, I believe that every one of them, who was open to receive, did receive! However, some of them lacked the faith to believe that they had! Maybe it is just that they refused to get out of the boat and practice their gift. Some may have wrongly thought that they were not worthy of the gift of prophecy, so they did not take me up on my invitation for them to prophesy over me and practice their new gift.

I sincerely hope that you enjoy this book.

## **LAURIE'S REFLECTIONS**

1. Introduction to the Prophetic Supernatural Experience

This is the perfect book for beginners. I wish I had, had it when I was first stepping out. As I read Matthew Payne's work on the prophetic, I am certain he has written a great book on the subject and another book to add to his previous written ones.

The prophetic connection between Matthew and I was made in 2011. In reflection, it was God's impeccable timing! Matthew stated to me that he had gone through some theological changes since I first tried to contact his ministry in 2009, and the Lord knows that I certainly have gone through my own changes as well.

Even though Matthew says that this book is not for those who have been moving in the prophetic for years, but only for the beginner, it is still a good read for anyone in the prophetic, or who wishes to be in the prophetic. It is gentle and simplified in its teachings, and may answer some questions or shed some light on the topic for you. This book is going to birth many people into the prophetic and it is going to guide and train those that are already involved that may need more knowledge or mentoring.

So, sit back and enjoy this book, and get ready for the ride of your life as you begin, or continue on in your prophetic journey.

## 2. Some Definitions used in the Prophetic

*"And the Lord said unto Moses, 'See, I have made thee a god to Pharaoh: and Aaron, thy brother, shall be thy prophet.'" Exodus 7:1*

The word "prophetic" describes a person who moves in the gift of prophecy. It is a derivative word that comes from the word "prophecy" or "prophet."

There is a gift of prophecy mentioned in 1Corinthians 12:10. There is also a gift called the 'word of knowledge' in 1Corinthians 12:8 *"...to another the word of knowledge through the same Spirit."* A 'word of knowledge' is supernatural information that you would not ordinarily know about a particular person. Jesus used this gift in John 4, when He said to the woman at the well that she had spoken correctly in saying that she had no husband. He added however that, though she had five prior husbands, the man she was now living with was not her husband.

Again, in John 1:47 we read: Jesus saw Nathanael coming toward Him and said of him, *"Behold, an Israelite, indeed, in whom is no deceit!"* Both of these examples were words of knowledge spoken by Jesus.

The 'word of wisdom' is different; it is a directional Word of God. (1Corinthians 12:8 *"for to one is given the word of wisdom through the Spirit..."*) Often, in the Old Testament, a King would seek a prophet and ask whether the Lord was on the side of his army in a particular battle, or should he make peace? God's prophet might say: "The Lord is with you and this is His battle plan." The ensuing battle plan would be God's directional words to the King. God still gives directions to His prophetic people and they are called words of wisdom.

Many Christians, who are not charismatic, believe that today's prophecies are restricted to the set-down prophecies contained in the Bible. They also insist that the preaching of the Word of God is prophesying, or acting in a gift of prophecy. They believe that a word of knowledge is knowledge of the Bible, meaning studied and imparted knowledge of the Bible, and that a good preacher moves in a wonderful "gift of knowledge."

Non-charismatic Christians also believe that the "gift of wisdom" refers to God's wisdom. However, in the Bible, God's wisdom and a "word of wisdom" are not the same! One is the supernatural wisdom of God to make decisions and do things correctly, while the other is the direction of God on how to move in something coming through a prophet or a person with the gift of prophecy, or a direction received personally from the Holy Spirit directly to a believer.

The term 'prophetic,' therefore, refers to believers who supernaturally move in the gift of prophecy with the ability to also operate in the gift of wisdom and the gift of knowledge, as the Lord directs. These three gifts are to have a positive impact on both the church and others and they will be discussed in detail in later chapters.

Whilst a prophetic person is someone who moves in prophecy, there is also the term "prophet" in the Bible. It is important for you to know that someone who has the gift of prophecy, or can move in the three gifts of prophecy that I mentioned above, is not necessarily a prophet! However, everyone, who has received the Holy Spirit in his or her life, ought to be able to move in the "gift of prophecy" – for it is merely just passing on a message from God to another person.

Jesus says: *"My sheep hear My voice, and I know them, and they follow Me," John 10:27.* If you can hear from God in your born-again spirit, then you can also hear a message for someone else. Just like the Post Office employs staff to deliver mail to individual suburban homes, God wants His people to personally deliver His spoken word!

As I have said, a prophetic person is not necessarily a prophet. Whilst a prophet is gifted in the prophetic gifts, they are also set apart by God to perform other functions in the body of Christ. A prophet is a spokesperson for God, who has been appointed by Him with a "ministerial gift" in order to equip and to edify the church, together with apostles, evangelists, pastors, and teachers (Ephesians 4:11-12.) It is the responsibility of a prophet to bring messages from

God to people, whether through preaching, through prophetic declaration, through music, or any other form. A prophet has to be chosen – appointed and trained by God, often through a mentor – to do this work.

There is a negative term that regularly rears its ugly head in the world. This is the term, "false prophet." If you have walked in the office of prophet, or you are a training prophet and have made a wrong prophecy, or you have said something in a teaching with which people do not agree, often, people level insults at you and claim that you are a false prophet.

Actually, the Bible defines a "false prophet" as someone who leads people to serve other gods, rather than the one true God! He often does this by exalting himself and saying that he has a personal revelation from God. In reality, the revelation is not in line with the rest of Scripture, so it must be immediately classed as heresy. No true prophet of God would attempt to teach anything that was contrary to the principles laid down in the Bible. Jesus warned us of this danger and taught us how to discern such a person. *"Beware of false prophets, who come to you in sheep's clothing, but, inwardly, they are ravenous wolves. You will know them by their fruits," Matthew 7:15-16a.*

When people insult a true prophet of God by wrongly calling them a 'false' prophet, it can damage the reputation of the prophet and negatively impact their future ministry. A true prophet's heart motivation is to always bring glory to God.

Definitely, it is plausible that a contemporary unbeliever would be wary of a prophet of God! But, to my mind, it is not plausible for believers to accuse others of being *false* prophets, yet these same people deny that the New Testament Biblical "office" of "prophet" is in operation today! They obviously believe in Satan's prophets, but not God's prophets!

I see that particular mindset as extremely unbalanced and very sad! These same people would believe in evangelists, pastors and teachers, yet they quite often deny the existence of both apostles and prophets in the modern church. They say they were (one-off) works of God in the early church and are not relevant today, just like they say that speaking in an unknown language is not relevant today. There were many people saved and physically healed in the early church. Is healing, or the salvation of souls, relevant today?

Even though the spiritual dark side has existed before the creation of man, you may have noticed that it is becoming more and more prevalent in society to approach clairvoyants, psychics or, mediums, in order to receive information about one's life and future. In women's magazines particularly, the counterfeit occult activities confront the reader every week. Yet, God who is the source of all wisdom and knowledge is ignored, along with His representatives who operate under His prophetic anointing.

God's prophet, in Hosea 4:6, warns about the perils of lack of knowledge and this is certainly true in the realm of the prophetic. Satan delights to oppose God in every way that he can in order to deceive and to destroy. He will have his agents duplicate the supernatural by offering a counterfeit message from the dark side. Even uninformed believers may be tempted into seeking help from the wrong source, especially astrology, for their spiritual information.

When Jesus was on earth, demonic activity was very prevalent and, as we approach the second return of Jesus, occult practices will also steadily increase. The printed media, television, the Internet, and Hollywood are certainly not shy about highlighting the dark side! Occult themes are escalating in today's society. Satan preys on the natural curiosity of naïve seekers, who want answers for life's problems, and on the general public's interest in weird or scary supernatural activities. People from all walks of life dabble in the occult, and many label it as just having 'fun.' What they do not realize is that Satan has a totally different agenda for them *and it is not in the slightest bit funny*!

Christian, be warned! God has specifically listed various occult activities, in which His children are forbidden to engage – see Deuteronomy 18:10-14. Always bear in mind that God *always wants the best for us,* and the enemy always seeks for ways *to ultimately*

## 2. SOME DEFINITIONS USED IN THE PROPHETIC

*destroy us!* He offers a sweetener with one hand and robs us of the knowledge and peace of the one true God!

Now that we have briefly covered the terms *prophetic, prophecy, word of knowledge, word of wisdom, prophet,* and *false prophet*, we move along to other words that are used in the spirit realm. In a way, you can say that you are in a trance, or in a vision, or in a spiritual experience of God, and, in Christian terminology, it is referred to as the "anointing" of God. This term is particularly acceptable in Pentecostal circles.

The simplest definition that I have heard is that the anointing of God is the power to do the task that God has given you. If you are called to speak to a handful of people in a youth group, a Bible study, or home church for the purpose of weekly teaching the Word of God, you will receive a small anointing. In general, the larger the audience or task, the larger the anointing you will be given. Whenever the power of God is released in an anointing it is not meant to be wasted, because it is released according to the need. That definition is one way of understanding the anointing.

Now, as you go through the higher levels of authority with more responsibility, God will also fully meet that need. The Apostle Paul said that God supplies all our needs in Christ Jesus, and that would definitely include His anointing. It is important to understand that God's anointing is also needed *before* the actual time of ministry begins.

When you are prophesying to others, you need spiritual preparation so the presence of God or the anointing of God will come and rest on your life. Often, God just brings His supernatural anointing upon a person, but prayer is a very effective way to receive His prophetic anointing. Also, you can prepare through praise and worship or reading the Word of God. Train yourself to become sensitive to the fact that you need the preparation that brings the power of God and the presence of God over your life, so that you are spiritually aware of a definite change in the atmosphere in and around you.

## LAURIE'S REFLECTIONS
2. Some Definitions Used in the Prophetic

In my search I found all sorts of information that led me in various directions -- not all good, and because of my personality, I just had to experience them all (big sigh). Therefore, I experienced the unpleasantness in thinking that God speaks outside of "His Word." Pride was the culprit. I was one giant human PRIDEFUL self that needed to be brought down a notch or two and God knew just how to do it! Yes, God will "do a number on you" if you want to go down that road. (Here is a little hint: Let Pride fall, so you don't have to.)

I eventually find my way back to the Word of the Lord. The search was not necessarily a bad thing, and I had received a prophecy saying that I would experience this type of searching for God, and even be like Elijah in the cave, thinking as he did that he heard God first in the wind, then in the earthquake, and then in a fire, until finally understanding that God's voice is in the still small voice within. (1 Kings 19:9-13) Jesus confirmed this: *"For indeed, the Kingdom of God is within you," Luke 17:21b*. It has been a tough lesson and a tough road to travel, but it was of my own choosing. We all have the choice of deciding which roads we will travel. I count it all blessed.

You do not have to go anywhere to find God for He is within you. He is not lost. I am not saying that God cannot use other means in which to speak to you besides the still small voice, because He does. The problem arises when you think you can get the answer without consulting God – that's what the psychic network does.

Before I had received any training in the prophetic, God allowed me to experience prophetic words spoken over my life while I watched them come to pass. He was setting me up to be ready to receive the call when I heard it.

Young Samuel thought he heard his master Eli calling him three different times. Finally, Eli told him to respond out loud if he heard the call again by saying: "Speak, Lord, your servant hears." In the same way, God will use your mentor or earthly master to point you to your calling from God, your Heavenly Master. Once you have

## 2. SOME DEFINITIONS USED IN THE PROPHETIC

experienced the prophetic in your own life, it is much easier to "trust and obey." As a result, I have received many words of knowledge and words of wisdom, both from prophets and those who are able to move in the gift of prophecy.

As you study the Word of God and are involved in a prophetic ministry you will have more of an understanding concerning the different terms used in this area.

The distinctive activity of the prophet is that he or she expresses the Word of the Lord, as given to him or her from the Mind of God. It is the mission of the prophet to communicate the Divine Word.

The latter part of the word "prophecy" is derived from a Greek verb meaning "to speak," and the prefix "pro" usually means "before" or "beforehand," as in "procession" and "progress." A prophet, therefore, refers to the future or a before-teller. However, this is just one definition. The prefix "pro" in "prophet" also means "instead of," in the same way the word "pronoun" means a word that is used instead of a noun. A prophet is a man who speaks God's word instead of God Himself speaking it. In the Scriptural sense of the term, a prophet does not mean a *foreteller of future events,* but a *revealer of God's will to man*; though the latter sense may and sometimes does include the former.

This is the Hebrews' idea of a prophet, as seen in Exodus 7:1, where God says to Moses that he is to be as god to Pharaoh, and Aaron his brother is to be his prophet – his spokesman. It is a clear example for us to follow.

Christ works through His servants, so the office of His ministry of the prophetic office is continued through the spoken prophetic word of the prophet or prophetess.

### Questions:
1. What do we learn from Exodus 7:1 as to the meaning of the word "prophet"?
2. Define the difference between wisdom and words of wisdom.

*Answers are in the back of the book.*

## 3. Choosing the Prophetic Experience.

*"Many are called, but few are chosen." Matthew 22:14*

As the chapter title suggests, I believe that we have the ability to *choose* whether or not to walk in the prophetic. In fact, I sincerely believe that all Christians can be prophetic. (We deal with that further in chapter 4.) But now let me go more into *choosing* the prophetic experience. First, however, if you seriously desire to be able to walk up to a total stranger in order to pass on to them an encouraging word or a personal message from God to edify them, then you had better prepare yourself for spiritual opposition!

Satan opposes and intensely dislikes those who want to strengthen fellow Christians or to encourage saving "belief" in Jesus Christ. Satan loves gossip, slander, envy, and anger. In fact, he loves to manipulate every negative emotion and every lust of the flesh. His purpose is to pull people down, so that they feel weak and defeated. When a person feels that they can no longer cope with life, and are contemplating suicide, then Satan resists a rescue effort!

A person who moves in the prophetic actually ministers "spiritual medicine" to those who need it! God has specific and important messages He wants people to know. Being willing to be used as His vessel, to come alongside and to share His love and His special words with others is a precious ability that is definitely opposed to the devil's purposes, and something *he will certainly come against.*

The prophetic anointing may seem glamorous to you, or maybe it is something that you genuinely want to pursue, but spiritual opposition is a very real challenge! Often, on my prophetic website, a believer will come to join my team and start to minister in the prophetic, when suddenly all hell breaks loose in their life. Spiritual warfare confronts them: everything around them is opposition because they have now come under heavy assault from God's enemy.

Many quit the team because of the negative drama that has arisen in their life. When I started my prophetic website, I wondered why there was so much opposition. What was so wrong with me speaking

## 3. CHOOSING THE PROPHETIC EXPERIENCE

encouraging words to others? Why would Satan hate me so much? Why would he hate prophecy so much? Clearly, this is because Satan is a liar! He loves to discourage people!

Satan is the enemy of the Christian faith particularly. This is because he is the enemy of Almighty God, as portrayed in the Bible! Stepping out in the prophetic requires much faith and boldness, so this, of course, becomes very threatening to the kingdom of darkness: Satan and his demons.

When you are an ordinary believer, just going to church on Sunday and simply minding your own business, the devil feels quite comfortable – you represent no serious threat to his kingdom! Many Christians are happy to attend church each week and perhaps a mid-week Bible study and that may be their whole Christian life. These people may never lead an unbeliever to Christ. They may never really impact their area of influence. On the other hand, when you raise your hand saying: "I really want the prophetic gift" and you start to move in God's prophetic blessing by encouraging and helping people into breakthrough, suddenly you place yourself on the enemy's radar!

I must warn you not to enter the prophetic unless you are ready for a battle – a genuine gloves-off struggle with no holds barred. Spiritual warfare will come! Therefore, it is vital to have a close relationship with Jesus Christ because the enemy is real; this war is real! Satan and his demons have plans and methods to come against anyone who is prepared to take a bold stand for God, but be confident: we have the authority of God's Word that we are on the winning side – the Holy Spirit in us is greater than the devil, who is actually the spirit of the world. (1 John 4:4)

You can be mightily encouraged that Jesus has his own angels, pastors, support people, books, and helpful materials to assist you in your prophetic blessing. Most of all, we have all the incredible promises in the Word of God – these are the most powerful weapons to use. Satan may be an enemy, but God is the conqueror! In Christ, we are victorious! *"Yet, in all these things, we are more than conquerors through Him who loved us,"* Romans 8:37. God understands prophetic people: He is on our side! The prophetic is an exciting and rewarding arena to enter.

Personally speaking, the upside of the prophetic makes it all worthwhile. To have people write back to me or grab me with tears in their eyes, saying, "You don't know how much that means to me," is such a blessing! They say there is much enjoyment in the giving of gifts and it is true. It is more blessed to give than to receive. I have discovered that this is even more so when operating in the prophetic.

Moving in the prophetic is wonderful and exciting – it can even be an "addictive" way of life! ("Addictive" in a good sense of course.) I urge you to look at the Impartation Prayer in Chapter 55 and to move into the prophetic. I encourage you to go through each of these chapters carefully and to understand the operation of the gifts that you are going to move into when living the prophetic supernatural life.

## **LAURIE'S REFLECTIONS**

3. Choosing the Prophetic Experience

*"Many are called but few are chosen," Matthew 22:14.* All Christians are called -- and there are many, but few choose to answer the call. I heard the saying: "Destiny is not left up to chance, but is a matter of choice" from Bishop E. Bernard Jordan; your destiny is up to you. Just as you choose what field of education you will study and eventually work in, you must also choose to accept or not accept the prophetic call on your life.

There are many choices we all make in a lifetime – yes, indeed, the choice is always ours to make. When I was called to be a prophetess, I still had to make the choice to follow the life and discipline of the prophetic. God is calling people with a specific character – a character of integrity to carry His Word forth, to be spokespeople representing Him.

However, God may use whomever at His disposal to deliver a Word to someone. It could be the town drunk or that homeless person off the street that is actually a prodigal child of God who has a Word for

## 3. CHOOSING THE PROPHETIC EXPERIENCE

you as you walk by. Or maybe the drunk is the only person available at that specific time. God is God. He will use whomever He wills.

However, at this time, I am speaking more specifically of those who chose the prophetic *as their lifestyle.*

At the point when you choose this particular lifestyle, be prepared for every kind of adversity – the enemy knows which buttons to push to get you doubting your decision to be dedicated to the prophetic ministry. (Believe me, it takes dedication!) Do not doubt this God-given ability! It is the trick of the enemy to place doubt in your mind. He hates prophecy given in Jesus Christ's Name and, if he can distract you from the call on your life to prophesy in Christ's Name, he certainly will!

Bishop Jordan taught me that "the enemy" is the "inner-me," and that your mind will play tricks on you. One famous trick is to make you think that you cannot prophesy, but, because Satan hates you sharing the Word, the "inner-me" will cause you to start doubting yourself and the gift that God has given you. The "inner-me" may also tell you that you do not have that much time to invest in the prophetic ministry. That is the devil playing mind games with you, and he will, if allowed, cause real chaos for you.

Other types of challenges are more physical and can also cause personal chaos. Soon after my decision, my husband's work started decreasing, my phone was disconnected, and we had to move. These are just a few of the challenges that Matthew speaks of in this chapter. You must overcome the negative thoughts that run amuck when things start to happen – it is just the enemy trying to distract you, but, if you can remain focused on what God has called you to do, the chaos will pass and all will be well.

There is nothing like the prophetic. To encourage others with the Word of God is an awesome experience like no other I have ever had.

*Isaiah 30:20, "And the Lord gives you the bread of adversity, and the water of affliction, yet shall not thy teachers be removed into a corner any more, but thine eyes shall see thy teachers.*

When you know God you will know that the adversary is your teacher. I've always been taught to have respect for the teacher and the lessons.

### Questions:
1. Why does Satan hate the prophetic?
2. Will you choose to answer the call that God has placed on your life?

*Answers are in the back of the book.*

## 4. Can All Christians Be Prophetic?

*"For you can all prophesy one by one..." 1 Corinthians 14:31a*

I appeal to both conservative and Pentecostal Christians – please bear with me!

I believe that the "Baptism" of the Holy Spirit is a further impartation of the Spirit beyond being born again. Many of those who readily agree with this also believe that you cannot move in any of the nine gifts of the Holy Spirit before this spiritual baptism takes place. I have a personal problem with this belief because it has not been my personal testimony. The gift of prophecy, words of knowledge, and words of wisdom are three of the nine gifts and I moved in these gifts long before I received the baptism of the Holy Spirit!

For years, I had been moving in all the associated gifts of prophecy! Jesus was clearly giving me prophetic words for specific people before I even knew about the prophetic gifts and the baptism of the Holy Spirit. When I stepped out in obedience to the Lord's prompting, I was genuinely encouraged by the positive reaction of my hearers. Before I even walked into a Pentecostal church, I was a Baptist boy and had never heard teaching on the Baptism of the Holy Spirit, yet, I was moving in the prophetic!

As an example, I was on a train once in Sydney, and Jesus gave me a twenty minute message for a young Christian Anglican girl sitting next to me. I told her, "If Jesus could talk to you now, would you be willing to listen to what He has to say even if it were a somewhat lengthy message?" She replied in the affirmative.

I said, "Well, the next time I say my name 'Matthew' it will actually be the words of Jesus speaking to you." Then I said, "Matthew is very nervous about this but I want to say these things to you today," and Jesus launched into His message to her. At the end of that train trip, I asked her if she would like to move in the gift of prophecy just as I did. She said that she did, and I said, "Raise your hand and pray this prayer with me." I lead her in a prayer. Then I tested whether the gift had come upon her by asking her to prophesy over me.

It says in the Word that the Spirit of Jesus is the Spirit of Prophecy: *"For the testimony of Jesus is the spirit of prophecy," Revelations 19:10b.* I believe that this means that if you have the Spirit of Jesus, then you have the spirit of prophecy. If you can hear from the Holy Spirit – if you can hear from God – you can prophesy to another person.

People assume that prophecy is something mystical and magical, but it is a supernatural ability from God which makes you able to give a total stranger a direct message from Him. Satan will always counterfeit the good things of God. He gives gifts of destruction! A clairvoyant will give you supernatural knowledge but it is from the wrong source. Satan wants to rob you most of all, **of your need for God!** Whereas God equips His people to edify and strengthen the faith of others in Him and to direct them in the best way they should go.

The brother of our Lord said that all good gifts come from God and are perfect! *"Every good gift and every perfect gift is from above, and comes down from the Father of lights, with whom there is no variation or shadow of turning," James 1:17.*

Prophecies are something that every Christian can do because, if they are in tune with God's inner voice, they can pass on His personal message to another Christian or even to an unbeliever. It is just that the world likes to complicate things. Though there is much to learn in the prophetic, you learn easier by practicing it with faith and letting God guide you step by step. Like everything else, the more you practice, the easier it becomes and the more proficient you become.

I am not alone in my assertion that all believers should move in the gift of prophecy. The prophet Moses said in Numbers 11:29 that he wished that all men were prophets. The apostle Paul said: *"But covet earnestly the best gifts,"* 1 Corinthians 12:31. The NKJ translation is: "earnestly desire" the best gifts. Later, in Chapter 14:1-5, Paul clearly identified the best gift as being the gift of prophecy! However, in between these statements, he devoted a whole chapter on the importance of "love" because no gift is profitable without love.

Exodus Chapter 20 lists the Ten Commandments that Moses received from God. The last of these commandments forbids us to covet anything that belongs to someone else. To covet in such a way is wrong because it comes from a wrong spirit of selfish gain, but Paul wants us to covet the wonderful things of God with a pure spirit in order to edify others, and not to take from them.

Prophecy flows out of compassion motivated by love. To operate in the word of knowledge, in order to give supernatural information to a stranger, you need genuine love for that person! This is because, if you blow it and say something untrue of their life, then they will class you as a fool and no one wants that type of reputation! Therefore, whenever you value yourself more than others, prophecy will probably not be your desire.

Faith in God's goodness and boldness is essential! You need to have God's kind of love for people. My pastor once said to me that the best gift is "love" and that prophecy actually flows out of love. Essentially, love is the character of God and, as such, it is not a "gift," but the evidence of His presence in a person. If you do not have enough love, you cannot prophesy. Paul acknowledged: *"And though I have the gift of prophecy, and understand all mysteries and all knowledge, and though I have all faith, so that I could remove mountains, but have not love, I am nothing,"* 1Corinthians 13:2.

Here, Paul is insinuating that it IS possible to move in the gift without love, but prophecy given in that way is worthless. So, can all Christians be prophetic? Yes, they can! It is a choice – your choice.

## **LAURIE'S REFLECTIONS**
4. Can All Christians Be Prophetic?

We have access to God's mind, therefore we can be God's messengers and, yes, we can prophesy – you can prophesy! Not all Christians are called to the "office" of a prophet, **but all can prophesy**; everybody can be prophetic at times.

- *"And he gave some apostles; and some prophets..." Ephesians 4:11*

- *"God has set some in the church, first apostles, secondarily prophets..."1 Corinthians 12:28*
- *"Pursue love, and desire spiritual gifts, but, especially, that you may prophesy." 1 Corinthians 14:1*
- *"..., desire earnestly to prophesy..." 1 Corinthians 14:39*

If you *"desire earnestly to prophesy,"* then you must *"pursue love."* Pursuing love brings the gift of prophecy. It is a question of, "How *much* do you love? Do you love enough to prophesy?" How do you "pursue love"? Since God is Love, all you must do is pursue God and desire earnestly to comfort, encourage, and lift others up; this is prophecy at its best.

You have to love with the "love of the Lord." This love is an unexplainable love. You love without knowing the person; you love even if they may seem unlovable; you love God in that person and in their situation.

*"Do not despise prophecies" 1 Thessalonians 5:20* – Yet, the way some churches sparingly dole them out, you would think the Bible says, "Despise prophecies." But the Bible does not say that. Instead, it encourages prophecy by saying in 1 Corinthians 14:31, *"For you may all prophesy one by one, that all may learn, and all may be comforted."* I am not saying that church should be all prophecy, but prophecy does belong in the church as much as praise and worship, the message, tithes and offerings and fellowship. Each part of a church service is as important as the other.

I remember a time when a certain friend was explaining how someone they knew was talking about being a world traveler. She put them in their place, so to speak. I told her that the Word says "do not despise prophecies." "They were prophesying to themselves. It was a good thing. You should let them prophesy."

Often, you may be prophesying even when you do not realize it, or plan on it. You will be having a regular conversation with someone, but you will declare and decree that something will be – and it will be, because you are operating in the prophetic at that time. This happens to me a lot of the times.

## 4. CAN ALL CHRISTIANS BE PROPHETIC?

Simply by the virtue of our union with Christ, all Christians are made, in a sense, prophets.

*"Would God that all the Lord's people were prophets, and that the Lord would put His Spirit upon them!" Numbers 11:29.*

*"I will pour out My spirit upon all flesh; and your sons and your daughters shall prophesy, your old men shall dream dreams, your young men shall see visions. And also upon My menservants and upon the handmaids in those days will I pour out My spirit," Joel 2:28-29.*

You are going to be used mightily by God if you will absorb the Bible. This does not just apply to a special class of Christians; it is for all Christians.

All true prophecy (from the One True God) is a re-publication of Christ's message – the expounding of truth already revealed in Scripture. Do not think of prophecy as "foretelling" but as "forth telling." Do you see the difference? You are speaking forth the Word of God, as revealed in the Scriptures and as God reveals it to you.

A prophet must know the Scriptures.

### Questions:
1. Can all Christians be prophetic?
2. Do you need to be baptized in the Holy Spirit to prophesy?

*Answers are in the back of the book.*

## 5. If All Christians Can Be Prophetic, Why Not You?

*"A man's gift maketh room for him, and bringeth him before great men." Proverbs 18:16*

*Why not you?* We have established in chapters 3 and 4 that the gift of prophecy is open to all Christians. It is the Holy Spirit within you that gives you this ability and, therefore, there is no reason why you cannot do this. You can move in the gifts of prophecy, including the word of knowledge, and the word of wisdom. In chapter 3, I warned that spiritual opposition becomes part of the prophetic realm or the prophetic office. Therefore, consider spiritual opposition as a compliment, because, if there is absolutely no opposition, perhaps you are no threat to the dark side!

Of course, if you enter the prophetic, and the opposition becomes too much, you can always just quit! But I warn you, quitting is not much fun, because the operation of prophecy is an enjoyable and exciting life to live. To me, it is much the same as having the ability to be a doctor without going to medical school for six years. It is being able to just go and give people spiritual medicine for their wounds or for their burdens.

I received a prophecy once that has always stayed in my mind. I was told: "There are people everywhere searching for answers. There are people going through trials in their lives as never before. People are in search of the supernatural as never before!" (This earlier prophecy was again confirmed after I had been to a dream interpreter – see Chapter 1.)

Today, this prophecy is so true! I run a prophetic website and we receive five to ten requests per day for personal prophecies. These people want answers! They are troubled people, just asking questions of God. Reader, you could answer those questions if you moved in the prophetic. God can supernaturally impart His words to you. Would you not like to be part of the body of Christ who will let God use your mouth to speak His positive proclamations to others? Even in church, it is wonderful to walk up to a brother or sister, with your pastor's permission, and give them a personal message from God.

## 5. IF ALL CHRISTIANS CAN BE PROPHETIC, WHY NOT YOU?

Would you not like to be the bearer of good news? *And how shall they preach unless they are sent? As it is written: "HOW BEAUTIFUL ARE THE FEET OF THOSE WHO PREACH THE GOSPEL OF PEACE, WHO BRING GLAD TIDINGS OF GOOD THINGS!" Romans 10:15.*

Bringing good news of the kingdom of God is exciting! God wants you to be part of His Great Commission and to declare His love to the world. Being bold for Jesus Christ is all part of it! You could be a baby version of Jesus walking around your community, being an encouragement and edification to the body of Christ, as well as to non-believers! God has a message of hope for all people from every race and lifestyle. You could be God's delivery person, giving a personal message to those who need it.

As explained in Chapter 1, this book and the video series are the direct result of a prophetic dream I had. This dream was interpreted by a prophet, who gave me a prophecy saying I should write such a book. I sat and wrote the chapter titles of all fifty-five chapters by the inspiration of the Holy Spirit. There is absolutely no way for me to have come up with these chapter topics. This same Holy Spirit can cause you to be His mouthpiece to others. Prophecy is a great gift: it is not something that should be looked upon as "difficult" to do.

*Why not you?* Is it because you feel unworthy? Maybe you doubt that God would move in your life in a supernatural way – He has already done that, you know! How do you think you were born again? Was that not a supernatural work of God, or did you just do it yourself? Every Christian can testify that they are not the same person that they used to be. God did a miracle in your life! Step out in faith and trust God's goodness! He will not disappoint you. I know that ninety-five percent of people have spoken correctly over my personal life *even with their very first prophecy*! You can do that, too.

Go to chapter 55 and read the Impartation Prayer or watch the video of chapter 55, and pray to receive this gift. Then, you can prophesy over me, and I will *confirm* that you have the gift. I know that those who genuinely seek this gift receive it! The gift of prophecy is a beautiful, wonderful and exciting gift and is something that should be both desired and shared.

For instance, imagine that you were going through India and, in every village you visited, you found that people were dying of cancer. Then, you came to a solitary village where cancer was unheard of. Imagine that you discovered the only difference in this village was that they grew a specific plant, from which they made tea, and everyone drinks two cups of tea every day – one in the morning and one at night. You would want to take the plant back to the West where you would discover that there are qualities in that tea that stifle cancerous cell growth. Would you not share that plant with the world?

You would not need to make money or to become a millionaire from it, but would you not share the wonderful secret of that plant with the world? Prophecy is like that! You have an answer for people. You have spiritual medicine for them. Come on! Be part of the prophetic Bride of Christ! Be part of the prophetic army that is being raised in these last days! I welcome you! I encourage you. Receive the gift and walk in the gift.

## **LAURIE'S REFLECTIONS**

5. If All Christians Can Be Prophetic, Why Not You?

Believe, receive, and walk in the gift, it is truly that simple. Many are called into the prophetic, some come on in, but from those that come, few choose to stay. The few that do are the chosen few. Some are like Lot's wife, looking back and therefore, having to stay right where they are, as a pillar to the community in which they are trying to leave. Lot's wife was not able to go into her future because of clinging to her past. Forge ahead to what is in front of you, not looking back.

Spiritual opposition is a part of why few choose to stay, but the main reason why some people do not stay in the prophetic is because it requires *discipline!* It requires the discipline to stay underneath your covering; it requires being submissive to your pastor and mentor.

Sometimes, a person might view that as opposition, but it's not; it is just God grooming you for the prophetic.

The opposition comes from both inside and outside the ministry to distract you from preparing yourself for the commitment of prophetic ministry. Quitting the prophetic ministry is not an option for me because the opposition becomes even stronger when I think about quitting. If I think it requires too much of a commitment, the Lord is quick to show me what it will be like if I do not stay (and bloom) where He has planted me.

I know when the opposition is here; it comes as a distraction. I try not to be bothered and stay focused on what God has called me to do, which is to PROPHESY and teach the Word of the Lord.

Right at this very moment, He has placed me in a small town where you would think there is no room – not space, for there is plenty of space out here in the hills, valleys and long stretches of Tennessee – but no *place* for my gift, oh, but yes! God makes room for your gift wherever He places you.

I was once a part of a phone conferencing ministry, but, soon after I began, my phone was disconnected! When I was able, I reconnected my phone line. It was good for a while, and then, one day, it stopped connecting to conference calls because conference calling was no longer a part of my phone plan. That is opposition. It was God's way of telling me that I needed to understand that my blessings are for the ministry. I did not fully appreciate that before, but God will make sure I always do. Without asking, a dear friend gave me a phone and paid the bill for a whole year, just so I could get on the calls – still, I thought there were too many distractions. The phone was such a blessing; she will never know. However, that has ended; God will have me dependent on Him, and no other. *"I am the Lord your God, and none else,"* Joel 2:27.

> *"And though the Lord gives you the bread of adversity, and the water of affliction, yet shall not thy teachers be removed into a corner anymore, <u>but your eyes shall see your teachers,</u>"* Isaiah 30:20.

While we are here on this earth, we are to learn from our teachers, so do not allow opposition to stop you. Opposition is a tool God uses to bring you to the level where you need to be, in order for you to accomplish the things that He is calling you to do. Opposition is your teacher!

One day, a friend of mine was visiting, and, unbeknown to me, this friend was feeling very discouraged. The Lord instructed me to tell her to sow a seed towards the prophetic call on her life and to join the prophetic team at Zoe Ministries by enrolling in their School of the Prophets with Master Prophet E. Bernard Jordan. I learned later that she had planned on leaving my house and ending her life that very night, but, because she received that Word and was obedient to it, she is alive and well today, and is a trained prophetess, who prophesies and flows in the gift of prophecy.

Another day, this same friend and I were on the phone together and she told me she heard a newborn baby in my house. I responded with, "No, there are no babies here." At the time, however, my daughter-in-law was pregnant, but unaware of it. So, I told my daughter-in-law that the reason she was not feeling well was because she was pregnant. She went to the doctor soon after and, sure enough, the doctor confirmed it.

A pregnant friend came to me and told me she had a dream that her baby was stillborn. I told her "Everything is fine with the baby." Several months later she gave birth to a beautiful healthy baby. Thank God for the Word that everything was fine. The Word changes things. The Prophetic Word is needed. People need to hear an encouraging word to get through a difficult situation. And, sometimes, the Word just needs to be spoken out or birthed out onto a situation. Many times, a person just needs the Word you are carrying. Make sure you deliver on time.

> *"Surely the Lord God will do nothing but he revealeth his secret unto his servants, the prophets," Amos 3:7.*

I had a dream, in which another friend was packing boxes. I told her of the dream and, about a week later, she called to tell me she was indeed packing boxes to move.

## 5. IF ALL CHRISTIANS CAN BE PROPHETIC, WHY NOT YOU?

This book you are reading right now is a result of a prophetic dream of Matthew Payne's. God speaks to us through our dreams. If you have any questions you would like to ask God, ask, then be quiet and listen for the answer. Ask Him before you go to sleep, and, when you wake up, you will probably have your answer or a dream to meditate on until God reveals more to you. Everything means something, so pay attention! Everything is connected; everyone is connected. It is for you, the prophet or prophetess, to learn the way in which God speaks to you so you can be a spokesperson for Christ.

A lot of us cannot attend day school so we must attend "evening classes." These classes are held during our sleep with us remembering only bits and pieces when we awake. However, what we learn during these classes is retained unconsciously – that's how we know things but don't know how we know it. "I just know, I don't know how I know it, but I do." It's by the Spirit and we learned it during night classes that are not limited by physical knowledge.

It is not by chance that this book has found its way to you. When people or things show up in our lives, there is always a message from God to us in every situation. In God, there is no such thing as "by chance," "luck," or "coincidence." Such things are God's Divine Timing – it is God being visible; otherwise, how would you see Him? Most people think God is invisible but, if you look closely, you can see God all around you, in everything.

That reminds me of the song: *I Can See Clearly Now* (Johnny Nash)

> *I can see clearly now, the rain has gone*
> *I can see all obstacles in my way*
> *Gone are the dark clouds that had me blind*
> *It's gonna be a bright, bright sun-shiny day*
> *Look all around you,*
> *There's nothing but blue skies.*

Receive the message that God is sending you right now through this book. If you do not get the message, it does not mean there is no message; it means you may have missed it or that it is for another day. Put it on a shelf and, when you are ready, God will bring it back into your remembrance, but, at some point, do not miss this message: The prophetic is for you. You can prophesy!

And when you are ready, the teacher will appear before your very eyes – in the form of a person, CD, book, or some other way – either in a dream and/or in the physical form. It goes beyond the visible and into the invisible. As you study and do your homework during your waking hours, God will visit you during your sleep and give you information you could not know otherwise.

### Questions:
1. Is there anything that could keep you from receiving the gift of prophecy?
2. "Surely, the Lord God will do nothing but he revealeth his _____ unto his servants the _____."
Amos 3:7

## 6. The Gift of Prophecy - What Is It?

*"For the equipping of the saints for the work of ministry, for the edifying of the body of Christ." Ephesians 4:12*

The gift of prophecy is spoken of in 1 Corinthians 12:10, along with the gift of the word of knowledge, and the gift of the word of wisdom. There are separate chapters later on that specifically speak on these two associated gifts. As stated in Chapter 2, words of knowledge were used by Jesus as He spoke to the Samaritan woman at the well: *"for you have had five husbands, and the one whom you now have is not your husband; in that you spoke truly,"* John 4:18.

Here, Jesus spoke "supernatural" knowledge about this woman that a stranger could not possibly have known. This information came by the Holy Spirit. Therefore, the revelation written above in italics is called a word of knowledge.

A word of wisdom, however, is telling a person about something that they need to do! In prophecy, the word of wisdom might say: "You need to spend more time reading my Word and also to spend time with Me in prayer." **Prophecy is the link between the words of knowledge and the words of wisdom.**

People often rejoice that they have received a personal prophecy, but they may not realize that prophecy has other supernatural elements within it. First it has words of knowledge which gives the actual information about them or their situation. Second, it may have words of wisdom that give God's specific directions that they need to follow. Third, everything in between these two revelations is called "prophecy." Most people may not recognize these separate gifts and, instead, they call the whole message a personal prophecy.

Imagine, as a piece of visual symbolism, that in my right hand are the words of knowledge – in my left hand are the words of wisdom – and in between, connecting these two, is the third element, the person giving the prophecy. God is using all His prophetic gifting in you to pass on His Word. For what purpose does He do this? He does this to equip His saints for the work of the ministry and to build up the body of Christ. (Ephesians 4:12)

Therefore, when a prophetic person says that someone has the gift of prophecy, they are actually implying that they have the other two associated gifts as well. Prophecy is to edify: it is to be given for the sole purpose of encouragement or to build up. Everyone needs encouragement; some people more than others, because they may feel downtrodden or defeated by the demands of life.

Christian life is difficult at times and Jesus acknowledged that the righteous would suffer many persecutions and troubles but, because we are in Christ and He is in us, we can know His peace. *"These things I have spoken to you, that in Me you may have peace. In the world, you will have tribulation; but be of good cheer, I have overcome the world, John 16:33.*

According to Strong's Concordance, "The primary use of the word 'prophecies' is not predictive, in the sense of foretelling, but interpretive, declaring, or forth-telling, the will and counsel of God." God, therefore, is giving the message, but He uses a human mouth and vocal chords. A gentle prophecy would be:

> Draw near to me. I love you, my child. Haven't I promised you many things in the past about your future? Don't worry! I'm going to fulfill all these promises in My Word. Rest in Me. Depend on Me and I will see you through.

These words give present and future encouragement, but they are not specifically about the future! Instead, the message is a "now" word from Jesus Christ that embraces their future as well.

A prophecy, occasionally, does talk specifically about a person's future. However, I, personally, would be reluctant to place a "sell-by" date on such a prophecy, except, of course, if the Holy Spirit strongly urged me to do so. I say this because, if a date was misinterpreted, then the person receiving the prophecy may conclude that the entire message was a false prophecy! They would disregard it altogether! However, with no date, it can come true at any time! This, in turn, encourages and strengthens a person's trust in the fact that God cares and that He is in control of their future, no matter what may happen.

I never tire of receiving a prophecy. Walking in this gift needs to be lived for it to be understood. This gift can do mighty exploits for God, because there are so many struggling Christians and non-believers in the world today. Many believe that we are living in the last days and creation itself is groaning, waiting for the second return of Jesus Christ. People need to be encouraged in these days and to be told that God has not abandoned them, or in fact the world.

If Jesus came *physically* to visit you in your daily life – maybe He would just come to a café, sit and introduce Himself by saying, "Hi, I'm Jesus." I am sure He would share many beautiful things with you. I am also sure that He would answer all your questions and cause you to re-prioritize your life. Prophecy is, therefore, the ability for Jesus to speak through you to another person.

Are you feeling discouraged? Jesus would give you a message of encouragement. Do you need to make a decision about something important? Jesus would give you a message with the direction and the decision you need.

## **LAURIE'S REFLECTIONS**

6. The Gift of Prophecy - What Is It?

This chapter expresses the beauty of prophecy and why it is the greatest gift of all, in such a simplistic and wonderful way that anyone can understand. God's voice is a spontaneous voice that comes as an idea, a word, a thought, a dream, a vision, or maybe even a song. It is not from any of our reasoning. That is the beauty of it! You do not prophesy on account of your mind and imagination, but on *God's* account of *His* mind and imagination, which He deposits directly into your mind, giving you the Mind of Christ.

We are made in the image and likeness of God – the image – the imagination of God! He imaged us and here we are!

There is no thought process to prophecy because it is what pops into your head at the moment God puts it there. "I thought I heard…" And you did! It was God talking! It is when you say, "I don't know where that thought came from." It could be a money-making idea, or a solution to a problem – take heed – God is talking.

Wikipedia defines prophecy as a process in which a message is communicated to a prophet, and then communicated to others. That is a good definition. We are specially speaking of divine revelation coming directly from the heart and mind of God. Prophecy speaks to the potential of a person; it is for confirmation of that potential and for things happening.

Recently, I was at a check-out counter in Wal-Mart, waiting for the clerk to make a correction to my purchase. While we were waiting for the supervisor I began talking with her. It was her first day on the job and she was very thankful that I came back to her instead of the store manager. I asked her, "How do you like it here so far?" Before she could answer, I heard someone behind me say, "It's a job." So I turned to see who had spoken, and there was no one behind me, but now she was saying, "It's a job." I thought: "Wow, Lord, I heard her loud and clear before she spoke." It's nice when God gives you the answer before hand.

The art of listening needs to be intentionally developed! Giving and receiving prophecy is wonderful. Personal prophecy is awesome! So again, pay attention to everything because everything means something. God is talking to you through everything around you; He's trying to get your attention. I can be stubborn at times, so, on many occasions, God has to "power-punch" me to get my attention – I am learning, however, to be more attentive to my surroundings. I am trying to follow His instructions, even if I do not understand them.

God will always prepare you for the ministry. You do not ever have to think that you are not worthy, or that you are unprepared. Your life has prepared you for this moment and ministry. God is preparing you. The prophetic ministry is not an easy life, so if you have not had an easy life, then you are most likely already somewhat prepared for this type of ministry. It is an ongoing process, always for the next level where God wants to take you; life is the continuing education process that builds you up with the help of great leaders within the ministry.

## 6. THE GIFT OF PROPHECY - WHAT IS IT?

Prophecy is delivered in many different ways. For example, with some prophets the Word flows out of them like a bubbling brook in a non-stop stream. Others see visions and interpret them or just give the vision and leave it up to the other party to seek God for the interpretation – these prophets are called seers. Some prophets, like myself, give prophecy during regular conversation, just in speaking things out. For those prophets, personal prophecy comes forth during counseling or coaching sessions as it is also called.

However, if I am involved in a ministry other than my own, the anointing of that ministry falls upon me and I will prophesy according to the specifications the leader of that particular ministry has called for – be it long five minute video prophecies, short one minute telephone prophecies or writing several paragraphs in an email prophecy. God anoints those He appoints, but you must follow the leader of the ministry in which you are assigned.

Questions:

1. What is prophecy?
2. What are the three elements of prophecy?
3. What are some ways in which God has been preparing you for the prophetic ministry?

## 7. Using Prophecy

*"This charge I commit to you, son Timothy, according to the prophecies previously made concerning you, that, by them, you may wage the good warfare." 1Timothy 1:18*

This chapter is in two parts. The first refers to using prophecy as the person giving the prophecy. The second refers to using prophecy as the person receiving the prophecy: that is, using prophecy in your own life.

In a way, prophecy is like the Word of God, but it cannot be held in the same esteem as the Word of God, because we know that the Word of God is perfect whereas, prophecies can sometimes contain errors. (Chapter 12) Therefore, people would cut me to shreds for even suggesting that prophecy is like the Word of God. However, I still maintain that there is one powerful similarity.

Prophecy, like God's Word, is like a sword! Giving a person a prophecy can give them a sword with which to fight the enemy. The apostle Paul wrote to young Timothy, *"This charge I commit to you, son Timothy, according to the prophecies previously made concerning you, that, by them, you may wage the good warfare,"* 1Timothy 1:18.

How would young Timothy wage good warfare? He would do it by standing on (believing in and trusting in) the prophecies that he has received. Now, if the apostle Paul gave Timothy the prophecies in which he is to believe, this means Paul also gave him a weapon with which to wage warfare. Therefore, when you prophesy to a person by giving them a personal word from God, you are giving them something solid to stand on – you are imparting 'hope' into them and are strengthening their faith in God's love and His protection over them.

Heidi Baker's husband, Roland Baker, from Mozambique and Iris Ministries, suffered from full-blown dementia – so badly that he did not even know what country he was in, let alone what day it was. His mind was totally closing down. However, he said, in a recent conference, that he continued to remind the Lord of the prophecies over his life that had not yet been fulfilled. Although most of his mental skills were closed down, he could still pray and he continued praying that the Lord would restore him and let him fulfill these prophecies. The Lord totally healed him of the dementia and he recovered fully, and today these very same prophecies are now starting to be fulfilled in his life!

Roland waged good warfare by standing on the prophecies in his darkest hour. Therefore, *any person* to whom you give a prophecy can stand on that prophecy and wage good warfare as well. The Bible repeatedly tells us that God is no respecter of persons! What He did for Roland, He can do for you!

1. Prophecy can be medicine to someone who is suffering hardship or confusion; it can be a healing balm to the human spirit.
2. Prophecy can be a tool of encouragement to live a victorious life.
3. Prophecy can give positive hope and vision for a person's future by giving them an understanding of their destiny and purpose.

One of the major functions of a prophet is to recognize the specific call of God on individual lives. This is like a personal road-map showing God's destination and purpose for their life. This map equips them to make godly decisions. Prophecy is a logical tool that God wants to use! This book or the video series would not even exist if it were not for a dream interpretation of a prophecy. Great good can be accomplished by people standing on their prophecies and a prophetic person actually contributes to God's earthly harvest.

In summary: You can be an integral part of God's overall plan. Prophecy is a valid and crucial weapon in the arsenal of God! It is a strategic weapon, just like a sword. Prophesying over a person gives that person something to stand on. It gives them strength. It encourages them. It gives them a host of good benefits. Receive the gift, practice the gift, and release the gift onto others.

## LAURIE'S REFLECTIONS

7. Using Prophecy

In an earlier chapter I used an example to illustrate how giving a prophecy saved a friend's life – it gave her renewed hope and a new direction. You can prophesy to dry bones (dead situations) and they can live! (See Ezekiel 37:4-10.)

The fact that you are reading this book is an indication that the Lord is calling you to the prophetic. Answer the clarion call by surrendering your will and saying "Yes, Lord." Once you have received the gift of prophecy, the best way to grow in it is to actually use it by prophesying to others. The more you prophesy, the more you will hear the voice of the Lord. Practice does make perfect.

The "How to" of prophecy cannot be taught; instead, prophecy is a gift that is "caught" from being around other anointed prophets. It pays to be in an anointed prophetic atmosphere.

Training is important. Do not just go off by yourself on a wild tangent, thinking, "I'm a prophet now! I don't need anyone telling me what to do or how to do it! 'Come here and let me prophesy to you,' or even, 'God told me to tell you this...'" Every beginner needs fine-tuning; a little bit of training goes a long way. Humble yourself and submit yourself to a seasoned prophet and let them instruct you *"in the way that you should go."*

Prophesying is a powerful tool for evangelizing. Just listen to what God's Word says concerning the effects of prophesying to an unbeliever: *"But if all prophesy, and an unbeliever or an uninformed person comes in, he is convinced by all, he is convicted by all. And thus the secrets of his heart are revealed; and so, falling down on his face, he will worship God and report that God is truly among you,"* 1 Corinthians 14:24-25.

Prophecy is, therefore, for the believer and the unbeliever.

K-Mart used to indicate their store specials by flashing a blue light so all their customers could find the great deals. K-Mart began to be known for their "blue-light specials." Recently, I was giving a prophecy and the Lord said "blue light" and then instantly I was reminded of the K-Mart blue light specials. I told her that I heard "blue-light" and it meant she was special.

She thanked me and said lately, she had been seeing a blue light in several rooms of her home. Well, frankly, I had never received a word like that for anyone before, so I thought it was a bit "crazy," but I gave her the Word anyway. What a blessing it was for her! Can you imagine going through your house seeing blue lights? You might think yourself crazy if not for the Word of the Lord through the prophet.

So, please, if you are hearing or seeing anything – no matter how crazy it seems – give it out, because it may be "just what The Doctor ordered."

### Questions:
1. Give two good reasons why we should all prophesy.
2. Who is prophecy for?

## 8. The Gift of the Word of Knowledge - What Is It?

*"And to another is given the word of knowledge through the Spirit."*
*1 Corinthians 12:8*

As said before, the gift of the word of knowledge is mentioned in 1 Corinthians 12:8. Also, to recap the encounter Jesus had with Nathanael, Jesus said: *"Behold, an Israelite indeed, in whom is no deceit!"* which means he was a pure-hearted person. Nathanael was astonished that Jesus even knew him, and Jesus went on to say: *"Before Philip called you, when you were under the fig tree, I saw you," John 1:48.* Jesus had "seen" Nathanael praying, and that was given to Him by a prophetic vision or word of knowledge, of Nathanael under the tree.

Here is a personal example of a word of knowledge: I was in a taxi, driving home with a client, when Jesus prompted me to ask my passenger how long it had been since he had spoken to his brother. He muttered: "I no longer talk to my brother!" The Lord then told me that this man was unaware that his brother was dying of cancer and desperately wanted to phone him and make peace with him, but his mother would not allow it because of the bad blood between them. I then passed on this message to him.

Knowing that the brother was dying of cancer is a word of knowledge. It was information about a person's life that I could not had possibly known. I watched as the man first rang his mother, and then his brother, so that they could meet with each other. As he did this, I was wondering – here I was, just a Baptist boy, yet God was giving me these messages! I had no idea at that stage what prophecy really was, but I learnt that God is more concerned about family relationships than our understanding of theology!

I will give you another example of sibling fallout being restored by prophecy. The Lord prompted me to say to a stranger: "When you were thirteen, your brother pushed you off a push bike, and you could no longer play cricket."

Most times, when you give a word of knowledge, that person is shocked! They ask, "How do you know that?" and you reply: "Don't worry, Jesus told me." In this example, I continued through the inspiration of the Holy Spirit: "Your brother was just playing – it was not intentional. You must forgive him. He did not mean to wreck your cricket career! He was just messing about, playing a game! He did not want your knee to break! You really need to forgive him."

So far, we have not talked about words of wisdom, but the words "You really need to forgive him," are directional and are words of wisdom. The fact that he was pushed off his bike at thirteen and broke his knee – that is a word of knowledge. When you give a word of knowledge to a total stranger, or even to someone you know, it always shocks them! This is the supernatural part of the prophetic experience. Words of knowledge are powerful things!

Once, I was in McDonald's, and Jesus told me to talk to a particular girl and say: "Jesus knows that you do not want to talk to Him, unless He gives you answers about why your mother is dying of cancer." Seeing her shocked look, I added: "Seeing that Jesus is not visibly here, I want to ask you what questions you have for Him and I will pass on His answers to you."

That was a word of knowledge and with some direction from the Lord, I passed on the message to her, and she started asking questions. She was in tears, but she *did start asking questions*. As stated before, prophecy brings healing.

A favorite pastime of mine is to pass on to people a couple of their positive personality traits that come from words of knowledge. These supernatural words certainly grab people's attention. However, the devil knows this too! He will use a clairvoyant to speak about personal things or situations in a person's life in order to draw them to the dark side. I have never been to a clairvoyant, but that is what they do and it works – people are impressed!

Most Christians want to make a difference in their area of contact. If you seriously want this, there is no better way than to move in the gift of prophecy, using the word of knowledge, and the word of wisdom. These are extremely effective ways for getting another person's full attention on what God, our Creator and Savior wants to say to them! God always has many things that He wants his people to know through the prophetic gifts.

God often tells me about a problem in a person's life and I go to them and reveal it to them. A word of knowledge never fails to get attention! Then the Lord gives me a word of advice or direction for them to put into practice. Once, I had a problem with approaching men because I had seen plenty of violence in my life. One day, I had just walked past a young man with his girlfriend – I did not intend to give him the word I had received, but the Lord wanted me to go back to the couple. I rather reluctantly approached the young man and said:

"Excuse me Sir I have a message for you!"

He angrily retorted: "I don't want to hear your message."

I nervously laughed and then said: "Come on, man. I have a gift. This gift allows me to receive a message for a person – but if you don't like the message after I've told you, then you can just throw it away – but at least listen." I directed my attention to his friend and asked: "What do you reckon? Do you want to hear the message for your friend?" She said she did.

I then told him that there was going to be an offer, something of a breakthrough coming into his life in the next six months and others would be saying: 'That's too good to be true.' I then added as a final statement: "Ask your girlfriend, and she will remind you of this conversation. You need to take up that offer, because many people will call it 'your breakthrough!' It will happen within the next six months and you will be offered something!"

That was a word of knowledge plus a word of wisdom about what he needed to do with the breakthrough. Words of knowledge can be extremely effective! What would you do if someone came up to you and said something similar?

Then, within a few months, a friend of yours makes you an offer to go into business with them with no personal cash outlay and all your friends tell you it is too good to be true! What if you talked to your girlfriend about it and she reminded you of the stranger who had told you these things. What if you took your friend up on the business venture and it had great success – would you not give God all the glory?

## **LAURIE'S REFLECTIONS**

8. The Gift of the Word of Knowledge – What Is It?

When I was ten years old or so, I recall going to some sort of school carnival where I walked into a 'Palm Reading' tent (gasp!) I really had no idea what I was doing, but all my friends were doing it. The lady told me things that later came to pass. She was definitely spot on with her predictions. She was having clear vision, which is what the word "clairvoyant" means. She did not, however, give God the glory. Do you see the difference?

But I have never forgotten her looking at my palm and telling me what I would receive for Christmas that year. I mean, I forgot all about my encounter with her until after I opened my Christmas presents and received exactly what she said I would! Years later as an adult and a Christian I say: TO GOD BE THE GLORY because it revealed to me the opposition's prophetic abilities – and the ability to take credit where credit is not due. She never mentioned the Holy Spirit, God, or Jesus.

A couple of years ago at a prophetic conference, I received a Word of knowledge that I would be visiting an elderly, balding man in the hospital and a specific car was mentioned. Later, I told my husband about it and we prayed in Jesus' name that everything would be all right. About a month later, my father-in-law was in a terrible car accident that normally would have been fatal. He drove a car like the one described in the prophecy (and he is a "bald man.") However, because I had received that Word of Knowledge in advance of the accident, we were able to pray about the situation "ahead of time," and so, the accident was not fatal, thank God.

"Tonight's the night," I prophesied to a fellow seeker.

She looked at me blankly and said: "What does that mean?"

I replied: "I don't know but that's what I hear, 'Tonight's the night.'" (A song by Rod Stewart.)

I could tell by her expression that she was *not* impressed. Obviously, she did not particularly care for my strange announcement. Later, that evening, there was a ceremony during which she received a very significant certificate. I looked across the table and she had a big smile on her face as she repeated the words, "Tonight's the night!"

Another time, I had to give a word that seemed kind of harsh and it came to me as, "Don't rock the boat." like a particular song says, and so I said, "You don't have to rock the boat all the time – don't be so fussy." The lady shook her head in acknowledgment as if to say, "Okay, I understand. I know the Lord is talking to me."

During the month of February, I was prophesying to a young lady and the Lord said, "You are my valentine."

So I said, "This might sound strange to you, but the Lord says: 'You are *My* valentine.'" She was so pleased; she smiled and said that she understood why she received that Word. Prophecy really does comfort and encourage others.

Information that suddenly comes upon you, spontaneous words made known to you by the Holy Spirit – are Words of Knowledge. If you are sensitive to these spontaneous bits of information, you have the gift of the Word of Knowledge.

### Questions:
1. What is the difference between a Word of Wisdom and a Word of Knowledge?
2. How does the Word of the Lord come to you most often?
3. Why is the gift of Words of Knowledge a valuable gift?

## 9. Using the Word of Knowledge - A Risky Gift.

*"For you have had five husbands, and the one whom you now have is not your husband; in that you spoke truly." John 4:18*

You would know by now that a word of knowledge is supernatural information that you would not ordinarily know about a person's present or past life. I have repeated this fact a few times, but, for those only watching the video episode or reading this particular chapter, Jesus used a word of knowledge to the woman at the well in Samaria. He said, "Bring your husband here," and she said she had no husband. Jesus said: *"for you have had five husbands, and the one whom you now have is not your husband; in that you spoke truly," John 4:18*.

Fifty years ago, it was not socially acceptable for an unmarried couple to live together. People would whisper and comment about such a situation in a very negative fashion. Well, you can imagine how it was two-thousand years ago! Jesus had put his finger on something *delicate*! The woman was embarrassed and needed to change the topic away from her private living arrangements.

After that word of knowledge, she said to Jesus: *"Sir, I perceive that you are a prophet," John 4:19*. Instantly, she had jumped from Jesus being an ordinary person to Him being a prophet! What caused that shift? Words of knowledge do that to people! But there is a risk in having a word of knowledge.

In Chapter 8, I talked about the man who had been accidentally pushed off his bike when he was only a boy. If I had been wrong when I said that, I would have blown it with that person – but I was not wrong because, normally, when you receive a word of knowledge, it is right! However, it can be risky because if you are talking to a stranger, or even someone you know, and you plunge in with a word of knowledge and "if" it proves to be wrong, then you blow all credibility with that person. Suddenly they accuse you of being false and they do not want to be bothered with you.

By the same token, when you are right, that person pays you much attention! It is like cheese in a mousetrap, with a word of knowledge being the cheese. Once a person accepts the word of knowledge, they are ready and open to accept everything else that you have to say.

Rick Joyner, a wise and famous American prophet, wrote in one of his books that whenever an unproven person prophesies over his ministry with major words of wisdom about changes he needs to make to his ministry, he does not pay any attention to the prophecies unless they have many words of knowledge in them. Like anyone, Rick needs to verify that a person is truly hearing from God before he acts on any directions he receives from a stranger.

Many people who move in the prophetic gifts give safe, bland, or generic prophecies because they lack words of knowledge. They lack the necessary courage to step out in a word of knowledge with specifics about a person's life. Lack of courage, therefore, causes the prophecy to be weaker. As an example, when my wife left me over sixteen years ago I was barely three months into the breakup and was still in a hurt condition, when a senior pastor of a Pentecostal church said to me in a prophecy:

> "You are in a dark tunnel at the moment and you cannot see light at the end. You are wondering if there is actually any light at all. One day, there is going to be light, and God is going to restore and heal you. Then, you will move into ministry. On that day, you are going to be mighty in the world."

The fact that he knew I was in an awful dark place certainly impressed me. Through the years that prophecy was with me and I have improved. I had been given hope of future healing and restoration. That hope finally brought me to a place where I would be happy being single, because I knew that God loved me as someone very special. My hope for a good future had been restored with that prophecy. Imagine trying to build a brick building with no mortar! A word of knowledge becomes the mortar! As mortar gives strength to a building, a strong prophecy gives strength to a human being.

If you give words of knowledge, it cements in the mind of people that the prophecy was indeed supernatural and not just the ranting of someone wanting to gain personal attention. It is also vital for the sake of the Gospel message that people *know* that God is interested and willing to continually intervene in the affairs of humanity.

You are doing God, the church, and the general public a great disservice if you receive words of knowledge and fail to pass them on in your prophecies. As stated before, people need evidence in order to believe and to be strengthened. I am very much aware that giving words of knowledge can be risky, but take that risk! I promise you it will be worthwhile. According to my estimates, ninety-five percent of *beginners get it right!* Therefore, if you have God's answer, what is the problem?

## **LAURIE'S REFLECTIONS**

9. Using the Word of Knowledge – A Risky Gift

Some people are born musicians, but they still need to take lessons to help them perfect their gift. My son is a born musician when it comes to the guitar. After only a few lessons, his instructor told me that my son could play the guitar as well as his other students who had been studying under him for years. However, he added that my son still needed lessons to perfect his gift and talent.

It is the same with prophets. Once you receive the gift of prophecy, you have the gift, but you must submit yourself to the training. In the Bible, Samuel was a master at Ramah, the school for prophets, in which David fled to escape Saul. They both, then, went and dwelt in Naioth, another school of prophets (1 Samuel 19:19-20.) In 2 Kings 4:1, it talks about the "sons of the prophets," meaning a school of the prophets. And, believe it or not, here it is in the Bible, Daniel 1:1-4 – a school of prophets run by the government!

*Nebuchadnezzar, King of Babylon came to Jerusalem and besieged it and the Lord gave Jehoiakim, king of Judah into his* [King Nebuchadnezzar's] *hand."* The king represented the government and he requested that: *"the children of Israel who were well favored, and skillful in all wisdom, and cunning in knowledge, and understanding science, and such as had ability in them,* **to stand in the king's palace, whom could teach the learning and the tongue of the Chaldeans.**" The prophet Daniel was one of these selected men.

To further my point on proper training being necessary, you will also find other schools of the prophets or sons of prophets at Bethel (2 Kings 2:3,) Jericho (verse 5,) and Gilgal (2 Kings 4:38.)

A repeated word of knowledge in a person's mind is meant to re-mind them of things. Yes, indeed! We all need re-minding. We need to give ourselves a new mind in the Spirit.[1]

If you have a prophecy recorded in some way (video, CD, mp3, written, etc.,) it will allow you to listen or read it over and over to re-mind you of the specific word that God has for you.

This is why recorded prophecies are so important. They are worth you taking "the risk" of delivering the Word of the Lord as He leads, to others and yourself.

### Questions:
1. Why is the Word of Knowledge a "risky gift"?
2. How often do you need to renew your mind with the Word of God?

---

[1] Ephes. 4:23

## 10. The Gift of the Word of Wisdom - What Is It?

*"For to one is given by the Spirit the word of wisdom; to another the word of knowledge by the same Spirit." 1 Cor. 12:8*

Without instruction, this gift could be confusing when you casually read it in 1 Corinthians 12 because you might assume that words of wisdom are just words 'full' of wisdom. For example: You could say to a child: "Look to the right and to the left before you cross the road." That would be a word of wisdom from any mother. From experience you know this fact, but a word of wisdom is different from human wisdom or even the Wisdom of God!

Words of wisdom are the directions of God to a person through prophecy, as I outlined in Chapter 8. Here, an older brother had been accidently injured and had held bitterness toward his younger sibling. The specific word of wisdom was: *"You need to forgive him."* In the same way, any spiritual life can be crippled by un-forgiveness. Refusing to forgive, not only destroys relationships which are God's number one priority, but this mindset affects our prayer life, our ongoing maturity in the Lord and it totally prevents us from experiencing God's best! Our Lord Jesus had very hard words to say about holding onto un-forgiveness!

The word of knowledge, too, was important. It reached the core of breakdown in the relationship between the brothers. That is why a word of knowledge can be deemed as surgical! The word of wisdom is, therefore, the practical application of the word of knowledge. Again, in Chapter 8, I gave a word of knowledge to a reluctant gentleman who would be offered a wonderful opportunity. God's will was for him to grab that opportunity.

Proverbs 16:9, teaches us that we may plan our way, but the Lord directs our steps. This is a wonderful source of encouragement to people who are anxious to do God's will. I know that the Lord continually directs my steps, but risk is a constant factor, even now! On the positive side, passing on a word of wisdom to someone is a blessing to their life, which, in turn, blesses me.

Prophesying words of wisdom to a leader, *can feel very intimidating.* Know that the fleshly soul part of us will always shrink back from spiritual boldness! Feelings are part of our imperfect soul, which is in the life-process of sanctification. Our soul has run our lives since birth, but a Christian must, moment by moment, re-new their born-again mind and emotions by choosing to hand their individual "will" over to their new Master, the Holy Spirit.

Therefore, we must be actively determined to resist fear and lean on God to reign over our imperfect soul! This inward war between our spirit and soul becomes easier the more we allow God to rule our personal will. God will never ever override a person's free will, even though He loves us. If He ever did, then the death of His Son would have been in vain!

The Apostle Paul said that God is no respecter of persons, and neither should we be. People are people and they are all equally loved by God, regardless of the title or position they hold. Therefore, you need to activate faith and minister out of love. True faith operates out of love, but fear comes through perverse faith: it is from the devil!

*"There is no fear in love; but perfect love casts out fear, because fear involves torment. But he who fears has not been made perfect in love."* Again, *"God has not given us a spirit of fear, but of power and of love and of a sound mind."* 1 John 4:18 and 2 Timothy 1:7.

You must know that it is God speaking to you, and that words of wisdom are God's answer for that person at that time. Be obedient to God and confidently and lovingly share what He has to say. If you miss your opportunity, you will miss out on that particular blessing! God will have to choose someone else to make His word known. He may reveal it to the person through a conference, a DVD, or through another Christian who works in the prophetic. However, the point is: He chose you to be His mouthpiece and what a privilege that is!

It constantly thrills me to be used by God to speak to whomever He calls me to. Many of the prophetic words God gives to me have words of wisdom in them. I must admit, however, that I still must be a *respecter of persons to some degree,* because being used by God to

## 10. THE GIFT OF THE WORD OF WISDOM - WHAT IS IT?

minister to a special lady like Heidi Baker really blows my mind! It fills me with unspeakable joy that she can receive a directional word from my mouth!

In ancient Israel, a king would seek a prophet for important advice. The prophet would then seek God and return with His answers to the king. At that time, there were three highly esteemed offices: prophet, priest and king. These Old Testament prophets were judged by their words of wisdom and their words of knowledge that they gave to the King, or his authorities. If it was perceived that they got it wrong, their creditability and even their life were at risk!

Thankfully, today, no one will throw physical rocks at you! But, if you give people words of wisdom in a prophecy and they then choose not to follow them, it sometimes can hold up the prophecy, or even totally stop it from coming true in that person's life. Similarly, if someone has prophesied over you that you need to spend more time in the Word of God in order to rightly divide Bible truth, then you need to do this. God may have called you to be a great teacher or preacher! Disobedience, therefore, can rob or delay God's calling in your life.

Even after many years of prophesying, I could not sit and share the information in this book if I did not have firsthand knowledge of prophecy. Practical experience is a necessary teaching component in having a subject understood by others. Similarly, you need to take the practical steps that God gives in prophecy, in order to spiritually advance in the kingdom of God and in order to fulfill your destiny. Do not allow procrastination to rule your life. Words of wisdom are the practical steps that God gives for ongoing success.

I hope that you now have an understanding about the word of wisdom. Bear in mind always that prophecy moves out of love and compassion. Would you not like to receive personal directions from God? Of course! This should prove to you that many others would also want to know the specific directions of God!

## LAURIE'S REFLECTIONS

10. The Gift of the Word of Wisdom – What Is It?

My husband and I received a prophecy that really saved us financially. We were looking for a house to purchase and had settled on choosing one of two lakefront properties that were next door to one another. We were walking back and forth several times, trying to decide which house we liked best, when all of a sudden I stopped dead in my tracks.

I was reminded of a prophecy we had received several months ago that said "You will be looking at two houses, going back and forth between the two, trying to decide which one to purchase. Do not buy yet!" At the time of the prophecy, I was disappointed, but in hindsight it was a blessing because not long after that, my husband lost the contract that would have allowed us to pay for such a home, so that Word was an important directional Word from God. Prophecy will help you avoid the pitfalls of life.

A Word of Wisdom can be either a "do" or a "don't" word for you to follow, but choosing to follow it or not can be life-changing! I cannot tell you how many times I have received confirmation on a Word of Wisdom that was prophesied to me. It is very important to take these words (directions from God) seriously. Otherwise you go around that circle, one more time.

The Gift of Wisdom is being able to receive directions or instructions for yourself and others, by the Holy Spirit, and to act accordingly. Words of Wisdom are usually directional information that you would not normally know. Hearing what needs to be done in certain circumstances is a Word of Wisdom. When Solomon ordered, "Cut the baby in half!" he was giving Divine Instruction – Words of Wisdom – and then again, "No, stop!"

We may not understand the instruction, but it is not yours to understand, but to deliver or act upon. Ordering to "cut the baby in half" was not really wisdom but was a Word of Wisdom, divinely given to Solomon by God to reveal the true identity of the mother of the child. This particular Word was a revelation of knowledge that was applicable to this particular situation, which was brought before

Solomon. It carries the mark of the Wisdom of God – and God's wisdom surpasses all other wisdom. Solomon was able to use that Word of Wisdom (Instruction) to reach the Will of God in that situation. It brought forth the truth of the matter at hand.

Disobeying a Word of Wisdom leads to going around that same mountain over and over again until we decide to obey that Word.

We are *asking* to repeat the lesson each time we choose not to listen to the instructions of a prophet of God. We just don't get it so we have to stay on it until we do.

### Question:

1. What is the difference between wisdom and a Word of Wisdom?

## 11. Using Words of Wisdom

*"Wisdom is the principal thing; therefore get wisdom and, with all thy getting, get understanding."*
*Proverbs 4:7*

Using Words of Wisdom is twofold: it relates to two different people.

1. The person **giving** the word of wisdom.
2. The person **receiving** the word of wisdom.

**Number One**: The Lord has perfect intelligence. I am continually amazed when others discover this fact for themselves! It constantly thrills me! God sees the whole picture of their life. He is compassionate, loving, and all-knowing. With these qualities at hand, He truly understands how to direct a person's life so they can best fulfill their particular destiny.

Therefore, when you are prophesying to people, recognize that God knows exactly what He is saying to them. To be a prophet and fail to pass on the words of wisdom out of fear of "anyone" is wrong! Fear is perverted faith from the devil. The righteous walk by faith and God always rewards our faith.

God knows the steps of a righteous man. It says in the Old Testament: *The steps of a good man are ordered by the LORD, and He delights in his way.*" **Psalm 37:23**. Later, in Proverbs 16:9 we read: *A man's heart plans his way, but the LORD directs his steps.*

The Good Shepherd wants to direct His sheep. If you are going to be God's instrument in the prophetic, you had better direct them in God's way! It is no good saying to the Lord: "This person is too knowledgeable." Or, "I don't have the right to be telling this person what to do."

Trust me in this: When you are under the anointing of the Holy Spirit, it is not YOU telling them! God is telling them what to do *and He does have the right!*

## 11. USING WORDS OF WISDOM

Even in the secular world, a General receives his orders from his commander-in-chief, but he will also take advice from his fellow leaders. In war movies, you may see heads of an army studying maps, while surrounded by army experts in fighting in different terrain or weather conditions. Example: if the soldiers were in a snow covered area, the General would want directional advice from those experienced in fighting in snow conditions.

Even people in leadership positions want to receive God's directions! So, when God gives you directions through the gift of prophecy, make sure you pass them on. You are to be faithfully obedient to God. This will bring blessings to you and to others. It is up to the other person to choose whether or not they are going to receive and apply those directions. It is not up to you!

**Number Two**: If you have received a prophecy containing directional words from God that you need to do, then do them! As I said in the previous chapter: if you fail to put prophecy into action, by disobeying the words of wisdom in your prophecies you are delaying, or even nullifying a prophecy over your life.

The time you delay reading the Word of God, delay praying, or delay spending time in God's presence, this time period will determine the length of delay in God's perfect plan being worked out in your life! God will continue to remind you whenever you procrastinate, but if you continue to disobey Him He will just pass over you and use someone else.

Therefore, it is necessary to remember that, when you receive a prophecy, the most important aspects of the prophecy are not about your future, but are, in fact, *the directions that God is giving you to follow NOW.*

Using your mind, heart, and intelligence is good, but using the directions of God is perfect! He knows how to direct you! If you have received directions, act on them! Clearly, it is advisable to run every prophecy you receive past your pastor and obtain approval that this was truly God speaking. When you have obtained approval, you have valid confirmation that the Word is of God, so do exactly what it says! Do not be foolish and ignore His directions – it is a grave error.

## LAURIE'S REFLECTIONS

11. Using Words of Wisdom

*"Where there is no wise counsel, the people fall; but in the multitude of counselors, there is safety."* One translation says, *"...there is victory"* (Proverbs 11:14, NKJV and WEB). The Lord will show you the "way" to deliver a Word.

Prophecy is supposed to give: (1) Edification (strength)
(2) Encouragement and (3) Comfort.

You must "see" the situation all the way through to one or more of the above results. You deliver the Word and let God lead to the interpretation of it. You prophesy to reveal the divine truth that God is telling you to reveal. It is God speaking through you; therefore, you take no credit as long as you are following God's direction in speaking. Your direction here is simply to give direction.

Directions are very important, or else God would not bother to pass them on. Listen carefully to any and all directions you receive and "just do it!" I have missed many a blessing because I did not follow the directions as they had been given (sad to say, but it is the truth). In hindsight, I have missed out when God was trying to get a blessing to me. Do not make the mistake of saying, "What difference does it make if I do it this way or that way?" It makes all the difference in your world. Jesus is The Way, so the way you do a thing matters.

For example, one day I was in the process of ordering business cards on-line while I was listening to a personal prophecy on CD. The very word to me was: *"Do the business cards."* I remember sitting there, just amazed. I love personal prophecy! It is so on target. But do you know that when I went to pay for them, I did not have the money in my account so I did not order them. I did not even take the time to figure out how I could do it! Yet, at other times in the past, when I had not received a Word regarding business cards, I had taken the time to figure out my finances. We tend to get twisted in our thinking and actions. It is a form of perversion or perverted faith.

This time, I had received a direct Word from God while in the very act of doing the very thing that was mentioned in the prophecy, but I can be so stubborn sometimes. Paul said, *"When I want to do good, I don't, and when I try not to do wrong, I do it anyway,"* Romans 7:15 and 19. I can definitely relate with Paul on this.

Why do we believe in His promises, yet do not follow His commanding officers, the prophets, here on earth? This is, indeed, a grave error. In any war the orders of the commanding officer must be complied with completely with every "i" dotted and every "t" crossed. And we are in a spiritual war. And God is a God of war according to Exodus 15:3, *The LORD is a man of war: the LORD is his name.* Also see Revelation 19:10-11 where it states that *"Jesus is the spirit of prophecy... and He is Faithful and True and in righteousness He does judge and make war."*

Master Prophet, Bishop E. Bernard Jordan has an excellent teaching and book called the *Spiritual Art of War*.

All spiritual gifts are to be used to build up the body of Christ. We must always follow God's guidance and command. In speaking words of wisdom, you must use wisdom, always lifting people up, encouraging them. There is a certain way of delivering a Word of instruction that does not cut or rebuke in such a way as to condemn. *"There is no condemnation to them which are in Christ Jesus, who walk not after the flesh, but after the Spirit,"* Romans 8:1.

I am reminded of the words in an old Beatles song called *Let It Be*:

> "Speaking words of wisdom, let it be.
> And when the brokenhearted people
> Living in the world agree
> There will be an answer, let it be."

And so, let the words of wisdom from God come forth and be, *"For it is not you who speak, but it is the Spirit of your Father who speaks in you.*[2] The Holy Spirit is more than willing to speak through you if you will simply open up and make yourself available to Him.

## Questions:

1. What can cripple your spiritual life?
2. What is the purpose of Words of Wisdom?

---

[2] Romans 8:1

## 12. Can Prophecies Contain The Flesh?

*"Am I now trying to win the approval of men, or of God? Or am I trying to please men? If I were still trying to please men, I would not be a servant of Christ." Galatians 1:10*

Is it possible that a prophetic word can contain some "flesh" words coming from the prophet and not God? Yes, of course it is possible! I know of a well-experienced prophet, who says that an immature prophet or a person new to the gift of prophecy will hear a message of God and add some of their own words in the prophecy. Obviously the inexperienced prophet subconsciously believes that even God needs their help!

In contrast, the well-experienced prophet will say only what God is saying and every word said by God comes through in the prophecy. Therefore, it does not fall to the ground. What God says happens.

In regard to the immature prophet adding his own words, I have to agree that this was true in my prophetic experience, but, as I grew in the prophetic, less of the "self" surfaced and I found myself pausing to take a breath before I passed on what the Lord was saying. Sometimes, you might foolishly imagine that it is all too heavy or too difficult to say, or even that the Lord is saying things that you think could be rephrased in a better way.

At the time, you may be unaware that the person needs to hear it in exactly the way God said it in order for it to have more meaning. Even a specific word the Lord uses can strike more resonance with a person because it is a word that they fully understand: it is a specific word just for them! If you change the words of the Lord, that special significance will be lost, maybe forever.

Therefore, certainly there are prophecies from people who are not experienced in the gift of prophecy that can contain some flesh words. So, should we disregard all the prophetic gifts? Not at all!

People have prophesied over me hundreds of times and, often, it is their first prophecy, but they are encouraging, edifying prophecies. Prophecies precious to my heart are those given to me by people who have just received the gift. They are stepping out in faith and have prophesied over my life as a test of whether they have received the gift. Would I say that I would not like a prophecy from someone who has just walked in the gift? No, not at all!

It is my decision whether I believe every sentence, but I would certainly choose to have immature prophets prophesying over me all the time rather than not have anyone at all. Having said that, I think I have answered the question. Yes, there is a tendency in prideful, immature trainee prophets to add their own words to a prophecy. They might speak presumptuously, but, because that is true, it does not nullify the gift in that person. They should be encouraged and bolstered just like babies as they slump to the ground when learning to crawl.

They should be encouraged to mature in the Lord. They should be instructed to follow the word-for-word instructions of the Lord. They should not be put down or treated harshly because they are immature in their gift. Get alongside of them and inspire them to go on, to do better, to do more, and have more of an impact with their gifting. I hope that I have covered this sufficiently.

## **LAURIE'S REFLECTIONS**

12. Can Prophecies Contain the Flesh?

Give the Word of the Lord exactly the way God gives it to you. It is not necessary to change it around or change the words so that you or the other person might understand it better. God knows what He is saying, and why, and how He is saying it, even if you do not. Most importantly, you do not have to understand someone else's word, even if you are the one delivering it.

As you grow in your prophetic walk by prophesying, (with lots of practice, practice, practice) you will become more proficient in the gift, just like any other gift or talent you practice, such as singing, playing a musical instrument, or teaching. "Practice makes perfect."

Training takes the flesh out. Be willing to receive instruction; it really helps in keeping the flesh at bay. A prophet is a prophet, no matter where they go, so keep this in mind and pay attention to all

## 12. CAN PROPHECIES CONTAIN THE FLESH?

things, because the Lord is speaking all the time through everything and everyone.

The flesh comes into play when you begin thinking you do not need any more training or that you know everything there is to know about prophecy. That is immature thinking and will never be the case. If you walk according to the flesh instead of the Spirit, it means that you are offering your body (an un-renewed mind) to God instead of your born-again spirit. So, keep the flesh under control!

It is important to keep yourself under submission to someone who has had more training than you, someone who has done his or her duty as a servant of the Lord and now is in leadership. Bishop Jordan teaches that leaders are not born leaders; they must first serve. They have been where you are now. They were once a novice prophet themselves. They worked it out and walked it out and became strong in the Lord.

We have the tendency to follow or walk in our fleshly desires of comfort, nourishment, and selfishness. We tend to act out due to our jealousies, bitterness, and anger.

Your leader will help you bring your flesh under subjection through some stretching exercises. Submit yourselves to your leader's training. Jesus was a servant to His Father, and became a leader to the world in which we live.

Prophets are not called to be "people-pleasers." If you are more concerned about how people are receiving you than you are about how God is receiving you, then you are a people-pleaser and not a God-pleaser. As a prophet, you cannot be concerned about the look on their face – be it joy, disappointment, or confusion. Just deliver the Word of the Lord as given by the Lord.

## Questions:

1. What can take the flesh out of prophesying?
2. "The Lord does not make leaders; He makes _____ who become leaders." --Bishop E. Bernard Jordan

## 13. Are There Reasons Why Prophecies Do Not Come True?

*"Let us not be weary in well doing: for in due season we shall reap, if we faint not." Galatians 6:9*

Prophecy is an amazing gift, but it is important to know that the supernatural can be counterfeited by the dark side. Satan and his demons are committed to deception. Therefore, the prophecy could have come from a wrong spirit attached to that person or operating through them.

There are other legitimate reasons why prophecies fail, as covered in the last chapter. Some part of a message may not be of God, but of the flesh!

A third reason why a prophecy may not come true is because the *receiver of the prophecy* failed to do what the Lord told them to do. As we covered in *Using Words of Wisdom*, it is important that you obey the prophetic directions.

This was certainly true when the prophet Jonah disobeyed God. God had given him specific instructions, which just did not sit with Jonah's idea of justice! He was to go to the pagan city of Nineveh with a message of repentance, but instead, he purposely went by boat in another direction. He had rejected God's instructions, so the Lord sent a severe storm that threatened the vessel.

As a result, even the pagans in the boat suspected their new friend had a spiritual issue! Jonah knew he was the cause of their calamity and told them to throw him overboard. They subsequently drew lots, threw him off, and the sea immediately calmed. (God uses unbelievers and even nature itself, to fulfill His will.) God was still merciful and caused Jonah to be swallowed by a "prepared" fish that eventually spat the exhausted prophet onto land. Even when the sinful people in Nineveh repented, Jonah was still angry with God for showing them mercy. We can be so self-righteous at times!

Just as it is possible to live outside God's perfect plan, in the same way it is possible for a true prophecy not to come to pass. A delayed prophecy may be perceived as a failed prophecy, whereas it may have been delayed because of human disobedience.

## 14. WHY SOME PROPHECIES YOU THINK ARE FALSE ARE NOT

Lastly, a prophecy will be fulfilled in God's timing, not our own! You may be just "assuming" that the prophecy has not come true! Maybe it is not yet the right time! Maybe it is because of something you are doing, or God is delaying it for His own very good reason!

David was appointed and anointed king of Israel, yet many years passed before he sat on the throne! Joseph had seen, in a prophetic dream, his brothers bowing down to him, yet it took many years before this actually happened!

When prophecy is delayed, it does not mean that it will not come true. Way back in Genesis 3:15, it was promised that a "Seed" of a woman would one day crush Satan's head, yet it was not until thousands of years later that this was accomplished at Calvary! That was a very triumphant answer to prophecy!

Therefore, let us recap why prophecies fail or are delayed.

1. Words were spoken partly by the flesh.
2. A wrong spirit may have influenced the prophecy.
3. Words of wisdom in the prophecy were not obeyed.
4. Personal character traits may first need to be developed before God allows the prophecy to come to pass.

Prophecies you receive should also be confirmed in your life. Prophecy should confirm itself. Sometimes other people and other prophecies confirm the major things in your life that have been prophesied.

Many times it would be a mistake to rush out and make a major decision purely based on one prophecy: things sometimes need confirmation. The Bible says that we should act on the words of two or three witnesses, so it is a good practice to do this. I have mentioned it before, and I will mention it often that it is a good practice to run your prophecies past your spiritual leader and receive confirmation that it is a true prophecy of God.

If your leaders suggest that parts of the prophecy should be put on the shelf, that is, not to place your faith in, then you should pay attention to your leaders. Why? You are to listen to them because they are anointed by God to direct you in spiritual matters.

## LAURIE'S REFLECTIONS

13. Are There Reasons Why Prophecies Do Not Come True?

A delay is like missing your plane at the airport because you did other things instead of arriving at the gate on time. You have to wait for the next flight out. You missed the first flight because you were too busy and did not pay attention to the time and are now delayed. You are the cause of your own delay.

My husband and I have experienced many delays. One time we were given a specific word of direction, but we procrastinated, for about a year. Finally, I suggested to my husband that we should do what we were told to do over a year ago! It was a simple thing – mail out a package. We let the package sit in our living room for over a year, like we were paralyzed or something, and could not get to the post office. We were paralyzed -- Paralyzed with the spirit of procrastination! (Some may call it the spirit of laziness.)

When we eventually got around to responding to the directional word, we both felt a physical "push" in the spirit, as though we had been literally pushed forward. Until then, our flight had been delayed; our next level in life had been put on hold due to our own action of sitting on our humps.

Finally, we were able to board the train (we had missed the plane which travels much faster.) It was a relief to be back on track. God's schedule for our lives had been put on hold while we remained in limbo due to the disobedience of a simple command.

If the Lord cannot trust us to do the simple, small things, how on earth can He trust us to do the more complex, larger things? Start with the smaller, easier things and God will gradually test you and graduate you to bigger and better things. He is not just going to throw you out there with a heavy load on a weak little limb. No, He is smarter than that! There is no one smarter than God: He always knows what He is doing. He knows the how's, when's, why's, and where's of every thing. He knows what's best for you and me.

Prophecies cannot be fulfilled if everything has not lined up for it to come to pass. That is why it is so important to follow the specific directions of God. A prophecy coming to pass is like a huge complicated machine that works only when everything else on the machine is working correctly. If one little screw or link in the chain is off or broken, the whole machine shuts down! The whole prophecy is delayed. You have to investigate and check everything on the unit to find where the problem is and fix it before the assembly belt starts back up, and the fulfilling of a prophecy is like getting to the end of an assembly belt where the final product is completely put together, packaging and all.

My husband is a master at mechanical systems – especially heating and air conditioning and refrigeration systems. When he has a repair call, he has to do a complete analysis on the unit. The unit is not going to operate properly until everything is in its proper working condition. Prophecy works in the same manner. Everything must be in the proper order, or otherwise you will have a messed up situation. It may even look to be going your way, when - BAM - something else goes wrong.

That's the enemy come to kill, steal, and destroy your belief system that "all is well."[3] That's why it's called B.S. for belief system.[4] What's your belief system? Faith and trust, or doubt and mistrust?

Sometimes wrong can be right in the grand scheme of things. We think of wrong as mistakes, but sometimes wrongs are "blessings in disguise." Wrong can help make things right. Do not think of them as mistakes, but as miss-takes or lessons you are learning. Now, head up, shoulders back, forward -- march!

> *"And we know that all things work together for good to them that love God, to them who are the called according to his purpose." Romans 8:28*

This verse is not an open promise for everybody to claim! Always keep in mind that the decisions of others and the work of the devil in many people's lives can cause terrible grief that is outside God's perfect will. But somehow God works it all out for His purpose – TO

---

[3] 2 Kings 5:22
[4] Bishop Jordan's teachings

THEM THAT LOVE GOD, TO THEM WHO ARE THE CALLED ACCORDING TO HIS PURPOSE.

Let us talk about "living out your destiny." This term is the same as living out your dream. Bishop Jordan teaches, "Destiny is not left up to chance, but is a matter of choice." You must choose to walk out your destiny – it does not happen by chance. You do not just *happen* into your calling. You choose to be led by the Spirit. Do what you love to do – that is your destiny! Microsoft Word Dictionary says that **destiny** is:

1. Somebody's pre-ordained future.
2. The inner realizable purpose of life.
3. Something that pre-determines events.

We are all conceived then by the Holy Spirit because of our pre-destination as stated in Ephesians 1:11:

*"In whom also we have obtained an inheritance, being pre-destinated according to the purpose of him who works all things after the counsel of his own will:"*

Your destiny is calling you out. Your dream is God's will for your life. Do not go to the grave with your life unlived.

We need to learn to live our life to its full potential. We are all destined to be great because we are God's and gods, according to Psalm 82:6, and, also, the words of Jesus in John 10:34. We belong to God, which makes us God's, and we are God's children, making us gods. Mr. Smith's children are little smiths and God's children are little gods, but we must follow His directions, because Father really does know best. You will not know where you are going if you do not listen and follow directions as given.

Have you ever tried to put together a model airplane without using the directions that come with it? Or have you ever tried to assemble a bookshelf using the directions for a crib? It will not work. The goal is never achieved. Do you ever feel that you are just "spinning your wheels," working hard, but never getting anywhere? Start following God's directions and see if that helps.

## 14. WHY SOME PROPHECIES YOU THINK ARE FALSE ARE NOT

How are you at following other people's directions – people of authority? Do you follow the speed limits and traffic lights while driving? Do you follow the ushers in church, or the parking lot attendants? Learn how to play "Follow the Leader." It is practice for following the Great Leader. Once you know how to follow, the rest just falls into place. One tip, however, is to make sure you are following the right leader!

Pastor Debra Jordan taught me that, "Delay does not mean denial." Just get in line 'cause your blessing is coming down the pipe! What happens to most people is that they get tired of waiting, but we have Scriptures for that too.

- "<u>Wait</u> on the LORD, and keep His way, and He shall exalt you to inherit the land......" Psalm 37:34
- "<u>Wait</u> on the LORD, and He shall save you." Proverbs 20:22b
- "Because their office was <u>to wait</u> ....."1 Chronicles 23:28

Just because a word has not come true does not mean that the word given was by a "false prophet," or that the word itself was false.

Jonah preached that within forty days, Nineveh should be destroyed; the people repented at his preaching and Nineveh was not destroyed; yet, so far as we know, the people were not told that if they repented the judgment should not fall on them. So was Jonah a false prophet?

There are numerous prophecies like this, where God departs from literal fulfillment of the prophetic utterance – because the *circumstances* had changed – not that the prophecy or God's Word had changed or was false, or that it just did not come true. No, it was because the circumstances changed. Had the people continued as they were, the prophecy would have gone forth, but thank God, their system failure was repaired with repentance!

*"At what instant I shall speak concerning a nation and concerning a kingdom to pluck up and to pull down and to destroy it, if that nation against whom I have pronounced turn from their evil, I will repent of the evil that I thought to do unto them," Jeremiah 18:7-8.*

> *"And at what instant I shall speak concerning a nation and concerning a kingdom to build and to plant it, if it do evil in My sight that it obey not My voice, then I will repent of the good wherewith I said I would benefit them," Jeremiah 9-10.*

Then you have this: *"The Lord has sworn and will not repent," Psalm 110:4.* (In some translations it says the Lord will not change His mind.) The Lord has made up His Mind.

The gifts and callings of God are without repentance: they are irrevocable.[5] No sin of man can bar the way of God's great purpose in Christ. It is irreversible. The irreversible promises do not depend on man's goodness, but on God's. They are absolute in their fulfillment, even though they may be conditional as to the time and place of their fulfillment.

False prophets and false prophecy, if you check the Bible, is speaking of the prophets of Baal (the mythical god of rain, crops, and livestock) – the false God. The Israelites added the worship of Baal to their worship of Yahweh (God). They had one God for their crises moments and another god for everyday living. God alone is God,[6] and no other can be mixed in – you cannot worship both God (Yahweh) and Baal or money or any other thing, else you are worshipping a false god. Worshipping a false god leads to false prophets and false prophecy.

All you need to know is if it lines up with the Word of God. That's the judging that needs to be done. Does the prophecy line up with the written word of God?

Timing is everything, *"in due season we shall reap."* Trust God to bring about what He said He would. God does not lie. If you miss out on your prophecy – your destiny – because you did not do what God called you to do, it will be passed on to another, maybe in another generation – to your children or grandchildren. The "G" in

---

[5] Romans 11:29
[6] Deu. 6:4

## 14. WHY SOME PROPHECIES YOU THINK ARE FALSE ARE NOT

God stands for "generations." Prophecy sets up blessings for generations to come.

Do not spend too much time worrying over "missed opportunities." God is a God of second chances. Nothing is lost in the universe; not even a prophecy. New opportunities will come back around and you will know better next time. It is called a lifestyle of learning in the circle of life. You have had your lesson and now it is time to be tested. If you pass, you will graduate to the next level *of lessons*. Life is about building character, one lesson at a time.

God's word does not return to Him void and the prophecy shall be seen in time to come – as it has in the past. Above all things, there must be faith in God. Paul says, *"I believe God that it shall be even as it was told me,"* Acts 27:25.

God is, by the necessity of His own nature, faithful and true. His Word stands forever. He calls us to be faithful (full of faith) because He is faithful. If we refuse to believe Him, we are sinning against one of the deepest laws of our own nature – believing. When we choose to believe that God has spoken, we have nothing to do but to stand on that belief and – MAKE BELIEVE! Haven't you ever played make-believe about something and it eventually became real?

### Questions:
1. What are some reasons why a prophecy might not come true?
2. What is the difference between the psychic network and the prophetic ministry?

## 14. Why Some Prophecies You Think Are False Are Not

*"Therefore I say unto you, what things so ever you desire, when you pray, believe that you receive them, and you shall have them."*
*Mark 11:24*

It is not unusual for someone to receive a prophetic word over their life and choose not to believe it. A modern prophet called Bill Hamon authored a book called *Prophets and Personal Prophecy*. There he wrote that he had received almost two-hundred and fifty thousand personal prophecies in his life and he had not received one false prophecy, as far as he was aware.

He saw no error, because, as he matured in the Lord, he understood *more about* prophecy. He came to believe that many prophecies simply could not be understood until they had been fulfilled. The Word of God is our supreme example of this. We are often taught that the New Testament is the Old Testament revealed and the Old Testament is the New Testament concealed!

This is because, often, prophecies are written or spoken in a language that cannot be easily understood until the time has happened. If in doubt, look at Daniel, the Book of Revelation, or some books in the Old Testament on prophecy and you will realize that it is not until the things have happened that people understood the prophecy. Exact details of the birth, life, and death of the Jewish Messiah were given hundreds of years before they were totally fulfilled in every way. Yet, most Jewish people remain in spiritual blindness even today and are still waiting for their Messiah! Even the religious leaders did not recognize prophetic fulfillment in the life of Jesus and they plotted His death.

Both historic and Messianic prophecies came to pass as precisely as predicted, because they were all true prophecies of God! Therefore, if these prophecies were once considered false, is it not also possible that a misunderstood personal prophecy could be deemed false, though it is true?

A novice may claim that anyone giving a false prophecy is a false prophet, yet if I was a betting man (and I have been in the past), I

*14. WHY SOME PROPHECIES YOU THINK ARE FALSE ARE NOT*

would stake my money on what Bill Hamon has said. Even though I estimate that I have received only about one percent of the personal prophecies he has, I too must assume that, out of my fifty printed out ones, none are wrong either. If some people fail to understand what God is saying until after it has happened, then it is possible for you also to think you have a false prophecy when in fact it may be true.

Even a word of knowledge in your prophecy could be wrongly interpreted by the receiver of the prophecy. I want to encourage you on two fronts. First, when you have received a prophecy and you do not believe all of it, just put the part you do not understand on the shelf – place it on the back burner and do not worry about it. Check on it later down the track and you may be surprised at what you discover.

Second, do not worry if some people accuse you of false prophecy because most of your prophecies *will be right* and maybe that disgruntled person just does not understand their prophecy correctly. I hope that you are learning new things and are being encouraged.

Update in September 2014

It seems that a couple of people have been confused by this chapter. It is possible for people to add flesh to a prophecy, or to prophesy from a wrong spirit and therefore some prophecies can be wrong. I have already covered that in a previous chapter and so in this chapter I was not saying prophetic people are infallible. I am simply saying that you should not assume your prophecies are wrong simply because you can't understand it or it seems impossible. All prophecies that you can't understand should not be dismissed therefore, but simply put in a place in your heart until it manifests.

## **LAURIE'S REFLECTIONS**

14. Why Some Prophecies You Think Are False Are Not?

Most people are prone to believe the negative over the positive, so if you are giving prophecy based on Biblical reasons, that is to strengthen, encourage, and comfort, then people may struggle believing in all this positive stuff you are telling them. Most people have a hard time believing that they deserve the best for themselves. However, Scripture says to *believe* and you *shall* receive.

If you believe the worst, you receive the worst, but the prophet said the best, so get on board the right train and stop derailing yourself. A prophet comes to bring instruction with a blessing. You follow the instruction of the prophet and the blessing follows. You speak the words of the prophet over yourself until they come to pass (manifest.)

How can you prophesy the best over someone when you do not believe the best for yourself, much less for anyone else? How can your prophecies come true if you do not believe in them? You have to believe for yourself before you can really believe for someone else. You have to receive for yourself before anyone will believe in what you are prophesying to them. Notice how we say, "Believe it and it will come true." Maybe a word cannot come true for you until you believe it to be true? Believe it is true so it can be true. Jesus said, "…I am the truth…" Believe it true and it will be true. You make it come true with all your "make-believe!"

Sometimes it takes quite a while for things to line up perfectly for the prophecy to manifest. This is what seems like the biggest delay, but delay is not denial, because it is not really a *delay* the way we think of delay, but it is the *process* of the thing, and you have to trust the process.

We all go around our circles, thinking that we missed the mark of the high calling of God – the prophecy. That is why people begin to doubt the truth of the Word of the Lord in prophecy. This is why prophecies you think are false are not – they just have not come to pass yet. God has said: *"So shall My word be that goes forth from My mouth; it shall not return to Me void. But it shall accomplish what I please, and it shall prosper in the thing for which I sent it,"* Isaiah 55:11.

The more you believe in the prophecy and hold your tongue – birthing it before it is time or aborting it with all your doubt – the more likely you will see the prophecy come to pass in your lifetime. *"Death and life are in the power of the tongue."*

## 14. WHY SOME PROPHECIES YOU THINK ARE FALSE ARE NOT

**Questions:**

1. Is it possible to think you have a false prophecy, but you do not?
2. How long does it take for a prophecy to come to pass?

## 15. The Gift of Encouragement

*"And though I have the gift of prophecy, and understand all mysteries and all knowledge, and though I have all faith, so that I could remove mountains, but have not love, I am nothing." 1 Corinthians 13:2*

During a recent Bible study on the spiritual gifts, our group prepared a list of about twenty-two or twenty-four spiritual gifts. Next to each name we had to give a short description of that particular gift. We were told to take the list to ten people in the church, who knew us well. We each had to give these people a pen and a separate sheet of paper on which they were to write down the three most obvious gifts they saw in our life. We were not to show any of the ten people what the others had observed, but we were to keep a tally of the individual pieces of paper.

When I received the papers back, all ten said that I had the gift of prophecy. (I have a prophetic website so that was not news to me.) However, it was a blessing for me to know that all ten people confirmed that gift in me, even though most of them may have been aware of my website, but what really thrilled me the most was that seven out of the ten people also listed the gift of encouragement. Prior to our study, I had no idea there was such a gift so I certainly had no idea that I had it! It was strange, because at the time of this test, I was going through a difficult time of personal suffering. Inwardly, I was in a bad way, but others obviously saw me as a happy and encouraging person – in fact a relatively nice person to know.

If you have this particular gift, known also as the gift of exultation, you will discover that it works well with the gift of prophecy because most prophecies are just encouragement. Prophecy is meant to build up people in the Lord and to give them godly answers or directions. Therefore, if you like to encourage people, you will love to move in the prophetic.

Prophecy and encouragement fit each other like a glove ("they go together - like a horse and carriage.") Along with prophecy, you need love – unconditional love. You cannot move in words of knowledge effectively unless you have love for people. You need to love the person over whom you are prophesying more than your own reputation because if you get a word of knowledge wrong, you have blown your reputation with that particular person.

To exercise and walk in the gift of prophecy, encouragement motivated by love is ideal. Paul said: *And though I have the gift of prophecy, and understand all mysteries and all knowledge, and though I have all faith, so that I could remove mountains, but have not love, I am nothing.* 1 Corinthians 13:2

This is true! Although I tend to believe that a person could operate in the gift of prophecy without the gift of encouragement, or without love in your personal life and still do a moderate sort of job, a humble motivation from a good heart allows prophecy to readily flow! Therefore, if you are an encouraging, loving sort of person, you will move in the gift more often than a self-centered person who only wants to build "self" up. God is no respecter of persons, for there are more than enough "needs" to be addressed and there are more than enough "people" that God wants to speak to.

As you grow in the Lord, He will motivate you to talk and move in the gift of prophecy with many people, but the ability to move in prophecy with these people without hassles comes from your love for all people and the gift of encouragement residing in you.

## **LAURIE'S REFLECTIONS**

15. The Gift of Encouragement

The gift of encouragement comes straight from God, and if you want to walk in the anointing of the prophetic, you have to overcome pride and stop worrying what others will think, and just encourage the people.

It's all about love, because God is all about love; God is love. I know this, not just because the Bible expresses it, but also because the Holy Spirit told me early one morning after I had been tossing and turning all night with excruciating pain from my sciatic nerve. I could not sleep or even lay comfortably on either side. I was crying out to Him why, why! Why did I have this pain?

If you do not know anything about sciatica, it is a shot of pain from the largest nerve in the body, which, when irritated, is painful from the roots in the spinal cord in the lower back region radiating down to below the knee. Can you say "Ouch" in sympathy?

The only other time I have ever suffered with this kind of pain was during my pregnancies, which is a common occurrence during pregnancy, but I was not pregnant at this time, so I did not understand why I was experiencing it. The God-thing about this is that we had houseguests during this time and two other adults in the house were experiencing this same pain. We were all limping around, trying to "walk softly" so as not to cause any additional or unnecessary pain to ourselves.

That night I cried out to God, "What is it? What is it! Why is this pain here? What is this all about?" As dawn approached, I clearly heard the Lord say, "It's all about love - My love. Not your love, not man's kind of love but My kind of Love." Then I fell asleep.

When I woke, I put my feet on the floor, fully expecting pain, but praise God, there was none. The pain was completely gone. So I went to my houseguests and repeated what God had said: "It's all about love. It's all about His love, not man's definition of love, but of God's pure, unadulterated love for Him and for one another, as we express that love from god to god.[7]

If we are made in God's Image, then every one of us is an individual cell of God, with all of us making up the whole Body of Christ. God loves us in an unconditional way and that is how we must love others and ourselves. We all have His DNA and therefore, are all related to each other. *Love one another.*[8]

But can we do that? God's love is a love that withstands lying, cheating, stealing, and adultery. He does not stop loving us, even if we cheat on Him. He does not start loving someone or something

---

[7] Ps. 82:6 and John 10:34
[8] John 13:34

else. No, He keeps on loving us and calling us to return to him. This is how we are to love one another.

This is also why Prophet Hosea was called to marry a prostitute (symbolic of Baal worship or the mixing of faiths), to give us the example of God's love. The marriage of Prophet Hosea and Gomer was an image of God's relationship with Israel, which often betrayed its spousal covenant with the one true God by worshipping the false gods of the pagans. Hosea was to manifest God's patience and love while he had an unfaithful wife – The faithful married to the unfaithful.

(God often asks prophets to do difficult tasks. Isaiah had to walk around naked for three years as a warning to Egypt and Ethiopia.[9])

I heard Pastor Nasir Siddiki say during a marriage seminar that God loves us, even when we are unlovable, and that we need to do the same for our spouse. This also applies to everyone else, to our neighbors, friends, and loved ones – and strangers too. We need to love others even when they are unlovable.

When you walk in God's love, you will only be able to speak encouraging, loving words. I understand that God had me experience the pain with my sciatic nerve as a way for Him to communicate His message of Love. I needed to come to the point of asking Him what all the pain is about, and it's all about love. If you are having pain in your feet – check the status of your love. Start forgiving others; start excepting others. Walking in God's love straightens out everything physically and spiritually. How's your love walk?

Encouraging others is an act of expressing God's Love.

Every now and then I will feel a twinge of pain developing in my hip area and I immediately know what that means! I need to check my "love walk." Oh those bones! "The backbone connected to the hipbone, the hipbone connected to the ..." – I start loving people immediately so the pain doesn't have a chance to connect.

---

[9] Isaiah 20:2-3

Trouble walking is symbolic of you loving in a natural way with your own weak strength, not in the spirit, with God's strength and love. You have to learn to walk in love with the love of the Lord, pure love without any hidden motive or agenda. When I walk in love I am in alignment with God. (And will not have to visit the chiropractor!) Loving someone only if you feel like it or if they are nice to you can cause you a whole lot of pain in the hip! Only some people call it a pain in the a-- because the pain radiates all the way down, through and through. The dictionary says this kind of pain is a discomfort. I'm here to tell you, it's a big discomfort. The only problem causing this big discomfort is you being a pain in the a--, not anyone else but you. Straighten your heart out and the pain in your a-- will go away.

I hope I made that clear, if not: Don't worry about it because the Lord makes the *"crooked things straight," Isaiah 42:16.*

Learn to operate in the gift of encouragement with God's gift of Love.

### Questions:
1. What other gift goes well with the Gift of Encouragement?
2. What do you need for both the Gift of Prophecy and the Gift of Encouragement?

**PART 2: The Prophetic Person**

## 16. My First Experiences with Prophecy

The first prophecy spoken over me was by a Baptist pastor in my hometown, who had definite Pentecostal leanings – a rare find in a Baptist church. He prophesied that if my desire was to go and preach, then one day I would receive the opportunity to do so. I never knew at that time that his statement to me was an actual prophecy, but it certainly sparked hope within me. My next prophecy came from a Pentecostal church where I was told that I would be powerfully used by God in ministry.

In Chapter 4, I shared my early experiences in the gift of prophecy, before being baptized in the Holy Spirit. Many people assume or they actually teach that this is not Scriptural, but I can only give my testimony! To my mind, there is much confusion about these things, so I want to say a few basic things about Salvation, Water Baptism, and Holy Spirit Baptism as I see it from Scripture.

**Salvation**: This supernatural work of the Holy Spirit brings a seeker of God into spiritual union with Christ Jesus. *The Holy Spirit baptizes us into the Body of Christ.* We are "Born Again!" Some relevant passages include John 3:3-5, Romans 10:9-10,13, and 2 Corinthians 5:17. *The indwelling presence of the Holy Spirit* guarantees our new status – we are adopted as children of God, having the full royal privileges and inheritance that are legally ours in Christ. 2 Corinthians 5:21 says that Christ took our sin and exchanged it for His righteousness - we have been cleansed and forgiven of all sin, past, present, and future, by faith in the grace of God.

**Water Baptism**: This is God's will for every new believer; it is an act of public obedience to God that testifies to the kingdom of darkness that we are under new management. This physical re-enactment symbolizes the *spiritual* death, burial, and resurrection that occurred at salvation when we were united to Christ and became a member of His Body. See Romans 6:3-10.

**Baptism in the Holy Spirit**: *Here, the Lord Jesus Christ baptizes a born-again believer with the "power" of the Holy Spirit.* His disciples had already received the "presence" of the Holy Spirit, but at Pentecost His dynamic power came upon them to supernaturally equip them to be victorious witnesses to the truth of the Gospel of the Lord Jesus Christ. (See Acts 2) Earlier, they had been timid disciples, who after the Cross feared the Roman authority.

The necessity of being spiritually baptized in the Holy Spirit has brought much contention in the Bride of Christ. For that reason, there is still much opposition between the Pentecostal and the traditional churches. This ought not to be so, for we are all members of Christ's Church.

The Holy Spirit is a Divine *Person*, and, as such, He cannot be divided up like an object. No! Believers are to hunger and diligently seek His anointed power in their life from a humble heart motive and they will not be denied this baptism. (Luke 11:9-13) His gifts are still in operation as *"Jesus is the same yesterday, today and forever." Hebrews 13:8*. People may level criticism at the gifts of the Holy Spirit and say that they are no longer in operation. On the other hand, Pentecostal Christians look at their siblings in the traditional church and say that they are missing out on the gifts which God has for them.

There we have it: I grew up as a Baptist and finished as a Pentecostal and now I attend a Salvation Army church, which has some of both beliefs. I am not going to try to pick a fight with anybody, but my point is that, for a full six years, before I was baptized in the Holy Spirit, I had been prophesying.

One of my first prophetic experiences was in a taxi. A young girl and her friend climbed into my cab telling me they had skipped the others in the line at the taxi rank, and had deliberately chosen my taxi. All the way home, the girl in the front seat chatted jovially with her friend in the back. Later, after I had dropped off her friend, I turned around to her and said, "You know, all that you have said to your friend is garbage! You are not as happy as you make out. When you get home you have planned to commit suicide with sleeping tablets."

That was a word of knowledge. The girl was shocked! Her bottom lip dropped. How could this taxi driver possibly know? Why had

## 16. MY FIRST EXPERIENCES WITH PROPHECY

they skipped all the other cabs at the rank and climbed into mine? God wanted her life saved that day and He laid it on my heart to pass His message on. We then spent two hours talking outside her place. Eventually, she promised that she was not going to kill herself. Prophecy had saved her life!

On another occasion, when two girls were my passengers, I said to them, "If God was here now, what sort of questions would you want to ask Him? Often, God gives me His answers for such questions." There and then, the girls started asking questions and God started speaking through me to the girls. God is interested in the lives of all people and I love passing on His words to people.

Once, in the cab, I had six prophetic assignments one after another. It was as if God was lining up particular customers who were open to spiritual things. When the last person was seated, I had become somewhat confident that God was on the move that day. As I pulled away from the curb, I said, "And why would Jesus have you hop into my taxi today?"

The teenage boy in the back looked at me and asked: "Why do you say that? Are you on my case?" I asked why he thought that. He replied, "My grandmother keeps telling me I should never play Dungeons and Dragons, and now I think God's getting on my case."

"It would be a good idea to throw that game out." I told him. On the way to his place, I led him to the Lord. When we arrived, I reminded him: "Throw out your Dungeons and Dragons and phone your grandmother. Tell her that you have just given your life to Jesus and ask her what you should do now."

I recall that, when I was eight and I first became a Christian, Jesus spoke to me, telling me to say certain things to people. Although I did not realize it, even at that tender young age, I was already walking in the gift of prophecy. Since then, I have discovered that it is not rare or uncommon for people to begin prophesying at a young age if they have been called into the office of prophet.

When I think about it, I must have been moving in the prophetic for many years before 1998 when I actually found out that I had been exercising the gift of prophecy. Even as a Baptist not baptized in the

Holy Spirit, I had been moving in the prophetic. I guess the Holy Spirit and Jesus Christ are far bigger than any limitations we might like to impose on God! I do not consider myself unique, therefore maybe this is good news for those who have not yet been baptized in the Holy Spirit – you can still receive messages from Jesus to pass on to your friends, and you can walk in the gift of prophecy.

It was not until after many years of walking in the gift of prophecy that I was actually officially called to walk in the prophetic – and that was done by a local pastor, but we get to deal with that in Chapter 17.

## **LAURIE'S REFLECTIONS**

16. My First Experiences with Prophecy

Back in the early 1990's, when I was attending a non-denominational church, receiving a prophecy was called "get in line for prayer." The term "personal prophecy" did not have any real meaning for me until 2007.

A friend once asked me if I had ever been in a room with a recorder while people spoke over me. If the words *prophet* and *prophecy* were mentioned, I don't remember them. I told her that I had not and she said it was an awesome experience. Indeed it is!

The first Word I can remember officially receiving was "Do not be weary in well-doing," and so I continued on in my "well-doing," trying hard not to get weary. God was gently moving me into the prophetic. It was not until I had experienced greater bouts of rejection that God could truly use me or really begin to mold me – He had to break me into pieces first. (See Isaiah 30:13-14.)

I remember receiving a few syllables of "speaking in tongues," but disregarded it as "nonsense in my head." This was in the late 1980's. It did not return until 2009. I was prayed over many times for "the baptism of the Holy Spirit with the evidence of speaking in tongues." Pastors and cell group leaders would say, "Open your mouth and just start speaking." I would open my mouth, but nothing would come out!

## 16. MY FIRST EXPERIENCES WITH PROPHECY

I remember one time I was "slain in the Spirit." The pastor laid his hand on my head and said, "Double portion." My legs just buckled under me and I slumbered down to the floor. I woke up crying, and not understanding why I was crying. My friend came up to me and helped me up and said that it would be okay. She explained that I would start to hear syllables, and that I should speak them out. I explained that I had already received a syllable, but nothing else. It was a simple syllable – da, da, da – one syllable repeated three times, that's all. I "tossed them out the window," thinking it to be crazy baby talk. God did not toss any more syllables my way for a long time after that.

My friend said, "Don't worry, you will hear them again." I did, about eight years later when I went for prayer, but this time it was more like receiving instructions. She led me into speaking in tongues, based on my earlier experience as I explained it to her.

There were no lightning flashes or thunder rolls, no sudden strong urge to run around the room. No, I just started speaking in an unknown tongue, starting with "da, da, da" and then adding other syllables that you might hear babies saying when they first begin talking, "da, ma, bo, su…" or what you might hear during a phonics lesson.

I do not know how long I spoke in tongues, but once I became conscious of it, my flesh got involved – and it broke the flow. I became very aware that I was speaking in sentences because I heard myself declare and decree some things! What, I don't know because it made no sense to me. It was not in English or any other language of which I am aware.

I am not saying that speaking in tongues will happen for you in the same way that it did for me. It was just my experience and I understand that everyone has their own unique experience, but, if you have been praying for the gift of tongues -- maybe this story will help you see that God uses *"the foolish things of the world to confound the wise."*[10] Let go of your pride and let God's language

---

[10] 1 Cor. 1:27

(sounds foolish to the world) flow through you. After you speak in tongues, just say, "Amen," and agree with God.

I am not saying that you have to speak in tongues before you prophesy either. I was prophesying before I even knew what prophecy was. I would speak things and believe them and they would come to pass. I love God and talk to Him all the time in English *and* unknown tongues.

What I have learned about prophesying is this: stay connected to the prophetic to keep the gift. It takes many, many hours of practice to become proficient at anything, including prophecy. Do not waste your gift by ignoring it. Get the training you need and trust it. Come forth with your gift when you are called. The more prophecies you give out, the more accurate seeing and hearing will become for you. Prophetic training builds a strong foundation for a strong tower that will not fall.

### Questions:
1. Are all experiences the same?
2. Do you have to be an expert to start prophesying?

## 17. My Call to Be Prophetic.

*"Before I formed you in the womb I knew you; before you were born I sanctified you; I ordained you a prophet to the nations."*
*Jeremiah 1:5*

Many people use the words of Jeremiah where it says that he was called to be a prophet while still within his mother's womb. Come to think of it, "we are all called" to a particular destiny in the womb of our mother. Scripture tells us that God knew us even before creation existed and that we are all predestined to become sons of God. The important thing is that we each must personally choose to take up God's call, but many do not!

*"For His eyes are on the ways of man, and He sees all his steps."*
*Job 34:21*

God knows a lot about who we are before we are born! If you have been called to either walk in prophecy, or to be a prophet, God certainly knows it. He has planned your parents and growing up years. He has planned the environment you have been in and, in fact, He has planned your whole life. He has done all this in order to fulfill His calling in you. So, when does a prophet become a prophet if it has already been pre-planned? A prophet only becomes a prophet after an apprenticeship and after God officially sanctions them into that office.

Just as a doctor goes to a medical school to study for six years and only then can he become a "General Practitioner." (This doctor is also known as a GP.) Then he can operate as a doctor and see patients and write prescriptions, and so on. He can also go on for another five or six years of study and become a specialist such as a brain surgeon. (Of course, by the time he has completed twelve years of university, he owes a lot in university fees, to the Government!)

Wherever you live, studies are a huge investment, which has to be repaid. When you start to earn an income, you have to pay all that money back. Similarly, with the office of prophet, you do not just receive the gift of prophecy and suddenly you are a prophet. Many people assume that because they can walk in the gift of prophecy, then they are a prophet. Wrong!

Many people walking in the gift of prophecy *are* called to be a prophet, but at that stage, they are a training prophet in much the same way as a doctor during medical school. Of course, a training prophet can walk in the gift of prophecy and prophesy over people, but a person in medical school cannot operate as a registered doctor until they are one. They are in a process of being trained, and similarly, a training prophet goes through an extended period of training.

My call to the prophetic began when I started to prophesy, but my "official" calling to walk in the prophetic only happened much later at the church I was attending. One day, they had an altar call for anybody who felt that they needed prayer. I felt in my spirit that I needed to respond – my heart was heavy, so I went down on my knees in front at the altar, and the pastor came along side of me and started praying for me.

He said, "The Spirit of the Lord says that you have been operating in the prophetic for many years. However, God does not want you on your knees anymore. He wants you to rise up and move powerfully in the prophetic from this day on." The pastor continued to pray over me, then blessed me and officially anointed me into the prophetic – and from that day, there was a sharp increase in my prophetic anointing.

At about the same time, I had an apostle staying at my house and he gave me the words of Jeremiah 1:5, saying that this scripture was a prophecy over my life. He gave me a further twenty scriptures that he said were relevant to my life – it was one big prophecy, with all of these scriptures applying to me. I recall that many of them were about prayer, and praying without ceasing.

One thing is important for you to remember and it bears repeating here. You cannot go to a prophetic school and "learn" to be a prophet! No amount of teaching can make you a prophet, much in the same way that constant visits to the garage can never make you an automobile. God calls you to be a prophet, much in the same way that He calls a pastor, a teacher, an evangelist, or an apostle. For example: pastors have the gift of shepherding, counseling, and looking after a flock, but there are more people with the gift of teaching. They may be even great teachers, but some are entering the office of pastor where they should not be because they have not been called to shepherd the flock. They should be itinerant teachers, teaching the Word of God. They do not have the skill-set to be shepherding a hundred people or even just twenty!

Similarly, someone can walk in the gift of prophecy and be very good at it, but has not been called to be a prophet. The calling of a prophet of God is something that God ordains and establishes in a person's life. Moreover, just as with any calling, you can reject it by not listening to God and so miss out on God's call. I was very happy when Pastor Brian prayed for me, but having an apostle say that I am called to be a prophet was good confirmation. I have had many prophecies since, saying that I am called to be a prophet to the nations. Because I believe that faith is essential in spiritual matters, I speak these prophecies over myself.

Dear reader, if you have been called to be a prophet, you will recognize it from the welling up within you, like a flame that cannot go out. You will know it in the deepest places inside you. God will place His people in your life to confirm your calling and to prophesy over your life. Also, if you do not believe you are called to be a prophet, but feel called to operate in the gifts of prophecy, as we have discussed, that too is a wonderful gift to have. Prophecy is something you should use as often as our Lord calls you to do so.

I always look forward to those days when I am travelling, operating in the prophetic, ministering, and teaching the Body of Christ all about our Lord Jesus as a prophet. I look forward to the day when you can join with me in helping to spread the Word of God.

## **LAURIE'S REFLECTIONS**

17. My Call to Be Prophetic

We are called by God before we know we are called, and the minute we are called, things are put into motion, and so begins our training.

My life experiences, up to this point, have made me who I am today. Keep in mind that God uses all things for the good of those who love Him and we are being trained for His use through our life experiences. What then can we really be upset about?

We need not think that God does not understand what we are going through, because He does. He knows and understands it all. He knows the parents we had, He knows our upbringing, and He knows all our other "issues." It is all a part of our training.

When do you think Joseph started his training? Was it with the dreams he had as a young boy? Was it the rejection by his brothers, which ultimately led them to throw him into the pit? Was it being sold into slavery? Was it being accused of rape? Was it his prison stay? The answer: It was all of it! Joseph's "darkness" was the place of development; his character was being developed, just like film in a dark room is developed by light. But light on the film before it is ready to be exposed will ruin the film and no picture will appear.

If the film (images, ideas, imagination) is exposed to light too soon, it will cause all the pictures to be ruined. In other words, you have to go into the darkroom to develop your pictures. Do not expose them; do not talk about your ideas or prophecies especially if you are surrounded by nay-sayers – this is called double exposure. You'll get a messed up picture. Instead, go into the darkroom of your mind and meditate (develop) on God's Word until it is manifested right before your very eyes, just like the picture on the negative.[11]

Jonah heard the call of God to go and preach to Nineveh, but he was not ready to answer that call. He set sail on the sea of his own desire, which caused a great commotion among the elements, resulting in a storm. And so, he was in the belly of a whale, called "hell" in Jonah 2:2 KJV.

Job experienced storms. David experienced storms. Isaiah spoke of storms, as did Ezekiel and Nahum. What about the typhoon Paul experienced? Jesus and His disciples experienced storms. Storms (trials and tribulations, chaos, darkness, "living hell") are all training ground for the greater good of God in you. Someone once said:

---

[11] Bishop Jordan, Zoe Ministries

## 17. MY CALL TO BE PROPHETIC

"Every adversity, every failure, in fact all heartache carries with it the seed of an equal or greater benefit."

I think I have always been prophetic, calling things into being, feeling God in my spirit telling me things. I can recall "knowing things" before they were confirmed. Several occasions stand out to me when I just stood up and prophesied things into being in a desperate moment – I just decreed and declared. And the next thing I knew – there it was, in living color! It was both easy and forceful, at the same time. The most important element is your belief in the words being spoken, but everything is voice activated whether you believe it or not. The Word says it is. God said, "Let there be light; and there was light."[12]

I remember having a horrific dream one night about some type of catastrophic event and the face of a fireman looking at me up close and personal. There was smoke everywhere, people in the background going here and there, looking frantic. When I awoke, I thought, "What an odd dream." I did not realize it was a prophetic dream.

Not too much later, when the news aired the horrible event of 9/11, I saw that exact frame or picture of the fireman in my dream on my television set. The firemen and the horrific event was taking place in living color on September 11, 2001. I had seen that exact frame or picture *before* the event happened and now on my television set was that same fireman looking at me.

The Lord has done that for me several times, letting me see a thing first; I think it is so I will not be frightful or too overwhelmed when it arrives. I thank Him for that. He is so nice to me. He reassures me ahead of time and lets me know that He is still in control and that everything will be all right.

As I said in Chapter 16, my first real involvement with an officially declared prophetic ministry was in 2007. It was not until 2009 that I was ordained as a prophetess by Bishop Jordan. His ministry changed my life. My calling as a prophetess has been confirmed several times by other prophets, concurring that I am called to the

---

[12] Gen. 1:3

prophetic. To be honest, when I found Matthew on the web, I was feeling weak in the assurance of the prophetic call on my life – me, a prophetess?

Matthew came highly recommended as someone who was right on target with his prophecies. I sent in my small donation just for support; I was not really expecting anything in return because of the amount so I forgot about it. But what do you know? When my YouTube prophesy from Matthew came in – the first thing he said was "Thank you for your donation. It helps with the cost of the ministry."  Although I am used to every seed being honored with a personal prophecy at Zoe Ministries, I did not think my small amount would receive anything except maybe a thank you, but I have heard the Lord say through Bishop Jordan's voice, "The amount doesn't matter," many times.  God was telling me now through Matthew Robert Payne's voice, "It's Me, God, talking to you – thank you for your donation; it helps with the cost of the ministry." God was thanking *me for my measly donation*! Then he went on to say that I was called to be a prophetess. He even mentioned that I had already been told that I was a prophetess, which is true. Matthew was spot on.

He went on to say that there was much opposition in my life and in my background, it has not been easy, but that I should just let it flow off me like water on a duck's back, the way he does.  Let the opposition flow off me and let the word flow out of me.

*"Believe in the Lord our God, so shall ye be established; <u>believe His prophets, so shall you prosper</u>." 2 Chronicles 20:20*

How about that? Prophets are seers and this verse just happens to be 20:20, (2 Chronicles.) There are no coincidences in the way the world thinks of coincidences; nothing is just by happen-stance; nothing happens all by itself. God is all in all. Coincidences are God and man coinciding, happening at the same time, being in agreement! It is no coincidence that man placed this verse about prophets precisely at chapter 20, verse 20, causing it to be 20:20. *Believe God's prophets and so shall you prosper* because God's 20:20 perfect vision is being voiced through them. Amen and amen.

## Questions:

1. When you are called by God, are you automatically a prophet?
2. When does training begin? When does it end?
3. Is it okay to have the gift of prophecy and not be a prophet?
4. Memorize so you can quote 2 Chronicles 20:20.

## 18. Being a Strange Fish and a Fool for Christ

*"But you are a chosen generation, a royal priesthood, a holy nation, a peculiar [strange] people." 1Peter 2:9a*

Jesus told a parable about some fishermen who were sorting their catch. Some fish were kept and others were thrown back into the water. I believe that being a prophet is similar to the second category of fish, because often a prophet appears to be quite strange!

Heidi Baker of Iris Ministries visited our country in 2010, and she prophesied that many "strange fish" are going to start coming into churches throughout Australia. In the context of her message, she meant "strange" kinds of people. These people would not be the average well-to-do Christian who enjoys a seemingly well-balanced life, a stable job, a house, a car, and who lives contentedly with a happy spouse and stable children.

I believe she was talking about people whose lifestyles were close to the edge. These people may include those with heavy addictions; people who cannot hold down a job; even clairvoyants; witches; homosexuals; drag queens. It could be a host of scenarios. Maybe just people with alternate lifestyles would infiltrate the churches, and the churches would have to love and accept these strange fish. But also, as stated above, being a prophet is like being a fish out of water. Yes, being called in to the office of prophet is something quite different and strange.

I know that, as a young prophet in training, you can read the Bible and receive understanding or revelation in it that goes totally against the current or predominant teaching in the church. Again, as a young prophet in training, you can spend hours reading the Old Testament prophecies and see similar things in the church you attend or the country you live in. You can even sit in a meeting at a church and receive revelation about what God thinks about that church, and this may be different from what the actual church members believe about themselves.

However, you must also bear in mind that your revelation can be totally wrong! In order to clarify this statement, bear with me, for I

## 18. BEING A STRANGE FISH AND A FOOL FOR CHRIST

talk about personal experience now, perhaps the scriptures that you are reading at that time are not read in the context of the finished work of grace that was purchased for us on Calvary. All this can make you feel sometimes that you are a strange fish!

When you spend endless hours reading the Old Testament prophets, you can see a patient loving God with arms outstretched to His chosen people, but also you read of a harsh angry God full of wrath towards these same people! Because the majority of humans are negative by nature, the positive aspect of God is often overlooked. Therefore, His wrath is magnified compared to His love. Then, with this negative mindset, if you apply those particular scriptures to the modern day, you will very soon become disheartened with your prophetic walk. I know this feeling very well.

It takes a long while to adjust your eyes and ears to the fact that you are a prophet, that you see things differently. As you grow as a prophet, it may seem as if you are definitely a fish out of water! When you are developing as a trainee prophet, it is even a strange experience just going to church. *"For you see your calling, brethren, that not many wise according to the flesh, not many mighty, not many noble, are called." 1Corinthians 1:26*

In the next verse, the Apostle Paul went on to say that God delights in calling the fools to confound the wise: *"But God has chosen the foolish things of the world to put to shame the wise, and God has chosen the weak things of the world to put to shame the things which are mighty." 1Corinthians 1:27*

Paul said: The Wisdom of God is foolishness to men and the things of the Spirit seem foolish to "natural" man. The term "natural" refers to unsaved man. This was because *"in the wisdom of God, the world through wisdom did not know God, it pleased God through the foolishness of the message preached to save those who believe." 1 Corinthians 1:21*

You may be quietly reading the Bible and the Holy Spirit begins to reveal a certain truth, or maybe when you are moving in the prophetic and you are receiving direct information from the Holy Spirit, it can cause no end of trouble because of the worldly mind-set operating even within the church. If you start to speak that new revelation too soon, by sharing it with others, it may bring you trouble. You may be rejected, maligned, or just picked on.

People can make snap judgments and call you a fool: they can say all kinds of harsh, mean things to you. However, that is just part of the life that God has planned for a young prophet. Now, many young prophets do not know other prophets, so they do not have like-minded people to share their insights with.

Sometimes the situation that you find yourself in is simply that you are receiving more revelation compared to the average believer. You start to believe that things just do not seem to be right somehow. What you read in the Bible and what you see in the Body of Christ are often out of alignment: they seem somehow not to quite fit. When you read the Word of God as a prophet, you start to see that the Western World is struggling and battling with the things of God. You see that people are not very passionate for Him or not very committed to Him. Most people are not very obedient because maybe they are ignorant of the teachings of the Lord Jesus Christ.

Now I confess that, personally, I have a war within me. One part of me is quite legalistic and seeks to earn my own righteousness by the works I do, rather than accepting the righteousness that comes through faith from Jesus as a free gift. This legalistic part of me thinks I have to do things to be right with God, yet I know that the Bible clearly says that Christ's righteousness is mine for free, by faith!

Perhaps this truth is such a struggle to me because I spent so many years in the Old Testament! Even though salvation has *always* been by faith, the introduction of the Old Testament Law put a huge emphasis on God's wrath and personal holiness! I am aware that this was God's intention in giving the Law in the first place. God wanted to bring His people to the end of themselves so that they would respond to a Savior! Yet, sometimes I still struggle because of my old legalistic mind-set, which of course the devil loves to bring to the surface.

On the flip side, even though Christ died for us and His righteousness is ours by faith, some people claim that we do not need to obey the commandments of Jesus, nor do we have to obey the directions of the Holy Spirit that are given to us. In this area, I most definitely differ! We have been made holy and we are to endeavor to imitate the walk of Jesus by the same power inside of us that He had inside of Him – the precious Holy Spirit.

I find myself constantly fighting not to be legalistic, and yet I find some people in the finished work of the cross camp, not too zealous to live holy, "set apart" lives in word and action. I see this as a bad witness and an obvious deterrent to unbelievers! I really do love the message of the finished work of the cross preached by Joseph Prince and Joyce Meyer, but I find myself also agreeing with the middle ground thinking of Rolland Baker, husband of Heidi, who says that "holiness" is not a swear word!

## **LAURIE'S REFLECTIONS**

18. Being a Strange Fish and a Fool for Christ

Prophets do not fit in with the crowd very easily. They are definitely the "outcast." People do not understand prophets and the life that they have to walk. Even prophets do not understand at first, and cry: "Why me?" But once a prophet comes into the knowledge and understanding that they are part of a prophetic ministry (the Lord's army), they can understand the "Why's" of the past.

Prophets have some very hard lessons to learn and God uses other people to teach those lessons – be it parents, siblings, spouses, bosses, co-workers, neighbors, or even strangers – then so be it. A prophet has to know that he knows – that he *knows* that God is his source, and God will take a prophet through many tunnels if necessary to teach what needs to be learned.

With each lesson comes a test to see if you will actually act on what God is telling you. If an instruction, (and there almost always is one), makes you look strange and foolish, do it. When you are standing in line at the grocery check out and the lady ahead of you can't pay for her groceries because her card did not go through and she is about to leave the counter – you step up and say you will pay for them – she and everyone else nearby will look at you strangely. *(But you are a chosen generation, a royal priesthood, a holy nation, a peculiar* [strange] *people…1 Peter 2:9.)*

Anything that seems foolish to others will also seem strange to you. Perhaps they will find the above Scripture and say, "Hey! We are supposed to be strange people!" "Strange" always gets people's attention. They will start to pay more and more attention to you and, before you know it, maybe they will buy into whatever it is that makes you strange! For, after all, strange seems to be working for you.

I am a strange fish and a fool for Christ.

### Questions:
1. Do prophets "fit in" usually?
2. What does 1 Peter 2:9 say that we are?

## 19. Learning Obedience

*"Though He was a Son, yet He learned obedience by the things which He suffered." Hebrews 5:8*

When we were children – well, when I was a child – I was dealt plenty of slaps. Moreover, if I was considered to be really out of line, the slaps became beltings. Does that sound familiar? As we mature and we become Christians, it seems you can casually participate in some sin and it seems you can get away with it. God does not appear to act the same way that my father once did!

Because there is no harsh or immediate punishment by God, learning to be an obedient Christian can be a difficult thing. In Hebrews Chapter 12 it says that God chastises those He loves by giving us warnings to repent and to change our ways. Sometimes, if we do not change our ways, we suffer because God allows something to happen in our lives that causes us a certain amount of discomfort. This may be God's way of training us and disciplining us to become obedient children. Just like an earthly father wants the best for his children, even more so, does God, want the very best for His kids!

Jesus told His disciples three times in John Chapter 14 - verses: 15, 21, and 23 that if we love Him we will obey His commandments. Love and obedience go together! Many people readily call Jesus their Savior, yet not a lot of them are like the Apostle Paul who identified himself as being a bondservant to Christ – a happy willing slave to Jesus Christ.

The idea of being a slave to Jesus does not appeal to many believers, but if you are going to walk in the office of prophet, then you must learn to obey the Lord. Only the obedient servants are raised in levels of anointing and promotion by God. A difficult part of a prophet's job description in the body of Christ is to bring correction where there is error. If you are not personally living a life of obedience, purity, and holiness, then how can you bring correction to a church that is in error?

I heard it once said, "That a prophet can only speak on things he has experienced and lived through." Certainly, a life of obedience combined with faith in a powerful and gracious God allows you to live the scriptures. If you are going to share the truth of the Bible, you first need to address your level of personal obedience. (In proclaiming that, I am certainly not advocating that you should live a perfect life because only our Savior did that!) We all daily fall short in the obedience department.

One day, the Bible says, I will be perfect and that *I already am in my spirit!* But perfection of my soul will not happen until the instant of my physical death or the rapture of the Bride of Christ! In the meantime, we are to be constantly aware of God's leading and His grace in times of personal repentance.

In the first draft of this book, I was using the fifty-five video series. These videos were never edited in any way: they are raw. (I believe the word today is "unplugged.") My only preparation for making the videos was a burning desire to share my love of the prophetic and to encourage others to be bold.

The only thing that I actually wrote down was a list of the Chapter titles that I believe the Holy Spirit gave me. I did not even have a list of Bible verses nor did I have any notes. In my mind, however, I had heaps of verses but not their particular addresses. Therefore this finished book has had a great deal of editing work. This is because there is a vast difference in unrehearsed spontaneous speech and actual typed words on a page. The videos simply gave me a book framework.

However, in both the video series and the edited copy of the book, I want people to realize that I speak from my belief that Jesus, in human flesh, would have had to learn things just like we do today. Scripture alludes to this fact: *"Though He was a Son, yet He learned obedience by the things which He suffered." Hebrews 5:8*

Obedience is always an act of personal choice! In the Gospels, Jesus made more than fifty commandments: things He said to do, or not to do if you are His disciple. Therefore, the life of obedience is to walk and live in those commands. He was our example: He loved His Father and always did only what the Father commanded. If you love God and have His love for your fellow man, obeying those fifty commandments of Christ is walking in obedience in the power of the Holy Spirit – just like Jesus did on earth.

To be an effective prophet – a prophet of change – you need to take directions from the Holy Spirit. You need to have a scripture or a sermon given to you by Him, so that it is right for that specific moment. You need to walk into a church, not with a prepared sermon, but in faith be willing and bold enough to speak the timely message from the Holy Spirit for that particular congregation.

In the same way, you need to approach a person and give them a message that the Holy Spirit has for them. In summary: you need to be obedient to the Holy Spirit when it comes to ministering God's love to people inside and outside of the church building.

If you are in tune with the Holy Spirit, He may call you to speak a hard message in a spirit of love! This "correcting word" is meant to edify and not to pull down, so that it will promote repentance which will lead to a change in outward behavior. The church may be having a problem in one particular area and you are to be willing to be God's tool for the job. If you are a person who just wants to preserve your good name, then you will not be able to do that! To obey God in the big things, you need to obey God in the little things. If you are called to be a prophet and you are obedient, this will result in the anointing and glory of God.

As stated in the very first chapter, the Lord told me to write a book through a prophecy interpreted by a dream. Because I wanted to be obedient, God gave me the enthusiasm to quickly begin on the project. I admit that I procrastinate in some things, but when I am excited about something, I am very different! Some things are difficult to do, but God never promised anyone a lazy or an easy life – He promised a bountiful life to all who obeyed His Word.

The Christian race is not run on a smooth stroll in the park. No, it is more of a steeplechase where you have to jump over some serious obstacles. In fact, Jesus will give you things to do that are difficult for your flesh. You cannot run around the obstacle, you need to jump over it! Obey the Lord, and do not even ask Him: "How high?" Jesus promotes His people according to their ability to obey His Word and the Holy Spirit. Your attitude determines your altitude!

You are never going to progress far with the great things of God unless you learn to be like Paul: a bondservant of Jesus.

## **LAURIE'S REFLECTIONS**

19. Learning Obedience

In the Old Testament, the prophet Daniel was miraculously kept safe in the lions' den in order to glorify God to a heathen people. But, in the case of the prophet Jonah, who was running away from God, a particular fish was appointed and prepared by God to bring about a work of correction or chastisement.

This ocean creature placed the prophet in "safe custody" but in a confined and uncomfortable way. Then, in due time: *"the Lord spoke unto the fish, and it vomited out Jonah upon the dry land."* Note: Jonah was not vomited out into the watery ocean but onto his own natural habitat! God is always good, even during times of correction!

In the New Testament, our Lord was kept safe "among the wild beasts" for the forty days of His wilderness experience. The Holy Spirit had led Jesus into this position because He had to first overcome the temptations of Satan before He could begin His public ministry.

Summary: Jonah initially disobeyed God's commission to go to Nineveh, but the prophet Daniel and our Lord Jesus Christ had both willingly been led by the Holy Spirit into the appointed place of testing.

Jonah's fish and also, the prophet of Balaam's ass, were two creatures used by God to bring correction to a human being and both prophets, Jonah and Paul, learned obedience as a result. Therefore, we know that God's prophets today can expect correction whenever it is necessary and in whatever form that is expedient.

We see from Scripture, that being "in the pit" brings us to obedience to the Lord. Obedience is a lifestyle that brings blessings with it.

## 19. LEARNING OBEDIENCE

Personally, in the past, I seemed to have learned obedience often through my disobedience (like Jonah.) Then, in hindsight, I always wished I had "simply obeyed" in the first place. I am working on learning to obey in the first place, and not as a final resort.

But regarding the blessings of obedience, I still miss the mark sometimes and a bunch of what feels like setbacks occur. In my spirit, I know that obedience is the only way to successfully reach my destiny, but my will is not yet perfected; I am working on it daily. The way to that next level is obedience. It is not always easy, but it is necessary. It is a setback as a setup for the way up.

The Word is God speaking, but only when you act upon the Word is the Word a Living Word (Heb. 4:12.) God sent His spoken Word (the Living Word made flesh, John 1:1, 14,) to show us the way, and He speaks through His prophets, *"Neither have we obeyed the voice of the Lord our God, to walk in his laws, which he set before us by his servants the prophets."*[13]

One of the first lessons a soldier learns is unquestioning and prompt obedience. *"He that is not with Me is against Me,"* Matthew 12:30. Our obedience is the measure of our allegiance and there is no neutral ground; you are either with Him or against Him. God seeks enlightened, willing, whole-hearted obedience, *"...bringing every thought captive to the obedience of Christ,"* 2 Corinthians 10:3-5.

### Questions:

1. What constitutes real obedience?
2. How did Jesus learn obedience?
3. Can you be lazy and still do God's work?

---

[13] Daniel 9:10

## 20. Developing a Deep Relationship with Jesus

*"If anyone desires to come after Me, let him deny himself, and take up his cross daily, and follow Me." Luke 9:23*

It is interesting that people often refer to a person walking in the office of prophet as a "friend" of God.

The Old Testament says: *"And it shall come to pass afterward that I will pour out My Spirit on all flesh; your sons and your daughters shall prophesy, your old men shall dream dreams, your young men shall see visions."* Joel 2:28

Even today, God makes Himself known by dreams and visions. A prophet should have such an intimate relationship with the Lord Jesus Christ that they are open to receive what the indwelling Holy Spirit is saying to them.

Most Christians talk about Jesus, whilst I prefer to talk with Him. A preacher may say in a sermon: "This is what I think Jesus was thinking." But I believe that, if a Christian comes across a puzzling passage in the Word, they can personally ask God about it. I often ask Jesus: "What were you thinking then?"

Many people know about Jesus as a historical figure. Also, many may praise Him for coming to earth and for His atoning death on the cross. They even praise Him for both the power of His name and for the power of His blood. They praise Him for all that His death and resurrection accomplished. However, when it comes to Monday to Saturday, some of these Christians do not live a life that shows that they love Him more than they love the things of the world.

Few of His disciples are doing the work that Jesus has told them to do! This includes being able to preach the Gospel or just sharing the good news of the grace of God and His love for all people. Some believers talk about Jesus, and their love and affection for Him, yet they choose not to obey Him. Jesus said: *"No one, having put his hand to the plow, and looking back is fit for the kingdom of God." Luke 9:62*

## 20. DEVELOPING A DEEP RELATIONSHIP WITH JESUS

I wondered for many years why people who are genuinely born-again cannot hear from God. John Paul Jackson solved this riddle for me. A believer may initially be able to hear the quiet prompting of the Holy Spirit within them, but over time, they lose this capacity to hear. There often comes a point in many Christian lives, when the Holy Spirit tells them to do something, and they do not do it. They are aware of the prompting within, but refuse to obey it.

At that disobedient point, they unknowingly switch off from the still quiet voice of the Holy Spirit. That is the same as taking your hands off the plough. John Paul Jackson went on to say that if they want to hear the Holy Spirit again, they should just remember what He told them to do, then go and do it, and the Holy Spirit will start to talk to them again, so that they will clearly hear. Earlier, Jesus had said: *"If anyone desires to come after Me, let him deny himself, and take up his cross daily, and follow Me." Luke 9:23*

Denying yourself is something relatively unknown in the Western world even among believers. It seems that self-denial is abhorrent to some modern Christians. A life of self-denial, of putting others first and the Kingdom of God before your own needs, lusts, and wants is just something strange to the West. Unbelievable!

You can only develop a deep relationship with Jesus through obedience to His Word and to His promptings. Obedience involves taking up your cross and doing what He says. Jesus was saying that we can only develop a deep relationship with Him by self-denial and following in His footsteps. What would Jesus do? Discover exactly what Jesus *did do* and then: *"Go do it!"*

A rather pious and self-satisfied Jewish Lawyer enquired of Jesus how to gain eternal life. Then he asked: "Who is my neighbor?" In response, Jesus told a parable about a merciful Samaritan who exercised godly compassion to a stranger, *in the same way that he himself would like to be treated.* Our neighbor is therefore anyone! Jesus wants us to adopt a similar attitude of compassion and mercy to others in need. Walking through big cities, you will see many homeless people sleeping on the pavements or shop doorways. A good neighbor would at least acknowledge such a person, or try to assist them in some way. They would not look the other way as if the person did not even exist!

You can develop a deep relationship with Jesus by obeying Him, by reading about Him, and by regularly talking to Him, not only in prayer, but in the everyday circumstances of your life! Involve Him in everything! Treat Him as your close and special friend and share everything with Him. These are the ways to have a deeper relationship with Jesus. If you truly love Him, you will automatically find yourself doing these things, just like two lovers share their innermost thoughts. God truly desires this level of friendship with all of us.

By developing a closer relationship with Jesus, you can help His kingdom principles of heaven to invade earth: you become part of the solution instead of the problem. Instead of being self-centered, you will make other people focused like Jesus did on earth. Walking in the prophetic office is just one way of ministering to others.

Becoming a close friend of Jesus allows Him to share with you the knowledge to build up His church and to repair individual lives. I genuinely believe that, if you do not purposely foster this type of relationship with the Lord, then you will not have God's kind of love and compassion in your heart and the mind of Christ will remain a mystery to you.

Also, the revelation of Jesus by the Holy Spirit comes by prayerfully reading the Bible. The Holy Spirit works first in your spirit, then in your soul area, which includes your mind, emotions, and decision-making ability, then lastly your body will come into line with God's will. You will want to become a worthy ambassador for God by becoming a "little Jesus" to your generation. Your area of influence will be enriched by both spending time in drawing close to Jesus and by simply putting into practice the things that He has commanded you to do!

To become a prophetic person, you need to develop a deep relationship with Jesus. He said: *"No longer do I call you servants, for a servant does not know what his master is doing; but I have called you friends, for all things that I heard from My Father I have made know to you," John 15:15.*

## LAURIE'S REFLECTIONS

20. Developing a Deep Relationship with Jesus

We have a brother in heaven; a brother who knows all and keeps up with everything, eventually making all things work together for our good. The eye of Jesus is upon us; the ear of Jesus is open to listen to our cries; the heart of Jesus is touched by our woes; and the tongue of Jesus is employed to intercede with His Father for us.

His strong arm will defend us; His merciful hand will supply us, and His tender heart will sympathize with us. He guides us and protects us with His counsel. We should expect Him to show a brother's love.

The deep relationship comes from being in His Word, by leaning on Him, by believing in His Word. The Word is Life. You cannot depend on someone else's relationship with Christ to get you through hard times, and you simply cannot depend on the pastor's relationship with Christ to get you through hard times either. You need your own personal relationship with Him. Once the introduction has been made, it is up to you to build on that.

When people stop talking to one another, the relationship dies out. If one day goes by and you do not hear a peep out of your spouse or your children, you will wonder where they are and go looking for them. You will search until you say, "Oh, there you are; where have you been? I've been looking all over for you."

It is the same with Christ, when you notice the silence, you must look for Him. The kingdom of God is within – You will find God deep within you, talking, for the Lord is always talking. He is waiting for you to hear Him and answer. Being a friend requires both listening and talking; that is how a relationship is started, and then you start doing things for Him because He has been doing things for you all along.

A prophet comes on the scene to change things. Everywhere in the Word, where you see a prophet, you see a problem, and the prophet brings the solution. Prophets and prophetesses fix things. Friends love to help a brother out of a difficult situation and there is no situation too difficult for your friend and brother, Jesus.

Back in the early 1980's, I told God that I would read his Word – if only I could understand it. Not long after that, an acquaintance walked up to me and handed me a Bible. It was an easy-to-read <u>Today's English Version</u>. She said, "I don't know why, but the Lord told me to give you this Bible. I have lots of Bibles at home and He told me to give this one to you. It's brand new."

I smiled and said thank you. I understood completely. Just tell God what you need and He will give it to you, even if it is an excuse you are giving Him – He will call you on it just to prove to you that it was only an excuse to get out of something you did not want to do. Bishop Jordan teaches that an excuse is nothing more than a guarded lie. Do you think I read that Bible? Only for a short while, because it was really just a lie that was guarded by a statement that sounded good. I would read the Word if only (here comes the lie) this, or if only that. THOSE ARE EXCUSES! God took away all my excuses, one by one, until I had absolutely no excuses left, and it was just me and my Bible.

I guarded the lie so well that even I did not understand that it was a lie. I just thought I didn't have what it took to do I what said I would do. I was not determined at all, that's all.

As God took my excuses, (such as the Bible is too hard to understand, there is not enough time in the day, I do not know where to start. I go to church every time the door is open, blah, blah, blah – excuses, excuses, excuses) I eventually began to understand that He was calling me to attention. He wanted me to attend to Him.

God's timing is perfect, and it is based on alignment. Is everything aligned for His perfect Will in your life? It was His Will that I join a prophetic church, but I needed to educate myself in His Word first, so the sooner I got busy studying, the sooner He would put me in touch with the right ministry. You have to know the Word to share the Word. You have to know Christ to share Christ.

## 20. DEVELOPING A DEEP RELATIONSHIP WITH JESUS

I took the long scenic route, but not everyone has to. Do not fight Christ; embrace Him. He will take you where you have never been before, if you stay close to Him and meditate on His Word (day and night), *"that you may observe to do according to all that is written therein: for then you shall make your way prosperous and then you shall have good success," Joshua 1:8.*

The Lord eventually took me out of church all together for one reason or another: I got my feelings hurt, church is just too far to travel, there are no churches near me that I care to attend. He finally had me where He wanted me – alone with Him and His Word!

As soon as the Word gets in you, you are developing a deeper relationship with Jesus. The minute you speak the Word or the Word has been spoken over you, the enemy tries to kill, steal, and destroy that seed – that Word; the Word is the seed of every solution to every situation. Reading the Word keeps the Word alive in you and keeps your relationship with Christ alive.

There is no better cleansing than the cleansing of the Word of the Lord. It's time to get washed by the Word.

### Questions:
1. How can you begin and continue to develop a deep relationship with Jesus?
2. Can you be an effective prophetic person without that deep personal relationship?

## 21. Getting to know the Father

*"I will be a Father to you, and you shall be My sons and daughters, says the Lord Almighty" Also, the Son said: "I am the Way, the Truth, and the Life. No one comes to the Father except through Me." 2 Corinthians 6:18 and John 14:6*

This second verse is probably one of the most controversial statements Jesus ever made of Himself. It is also an integral verse to the prophetic and to Christian life. Jesus is categorically declaring that He is the only way to the Father because He is the embodiment of all truth, and He alone is the source of eternal life. Unless you know Him, you cannot know the Father! Many people pray to the Father, but they do not know much about Jesus. These people "assume" that they have a relationship with God. However, John 14:6 nullifies that assumption!

People can know about Jesus, but when you really KNOW Him, you will see Him as the Bible proclaims Him: King of Kings and Lord of Lords. Jesus said: *"Why do you call me 'Lord, Lord' and do not do the things which I say?" Luke 6:46*

Jesus said: *"If you love Me, keep My commandments...He who has My commandments and keeps them, it is he who loves Me. And he who loves Me will be loved of My Father, and I will love him, and will manifest Myself to him...If a man love me, he will keep My words: and my Father will love him, and we will come unto him, and make our abode with him. John 14:15, 21 and 23*

If Jesus IS Lord of our life, our faith in Him will produce the obedience He desires. In fact, He will call us His friends: *"No longer do I call you servants, for a servant does not know what his master is doing; but I have called you friends, for all things that I heard from My Father I have made known to you." John 15:15*

In contrast, Jesus went on to say in John 14:24, *"He who does not love Me does not keep My words."* Earlier, in John 12:48 He said: *"He who rejects Me, and does not receive My words, has that which judges him—the word that I have spoken will judge him in the last day."*

## 21. GETTING TO KNOW THE FATHER

*"The word that I have spoken will judge him in the last day"* – I can testify that my Christian life had a definite turn-about when I saw in the four Gospel records that Jesus had spoken fifty individual commands to His disciples. These, in reality, call us to love God above all else and to love our neighbor as much as we love ourselves. You will not travel too far in the prophetic if you do not genuinely love God because you will not have His love for other people!

It is only through fellowship with Jesus that you can develop a relationship with the Father. You need to desire with all your heart to hear Him speak inside of you and to develop the sensitivity and the necessary discipline to take time to listen to His voice. It is wonderful to know the thoughts of Jesus and the Father about yourself, your loved ones, about His church, and in fact, His thoughts about all kinds of things.

Once, a few years ago, while I was in bed speaking to Jesus, He told me that in the future, I was to pray to the Father. I panicked for a second until Jesus told me I could still talk to Him but I had to start to address my Father in Heaven when I prayed. That night I tentatively spoke to the Father and simply said: "Hello." He replied, and we had our first conversation! I also took my petitions to Him. For years now, this relationship has been growing closer and deeper.

If you are called to be a prophet, then you are called to understand the things the Father has said. Moreover, the Father has spoken both through Jesus and the Word of God. Therefore, if you have a good relationship with the Father, the Word of God begins to make sense. You will receive more revelation about God's nature as you read and listen for Him to speak to you.

The more you understand and know God, the more you will understand the message of the Old Testament. Christians tend to major on the New Testament, but the Old Testament sets the platform for the New. It is very important to have the correct balance between the revelation concerning the "holiness" of God and His "Father-heart" of mercy and grace towards His chosen people.

For example: people who know me really well will understand my specific mannerisms and my unique Aussie vocabulary. They will understand my stories far more than those who do not personally know me. The latter may only hear the message, but miss out on the depth of meaning behind my stories or my message. In the same way, the more you know Jesus, the more you will understand His heart and His message for you.

People are always talking about God, but I have been in the Throne Room and have talked WITH God while I was there on three different occasions! I can tell you that it is exciting to know the Father. People often wonder if they are going to make it to heaven. When you have been to heaven as I have, then you KNOW that heaven will be your eternal home! I will talk about this in later chapters.

The Father is an exceedingly wonderful God! Many people are totally ignorant of His awesome goodness for why else would they disobey Him? Why else would they do the complete opposite of what He has said to do in the Bible?

*"Do you not know that friendship with the world is enmity with God? Whoever therefore wants to be a friend of the world makes himself an enemy of God,"* James 4:4.

Why do people constantly look to the world for pleasure, for recognition, for love and acceptance, for knowledge or satisfaction in life? People only settle for less when they are ignorant of the things that give lasting peace, fulfillment, and joy. The world was created for our enjoyment! God was very pleased with all that He had created. However, God has a spiritual enemy and sin entered the world. Therefore, the world is no longer as God originally designed it to be.

The closer you come to God, the more you can leave the troubles and wicked schemes of the world behind. In fact, you will begin to love what God loves and to hate what He hates. This spiritual change is called: "The fear of the Lord" and it is the beginning of all wisdom and understanding. The reverent fear of the Lord gives you freedom to be the person God wants you to be. You will become more active in your prayer life so that the kingdom benefits in Heaven will begin to transform your life on earth and also the lives of those you pray for. Also, the reverent fear of the Lord will lead to a life of obedience to the Son. This willing obedience leads to an intimate relationship with God.

In your progress toward becoming a prophet, you come to know the Father, and knowing the Father is an enjoyable experience. If you have not received a vision of God, then you need one, and maybe you need to ask God for one. You need to *know* Father God in order to come into the office of prophet.

My prayer for you: *Dear Father, Please reveal your presence to the reader in a way that they will understand. Please lead them in their prayer life so they will draw closer to you. Please make yourself known to them in visions and dreams so they can grow closer to you. Instill in them the passion to move in the prophetic and to move in your ways. In Jesus' name, I ask. Amen.*

## LAURIE'S REFLECTIONS

21. Getting to Know the Father

God is preparing you and has been preparing you since the day you were born for your ministry as a prophet or prophetess – it is all for the work of the Lord. *"We are the children of God: and if children, then heirs; heirs of God, and joint-heirs with Jesus Christ," Romans 8:16-17.*

We are not orphans! We have a Father. God, in all His glory and perfection, is our Father. He has adopted us for His own. He has regenerated us by His Spirit. He has called us out of the world, and has promised to do a Father's part by us. He says, *"I will be a Father unto you."*

People do not know what they do not know. When they know different, they will do differently. Until then, people are just people. They do what they think is right for them; they look to the world for pleasure, recognition, and acceptance. They look for love in all the wrong places.

Do you want advice? Consult your Father; He is a wonderful counselor. Do you have needs? Ask them of your Father; *He supplies all your needs according to His riches in Glory by Christ Jesus.* Are you tormented with cares of this world? Cast all your care upon your Father because He cares for you. Are your enemies "driving you crazy"? Your Father is an enemy to your enemies! God is not just a Father in name; He has a Father's nature. He not only calls us his sons and daughters, but He wants us to call Him – Daddy.

We should trust in God's Word; we should appeal to His paternal heart; we should look for our supplies in His Hand. In everything, by prayer and supplication <u>with thanksgiving</u>**,** we should let our requests be made known unto God. He loves to see us confide in His care, rely on His Word, expect His love and favor, and agree to His Will. I repeat: *"We are the children of God: and if children, then heirs; heirs of God, and joint-heirs with Jesus Christ," Romans 8:16-17.*

By expanding on John 14:6, we can see that Jesus was saying "I AM" is the **Way**, I AM is the **Truth**, and I AM is the **Life.** In the previous verse, Thomas had asked Jesus, "How can we know **the way**?" Turn to Genesis 3:24: *"So he drove out the man: and he placed at the east of the garden of Eden Cherubim, and a flaming sword which turned <u>every way</u>, to keep <u>the way of the tree of life."</u>* The way is the tree of life. The "way" is Jesus for He is eternal life. (See John 17:3 and 1 John 5:11.)

*"God so loved the world, that he gave his only begotten Son, that whosoever believeth in him should not perish, but have <u>everlasting life</u>," John 3:16.* Finally: *"<u>In Him was life; and the life was the light of men,"</u> John 1:4.*

Do you see the connection within these Scriptures? If you know the Truth, you know that I AM is the Way and the Life, and I AM is Truth. God told Moses that His name is I AM; God said: I AM THAT I AM. (See also John 8:58 where Jesus used the "I AM" name for Himself.)

## 21. GETTING TO KNOW THE FATHER

Who are you saying "I am" is? Every time you say, "I am…" You are declaring that God is that! Your "I am" should reflect your Father. Jesus said, *"I and my Father are one."* [14]

Do you know Jesus? Not so much His history of who His physical father and mother were, but rather, do you know what He stands for, His principles? The only Way of getting to know the Father is by getting into His Word, praying, and meditating on it, which is what is meant by "through the Son" – the Word made flesh.

I have been in church for as long as I can remember. However, it was not until I dug into His Word that I began to have an inkling of what it really means to be a Christian. I full well understood what it meant to be a religious freak – but not Christ-minded. I knew from many years of church attendance how to add a bunch of do's and don'ts to my life and the lives of my children, just like the Pharisees in Jesus' day. Only when I studied for myself and got under some great teachings, was I able to "get understanding." (See Psalm 119:104, Proverbs 4:5, 7; 16:16) and be set free from the bondage of religion! I had to become Christ-conscious.

I am certainly not church bashing because I truly believe each church I have ever attended has been a stepping-stone for where I am today. So praise God for them.

### Question:

1. Why do people constantly look to the world for pleasure, for recognition, for love, and acceptance, for knowledge or satisfaction in life?

---

[14] John 10:30

## 22. Getting to Know the Holy Spirit

*"I will pray the Father, and he shall give you another Comforter, that he may abide with you forever."  John 14:16*

I have been a Christian for thirty-five years. However, I must say that it is only in the last year that I have been really getting to know the Holy Spirit.

For many years, I really was not close to Jesus because I lived in disobedience and in a sexually immoral lifestyle. In those prodigal years, I had tried to overcome my perceived rejection by my earthly father. Therefore, like many others, I was not open to knowing God the Father. Only when emotional healing came, was I open to address and speak to Father God. However, over the years, I have become closer to Him, so now I know Jesus and the Father.

In the two proceeding chapters we spoke about being close to the Father and His Son. However, as I said, it is only in the past year or so that I have started to know the Holy Spirit. I look back now and realize that while I was talking to Jesus, it was actually the Holy Spirit conveying the words of Jesus to me and while I was speaking to the Father, it was actually the Holy Spirit conveying the Father's words to me. Isn't God good! God knows where we are at and lately I have been instructed to do things by the Holy Spirit. It has not been Jesus – it has been the Holy Spirit – and now everything is in order. It is a wonderful experience!

The Holy Spirit is the ideal personal assistant. Sleep patterns in the past have been a huge problem to me. But the Holy Spirit convicts me when I should be up and when I should sleep. He reserves a vacant seat for me on the bus I need to catch, in order for me to give a specific fellow-passenger a word of encouragement. He knows what time I should leave work. He knows what groceries I need and the people I am to speak to. He guides my daily conversations and plans my day perfectly. The Holy Spirit is truly a genius in personal organization.

Christians may be aware of the Jezebel spirit, but that is not part of our fifty-five chapters. Although I am not addressing this particular spirit, it is very much a part of a prophet's life. People with a Jezebel spirit come against the prophets all the time and I must say that the only way to outmaneuver this evil distraction is to continually walk in the Holy Spirit.

To have your life directed by the Holy Spirit is absolute genius – yet He is so humble. Just as Jesus always did and spoke the Father's will, the Holy Spirit always reveals the Lord Jesus Christ. He never, ever, glorifies Himself in any way, but gives all glory to Jesus or the Father. He is very gentle and patient. At the baptism of Jesus, the voice of the Father was heard and the Holy Spirit was depicted as a dove hovering over the shoulder of Jesus. All three members of the Trinity were present at that memorable and historic day!

The Holy Spirit is like a popular person who is important in the world's eyes, but who is reclusive or privately shy within. Maybe you perform publicly on the stage and do grand things because that is part of your job, but privately you are shy and reserved. You are quite happy to be silent at the table and let someone else take the stage. That is the Holy Spirit!

He is happy for God and Jesus to receive all the attention and glory, while He brings the anointing into the room so people can give their adoration to "Them!" As I have discovered, the Holy Spirit can direct your day. He can keep a personal diary and tell you where to go, what to say, and how to say it. The Holy Spirit has the answers to all your questions. He can remind you to do things and He can tell you how to do them.

The more you are in touch with the Holy Spirit; the more you can be directed by Him. For years, it was just Jesus telling me to perform specific actions. Recently, it has been the Holy Spirit because He has replaced the voice of Jesus.. So now, when I talk to Jesus, it is by choice. I ask Jesus a question. I talk to Jesus. When I talk to the Father, it is by choice, but all the other instructions now come directly from the Holy Spirit.

He performs mighty miracles! The Holy Spirit is the one who manifests the anointing of God and performs all the mighty miracles of God. As a prophet, you want to know the Holy Spirit and be sensitive to His voice. It is wonderful to know the Holy Spirit as a person moving in the prophetic – knowing that He wants all praise, prayer and worship to be directed to the Lord Jesus.

To me, the Holy Spirit is like a good actor in a film who always passes accolades to the director, the producer, and the writer of the film. The actor himself may stress that he had a great script to work with plus a good director. He gives honor where it is due. That is who the Holy Spirit is! He loves you. He led you to Christ. He led you to this teaching. He will lead you to better things. Always allow Him to lead you.

It has been a year now since I made the videos that became a platform for this book. Now I have known the Holy Spirit for a year. It is exciting to be told that you left your mobile phone at home before you are too far away. It is great to be directed around the place and have divine appointments continually. It is fun to talk to the Holy Spirit occasionally and to have Him as your friend. I pray that the Holy Spirit becomes more precious to you in your prophetic life than just His outward manifestations.

## **LAURIE'S REFLECTIONS**

22. Getting to Know the Holy Spirit

Jesus understands that our sorrows are sometimes so deep that human comforters are just not enough, so He promised to send the Holy Spirit to be the Comforter for His earthly family. The Holy Spirit is a Divine Person. He can search the heart, pierce the clouds, penetrate all recesses, and ascertain the true cause of all our sorrows. His tenderness and love are infinite, therefore He can console in the most efficient way. It is His work and delight to comfort.

Our earthly friends may fail us or prove to be miserable comforters to us; but the blessed Holy Spirit can and will comfort us to the end.

If you are busy with your own thoughts, it is hard to get to know the Holy Spirit because He is a "soft speaker," and cannot be heard over the rumble of your thoughts. So if you are being stubborn and refusing to acknowledge that the Holy Spirit is speaking to you, He just might cause a donkey to speak in a language you can understand! I bet that would get your attention!

The Holy Spirit is gentle; He keeps the flow moving in the gentle way He guides. There is no drama with the Holy Spirit. Have you got drama going on? Don't speak to it. It will always speak more drama back. Look around you, where is it coming from? Retreat within and seek God; meditate on His Word for a while. Let the Holy Spirit give you His Peace.

When there's chaos, you say, "Let there be peace." You tell a person you will get back to them later, that you need to think about the situation before you make a decision. Don't let someone called Drama pressure you into something you will regret later. Let the Holy Spirit guide you in all your decisions.

One day, the thought "orthodontist" popped in my head and about thirty minutes later, the orthodontist called to schedule an appointment. When you know the Holy Spirit, He will "drop" information in you so that you will have an idea of things that are headed in your direction and you can make plans accordingly or pray over a situation, or give a prophecy. The Holy Spirit is way cool.

The other day as I was turning a corner aisle in the grocery store, without thinking I grabbed a box of garbage bags. When I returned home I was so glad I did because I saw that I had used the last one that morning.

When you follow the leading of the Holy Spirit, you will be able to operate on auto-pilot. You will just go and do, following the Holy Spirit throughout your day. At the end of the day you will be able to review and see God's hand in your life at every turn.

My mother-in-law had accidentally packed her two cans of "Restor-A-Finish" before she had a chance to use them, so we made another trip to Home Depot and repurchased them, along with an extra can. She said she just felt like getting three. Later, when her sister-in-law came to visit, that extra can was given to her as a gift so she could finish a certain cherished piece of furniture on her own.

I told my mother-in-law that she was operating in the Spirit. Spirit knows all things and had prompted her to purchase that extra can of finisher, and because she did not question it, but just did it, she was able to be a blessing when her sister-in-law came for a visit.

Big and small, God is all in all. We are spiritual beings, being led by the Holy Spirit. You are at the right place at the right time for the right reason in the right season; your steps are ordered of the Lord. Keep your receptors on so you can hear what the Spirit is saying.

When you are ministering and the person is unsure if they have received the Holy Spirit (speaking in tongues is a gift; it is not the only manifestation and it is not a requirement of your being filled with the Spirit) – 1 Corinthians 12:3 says, *"...no man can say that Jesus is the Lord, but by the Holy Ghost."* If a person can say, "Jesus is Lord," then they are speaking by the Spirit. The Holy Spirit is leading them or else they could not have spoken those words. They may not be "filled" yet, but they are being led and that's the first step to being filled. It's just that simple.

Getting to know the Holy Spirit is such an essential part of being in the family of God. We know that God is the Father, the source of all authority, and Jesus is the firstborn of many brothers. Both are of the utmost importance in respect to our spiritual life, but we also need the Holy Spirit who is like a comforting mother – guiding, nurturing and comforting her child.

### Question:

1. What do you need to be able to say with all sincerity to receive the Holy Spirit?

## 23. Getting to Know the Bible

*"Study to show thyself approved unto God, a workman that needeth not to be ashamed, rightly dividing the word of truth."*
*2 Timothy 2:15.*

There are people who start blogs, YouTube accounts, or post various videos about false prophets and false teaching on the web. They are warning others about all types of heresy because people are being deceived, but if you know the Father, Jesus, and the Holy Spirit and you study the Bible then you cannot be deceived forever. If you have a healthy relationship with God and are walking in obedience, the Holy Spirit will give you revelation of the Bible that will correct deception in your life.

For much of my life I was a legalist. I believed that God loved me for what I did personally. Because of my work mentality, I was into rules and obedience as a way to please God. I argued that the Old Testament Law was very relevant to a Christian. I thought that my salvation depended on my own goodness. *(I must warn you that the actual videos from this book were recorded before I had emerged out of that teaching, so they have legalistic leanings.)*

Thankfully, since making the videos, God wonderfully broke through with His messages of grace and the finished work of Christ on the cross! But for most of my life, I was deceived. As I said: If you have a healthy relationship with God and are walking in obedience, the Holy Spirit will give you revelation of the Bible that will correct deception in your life.

It is easy to cast stones and pick on other people. Earlier, as a training prophet, I saw errors everywhere! As I matured, I have come to understand that it is up to deceived individuals to realize their own errors. We have been given the powerful and living Word of God to use as a spiritual weapon, as Jesus did against spiritual opposition. Our Lord did not debate with Satan; He defeated his temptations with God's own words in the Old Testament.

A wise Prophet of God told me that the secret of reading the Bible was to follow a balanced reading plan. His own daily plan was to read two chapters of the Old Testament starting with Genesis, then one chapter of Psalms, one chapter of Proverbs, and finally, two chapters of the New Testament starting with the Book of Matthew. If pressed for time, just read alternatively, once chapter of Psalms OR Proverbs, then read one chapter each of the Old and the New Testament. To our detriment, we tend to have our own favorite Books of the Bible and neglect others.

The Bible gives us hope in our problems: *"And we know that all things work together for good to those who love God, to those who are the called according to His purpose," Romans 8:28.* If you love and trust God, then everything that happens to you will ultimately work together for good! That is a comforting promise. The devil may try to abort God's plans for our future, but God will have ultimate victory in the lives of those who love Him.

Seriously, if that scripture were not in the Bible, I would have committed suicide at one terrible stage in my life! Getting to know the Word of God is an essential tool for a Christian. You can of course read books about the Word of God, but there is nothing as powerful as receiving YOUR own revelation directly from the Holy Spirit! Reading about the revelation of others does not guarantee that you will receive THEIR revelation. Also, reading the Bible is the only way that faith is developed! See Romans 10:17.

If you know the Triune God, His Holy Spirit will lead you from scripture to scripture to bring home a particular point. He will personally unveil that scripture so that it becomes part of you. He will repeat this process again and again with other scriptures so that you build up a personal arsenal against the enemy and a reservoir of verses to strengthen your faith in God's grace, holiness, mercy, love, and power.

It is the Holy Spirit who will lead you through the Word of God - passage by passage, revelation by revelation, so that you know your full inheritance as a child of God and the power of the Word, the power of the Name and the power of the Blood of our Savior. Without the presence of the Holy Spirit, much of the Bible is very dry reading.

## 23. GETTING TO KNOW THE BIBLE

So, what is meant by the expression: "the Holy Spirit's presence?" First, know that He is continually present with every believer, but we need to draw close to Him! It is rather like the way you feel at church, when you have been genuinely praising the Lord for half an hour in the atmosphere of corporate worship then suddenly worship and praise becomes very private as you are overcome with His awesomeness. You feel the sense of God's peace and joy, and His love and grace all around *and in you in a very precious way!*

You need to take time to consciously develop this spiritual awareness before you read the Bible each day. Spend time just quietly praising and worshipping the Lord, or be in prayer for about twenty minutes so that you feel that same presence come upon you. That is when you should open the Word of God and actually begin to read His Word. He will speak to you as you read.

Holy men of God inspired by the Holy Spirit wrote the Bible, and if you know the Divine Author, then you can understand more of what He says. Then, when you read God's Word, it becomes exciting, rich, and full of revelation. You begin to discover more about the Holy Spirit, Jesus and the Father and you will want to spend time with each of them. You can only understand the Bible by spending much time in it. The Holy Spirit's discernment and correct Bible knowledge stops deception in its tracks.

There are many deceiving voices today - there is even deception among those pointing out deceptions. Jesus said in Mark 13:22, *"For false christs and false prophets will rise and show signs and wonders to deceive, if possible, even the elect."* Why did Jesus say, "if possible?" Was it because the elect do not get deceived? If you know Jesus, the Father, the Holy Spirit, and the Word of God, you are in an excellent position to identify deception and expose it.

Be careful not to just study the Bible to simply acquire spiritual "knowledge" as this type of study puffs up, it creates pride in the reader. Actually, any knowledge can make a person prideful, but the practical application of knowledge in the right way is called *wisdom*! A prophet particularly needs the wisdom of God. Moreover, a prophet needs to personally apply the Bible by walking in the correct application of it before they can teach and bring correction to others.

Are you willing to pay the price of disciplining yourself? You must enjoy the Bible in order to teach it. You also need to enjoy spending time with God to be a good prophet.

## **LAURIE'S REFLECTIONS**

23. Getting to Know the Bible

God is a genius. The Bible is the Greatest Book ever written and always will be. He has spoken, and the ordinary language of our time is made eternal and spiritual. For example, Jesus took the word "bread," and gave it a holy and spiritual meaning. When we pray: "Give us this day our daily bread," we are seeking the nourishment that shall sustain us in every deed and need as He is the Bread of Life.

Make the Word of God your word and it will work for you. It is well worth the time and effort (work.) The New Testament will reveal the old to you afresh as you launch out into the deep thoughts of God.

Knowing the Bible is like being a farmer who knows his land. He should know how much land he has; how much is forest and how much is pasture; where he should plant his corn, okra, and potatoes. Once he knows all about his land, he can begin the work to produce a harvest and prepare to reap the benefits of knowing his land.

Fill your mind with "the great thoughts of God"; by knowing the Word, you will know your full potential, just like a farmer knows the full potential of his own land.

The Bible is awesomely self-interpretive if you give it a chance. Just start at Genesis and read the book. You will have to sit down and take the time to actually read it chapter by chapter, verse by verse. It takes time to get to know the Bible, but it is time well invested. There is no reason to feel overwhelmed or inadequate. The Lord leads, guides, and protects you when you rest in Him. He will bring the right teachers to you.

The Bible is the Library of the Grace of God. Looking back over the books of this library, bound together in a single volume, we find biographies, letters, lyrics and poems, speeches, histories, and all sciences. That's why a very good pastor friend of mine has written a Bible-based Christ-centered grade school curriculum.[15] "It bases every lesson on a passage of Scripture and brings all thoughts to Jesus Christ."

The Bible is the handbook of patience and comfort. Through this Book, we learn that it is possible to descend into the valley of the shadow of death, confidently declaring that you will not be fearful of any evil, *"for Thou art with me."* When there is no peace such as the world can give, we read: *"My peace I give unto you."* The Bible is a treasury of solace. It is a *"refuge from the storm, a shadow from the heat, when the blast from the enemy is as a storm against the wall."*[16] The wise go to it, and read it when the way of life is beset with difficulty because there is comfort in the Scriptures.

It took about sixteen hundred years to write the Bible. Think about it – this book took sixteen centuries to write. It was originally written in several languages (Hebrew, Arabic, and Greek.) Sixty-six books with one supreme subject – the Son of God in His varied forms – it is Christ-centered, a book of order, filled with life, love, and warfare, written to quicken the minds of the sons of men.

One way to get to know this Great Book is to compare Scripture with Scripture. It is written that in His light, so we shall see light. An illustration of this can be seen by comparing Revelation 19:15 and Ephesians 6:17. The sword out of His mouth in Revelation is explained by Ephesians to be the sword of the Spirit, which is the Word of God, and so the sword out of the mouth (the tongue) is simply the declaration of that Word reigning over the nations.

Matthew 25:1 is explained by 2 Corinthians 11:2, the virgins of Matthew equaling the assembly of Christ presented as a virgin in Corinthians.

You must study slowly. You cannot "cram" the Bible. You must chew your food well before you swallow it, or you will choke on it. *"Thy words were found, and I did eat them; and thy word was unto*

---

[15] Bedell Curriculum, http://www.bedellcurriculum.com/
[16] Isaiah 25:4

*me the joy and rejoicing of mine heart: for I am called by thy name, O LORD God of hosts."*[17]

Read carefully. Get all the light you can get. Examine every word and subject with a microscopic investigation – a fine-tooth comb; don't read over verses. Dig into the original if you can and get some help if you cannot.

Be patient. If you do not understand today, you may tomorrow. Put it on a shelf, as they say. The advancement in truth is in proportion to the use of truth. Reading the Bible is much like eating cooked fish – don't choke on the bones, but put them aside – difficult things will be revealed later. God will bring meaning to the bare bones of the Bible as you grow in maturity through your own life experiences.

When you are reading God's Word, His breath and presence are in it. Revere the Word. Obey the Word. Pray the Word. Live the Word for in the Word is Life Itself.

Finally, pray for illumination – for opening *"the heart to attend unto the things spoken," Acts16:14.* Endeavour to make it a daily practice to read and always to study something, no matter how unimportant it may seem. Please have a daily devotional even if it is only five minutes.

The Bible tells the story of Light, Sun, Moon, and Stars, of the deep Sea and melted Rock, before astronomy, or geology were ever mentioned; it waits patiently until Science stops all its hypotheses. It reveals to those who read it that the only opposition ever made from Science is not from Science, but from *"Science falsely so called."*

*"O Timothy, keep that which is committed to thy trust, avoiding profane and vain babblings, and oppositions of <u>science falsely so called:</u> which some professing have erred concerning the faith..." 1 Timothy 6:20-21 KJV*

*"Timothy, guard what God has placed in your care! Don't pay any attention to that godless and stupid talk that sounds smart but really isn't. Some people have even lost their faith by believing this*

---

[17] Jeremiah 15:16

*talk. 1 Timothy 6:20-21 The Learning Bible, Contemporary English Version (CEV)*

Christ is in every line. He is the key that unlocks every mystery! Christ and His Church point back to the First Man and his bride, and the river under the throne becomes the reality of the river of Eden!

*"Study to show thyself approved unto God, a workman that needeth not to be ashamed, rightly dividing the word of truth," 2 Timothy 2:15.* I cannot quote this Scripture enough.

Those that spend time getting to know the Bible will see the rooting of its unity in Genesis and the fruiting of its unity in Revelation.

**Questions:**
1. How many things work together for the good of those who are called according to His purpose?
2. How many things is God aware of?
3. Is there anything missing from the Word?

## 24. Being a Prophet in Training

*"I have meat to eat that ye know not of." John 4:32*

Wearing a diaper (nappy) as an adult would be terribly humiliating – but that is what it can be like for a prophet in training. Some people read the Word of God and spend much time in the prophets because they are attracted to their lifestyle – for there are many prophets in training who do not even know that they are called to be prophets!

These people have a burning desire to know truth and they particularly enjoy reading books on the prophetic. When they read about the prophets in the Bible, they begin to seriously departmentalize things around them. They may think: "Boy, this verse sounds like my family, or America, or the world! This whole chapter sounds like God is furious with the world, or the church, or my church! Wow, these verses describe a false prophet – it sounds just like some so-called prophets in the world today. This verse is talking about pastors, preachers, and priests in the world. This is amazing stuff!"

In hindsight, reading the Word of God and seeing the whole world through a prophet's eyes was extremely frightening to my legalistic belief system! My whole belief system was void of God's grace! My belief was HEAVY to carry!

I aggressively argued with anyone who proclaimed "once saved always saved!" I saw it as a cop-out for not living holy. I would read the Gospels but I did not bother with Paul's writings in the epistles of the New Testament. I was addicted to the prophets in the Old Testament and saw God as being an angry, vindictive, holy God causing pain and havoc and bringing judgment on people.

I thought: if He did it back then, He can do it now, and I was sure that He could do a number on me if I was not careful. I lived with fear of condemnation. I was desperately trying to achieve, yet I kept failing.

When reading Jeremiah 23, and Ezekiel 34, I was sure the prophet was talking about the modern church and contemporary preachers, and I was certain that God was going to pour out his wrath on all those people. It is dreadful, having all that "revelation" and people not understanding and refusing to listen to you! In my case, I was seriously out of order in my theology and also I was very sick for years. Despite all that, criticism from others does go with the territory! It is to be expected when you are a prophet in training.

A baby's behavior is accepted because of who they are. However, when you are a prophet in training, it is as if you have become a baby again. It is embarrassing. There is plenty of rejection. You feel as if you just want to get rid of the mindset and the revelation you have and you feel sick to your stomach. You feel that you are wired differently and you do not fit anywhere! You are different – you are very strange! People even avoided me.

We talked in Chapter 18 about being a strange fish. If you profess to talk to Jesus Christ – you are just strange; you do not fit the mold of a typical Christian. Things worry you; things start to get on your nerves. You start talking to God and God is talking to you. Yet it is amazing, the revelation, the pain, and the trouble that all this causes you. The more knowledge you receive, the more puffed-up you get – in your pride you think that you are better than anyone else, because you have all the answers and everyone else should listen to you. Looking back, I was an arrogant, angry, frustrated, self-opinionated man, before I was set free from legalism.

Being bound by legalism is like training to be on a football field, never allowed to play in the game, but always standing on the side lines. God has a reason for you being a prophet in training. God has a good reason! My mother was always insistent in sharing with me: "God doesn't care *what you do,* son - He cares *who* you are! He hasn't called you to *do*: He has called you to *be!*"

Doing things for God and pleasing Him had always obsessed me! It seemed that my mother's advice was illogical: to accept that God did not look at my achievements, but cared far more for my character development and loved me through all the necessary stages was crazy! But now I realize that the reason why God puts a prophet in training is that He wants to develop their personal character. Moses was over eighty years old when God called him to rescue His people. At the beginning of the exodus, young Joshua began to show leadership potential, but it was another *forty years* before he actually took over from Moses! (He had been constantly mentored by Moses for all that time.)

David waited a long, long time between the time when he was anointed as king and when he actually sat on the throne as a king. *"And the period that he reigned over Israel was forty years; seven years he reigned in Hebron, and thirty-three years he reigned in Jerusalem." 1 Chronicles 29:27.* His desire was to build a beautiful temple for God, but he was denied this because he was a fighting man.

Jesus, at the tender age of twelve, was holding his own in the temple, to the amazement of the Jewish leaders! (Luke 2:47.) Yet, even He had to wait until He was thirty before He could start His ministry. Eighteen years He waited, because it was not God's time for Him. Jesus returned home and increased in wisdom. Later when he was ready and was again teaching in the temple, it was said of him: *"Where did this Man get these things? And what wisdom is this which is given to Him, that such mighty works are performed by His hands!" Mark 6:2b.*

If you are a prophet in training and you have not yet been released into the pulpit, be patient. I can identify with you. You have not been able to do things for God, even though you have much knowledge! You are frustrated that no one understands. Listen to me, I understand. I have been there, *and I am still there!* I have only preached a few times aside from my videos on YouTube; I am still working through the process of coming into my office and becoming used full-time by the Lord. He is smart. The Holy Spirit, the Father, and Jesus, they are so smart: they know exactly what they are doing!

Like it was the case with me, God needs to develop your character, your patience, your love, and your compassion, so when He releases you into the pulpits, you will be pleasant and kind to people! Right now, you may at times, want to bring fire down from heaven on people in much the same way as the disciples wanted to smash people! Right now, you might be full of the entire wrath and judgment of God, but He wants to develop the fruit of the Spirit in you. This is an essential time for the prophet in training – that time between obtaining the ability to prophesy and actually prophesying in a pulpit. Waiting to be acknowledged by fellow prophets can be a long and painful training process.

For you to develop the character to be properly used by God depends on how sovereign God is in your life, how hard your head is, and how much knocking about you need by the affairs of life.

## **LAURIE'S REFLECTIONS**

24. Being a Prophet in Training

There are many adults running around in diapers… Diaper-wearers cannot swallow anything other than babies' milk. They can only drink milk and eat food that has been mashed to a pulp. We can forget about serving them with solid meat or strong drink (wine). They cannot handle it. Anything meaty is much too hard for babes in Christ to digest. They are unable to even chew on it for they have no teeth – how long will they remain babes?

*"For every one that uses milk is unskillful in the word of righteousness: for he is a babe. But strong meat belongs to them that are of full age, even those who by reason of use have their senses exercised to discern both good and evil," Hebrews 5:13-14.*

A prophet must be willing to chew and then swallow the meat and then the mystery of the Word of God. We must learn to stand, receiving a firm foundation, partaking of the meat of the Word of God. Jesus said, *"I have meat to eat that you know not of."*[18]

Yet, when a pastor starts to get into the meat of the Word, people want to get up and walk out of church. Notice how there is usually a smaller crowd on Wednesday nights? That is when the real meat of the word is preached. Only a select few Christians can handle the meat. And forget about the mystery; start preaching that and people will start calling you crazy! For more information on the mysteries of the Kingdom you should do a Strong's Concordance search of the word "mystery" and read each reference and cross-reference.

---

[18] John 4:32

It is time for the Church to grow up and begin eating the meat from the Master's Table and get off the bottle! You must eventually learn how to be sustained from a balanced diet. It is a new day, so do not worry that you are hearing things that you have never heard before! It is time for you to learn to "chew the cud" of your spiritual food – manna from heaven. Chew it really well, meditate on it, and then meditate on it some more.

The meat of the Word takes time to digest and produce fruit. You must learn to wait on the Lord; His timing is perfect. He knows exactly when to open and shut doors, but while you think you are waiting, you are really in training. There is no waiting – it's all training! Learn to be patient; it helps things go faster and smoother.

When the Lord gives, He gives the seeds of things. He gives, so to speak, the raw material. When He gives us bread, it is not in the form of a loaf ready for the table, but in the form of grain, which must be planted, toiled, gathered, grind, and baked, and so it is in the spiritual realm as well.

Someone with a natural ability and spiritual grace, rightly cultivated, would be of high service to the Lord. There must be development and opportunities for increase in this natural ability, making it supernatural. This is the reason for a school of prophets, whether the school is a physical school or the school of life. Schools of prophetic training are for the purpose of bringing increase.

One of the BIGGEST "helps" I can give you is to let go and let God. Just let the past pass you by so you can move forward in your training. Hanging on to the past keeps you stuck in the past but the future is now!

Being a prophet in training is like being in the pit with Joseph. It is a time of intense opposition and if you do not know if you are a prophet in training, a life in the pit is a sure sign that you are being prepared for the prophetic ministry.

"Prophet in training" may sound glamorous, but it is not! It is anything but that! Mostly, you may feel very unworthy or unqualified to be in the position of prophet. I mean it is just not the same as doing nursery duty or teaching children's class at church. I am not putting these positions down at all. I went beyond the call of duty when I was serving in these positions. They are important, indeed, and volunteers are always needed.

I missed a lot of opportunities to serve because I hesitated one second too long on the call for prophets and the moment was gone. With each missed opportunity, I realized I was feeling less and less like a prophetess because "what you don't use, you lose!" You really have to stay active in the prophetic to keep the flow going.

Just like any river, if there is no activity going on, no movement, the water gets stagnant. There must be a flow and the flow is from the head down. What is your leader calling you to do? Do not miss your opportunities to serve when the call is made. God is not going to force you to work for Him. He is ever so gentle; coaxing you, yes, but forcing you – never.

## Question:

1. If everything a prophet does or says must be 100% perfectly said and done, how are prophets to be trained?

## 25. Learning to Deal with Revelation.

*"Iron sharpens iron." Proverbs 27:17*

We have previously touched on this briefly, but we need more detail. As a prophet in training, the Bible will increase in richness. We all want more Bible revelation from the Holy Spirit. You want to understand the way God thinks so you can line up your thoughts with His.

In giving much time to reading the Bible, we become focused, driven, or very excited about God and His purposes. Also, the more the Holy Spirit reveals to you, the more passionate you may become. Therefore, it is very important that you learn to deal with the revelation that you have been given. Bear in mind that revelation is more often a growing process revealed over a lifetime.

Not being able to express yourself in the pulpit may result in overwhelming frustration! You may be denied the opportunity to teach on the revelation you have received because you still need to balance personal emotion with the insight God has given you. Over the past few years, I have found a wonderful way of expressing and expounding revelation. I have been writing articles and sermons online. Also, I have been producing various YouTube videos.

I hope that people will understand in years to come – while those articles and videos are still on the internet, that: "Yes, he *was immature* in his early days, but he has definitely grown a lot since then." I know that God *has* already forgiven me for the wrong things I've said in the past for He saw my passionate heart! In hindsight, I was "over-the-top zealous" about my belief system when trapped in ugly legalism! I am so thankful that God's grace has rescued me!

Since then, I have learnt that it is important to be part of a group of Christians, rather than a radical lone ranger! There are many precious revelations in the Bible, and faith is strengthened when you openly verbalize your views within the Body of Christ for *"iron sharpens iron," Proverbs 27:17a.*

I know now that spending all my time in the Old Testament was personally detrimental and also was to others. I had become too

## 26. CONQUERING PRIDE

focused on judgment and Law. I became an angry prophet until I truly embraced the grace of Jesus Christ's death for me. I recall that one day at a conference, I spoke to Rolland Baker, and he asked me why there were so many angry young prophets around. I testified of my own walk with God and told him that most prophets in training spend all their days in the prophetic books in the Bible. They then come away with a judgmental attitude.

I found it difficult to both read about holiness and to understand what it required as well as to deal with a whole host of Christians who seemed to have no regard for sin and righteousness. I struggled with this problem, yet in my heart I knew that I too, was a *dreadful sinner,* despite my claims of personal holiness. I was justifying my actions by comparing myself to others *instead of having Christ as my only benchmark and seeing my sin in the light of His purity*

How do you deal with new revelation? We know that one negative way is to become puffed up with pride. Because you genuinely think you have so much "knowledge", you constantly accuse pastors and whole churches of error! In fact, the country is wrong – everyone is wrong but you! This type of reaction can happen if you have a smidgeon of law mixed with grace. When you are of a legalistic leaning, you point a finger at everyone! What you consider revelation of the Holy Spirit *is very often imaginations of your own making!*

*"For whoever shall keep the whole law, and yet stumble in one point, he is guilty of all." James 2:10*

What do you do with a verse like that? I really detested it! Before I came into the revelation of God's amazing grace, I was an extremely difficult person to reason with. I wanted to delete that verse from every Bible! I truly thought I was right and everyone else was out of order, either partially or totally!

In my deluded state, I was the only one who cared: I was the only one with the right answers. Like me, some trainee prophets may go from church to church bringing down fire and brimstone judgment on Christians. This is all they know because this is what they genuinely believe the Holy Spirit is telling them to do. *Pride whispers: Christians need to be warned-don't they?*

Some Bible revelation can lead certain types of people to depression or it can lead to dangerous levels of passion and zeal, causing a person to be susceptible to a cult! In contrast, many young prophets I have seen on YouTube make great videos with tremendous insight and revelation. YouTube is just a fantastic place to share information with others in a practical way and to receive feedback for things you have said. Good feedback is encouraging, but even negative feedback causes you to ponder and dig deeper into things. So all feedback is useful!

You need to deal with new revelation in your life in a practical way. If it continually builds up and there is no outlet opportunity, it can cause depression, frustration, anger, judgment, pride, and all kinds of unhealthy and negative feelings or outbursts. Even writing a personal journal is a positive way to express revelation. Share with God and talk things over with Him. Deal with it somehow and do not just bottle it all up.

Try not to become a judgmental, fire-and-brimstone prophet going from church to church, being kicked out for making prophecies over the people and warning them of God's impending judgment like I did! In fact, I know of many people who have done the same thing. I pray that my confession may perhaps prevent you from this error. I have been totally honest with you and I pray that God will use my mistakes as a positive warning to others.

## **LAURIE'S REFLECTIONS**

25. Learning to Deal with Revelation

If you feel justified by the law, you have fallen from Grace (Galatians 5:4.) Yield to the Holy Spirit and feed your new nature. It is impossible to be feeding both the old and new natures at the same time. You must consciously choose one over the other. To do this, it is important to be connected to "like-minded" people, people who believe as you believe. Sometimes that can be hard to find, but you can find them, even if it is an on-line church or a conference call.

Stinking religion comes in when you mix law and grace. Grace replaced the law. Law is still good, yes. It is good to keep the laws, but it is God's grace that covers us. Law actually keeps us physically alive. It is good not to kill or steal; otherwise you end up in prison, but Grace keeps us spiritually alive. Pastor Joseph Prince does a great job teaching the harmful effects of mixing God's Law with God's Grace.

In the past, I have been overzealous when revelation is revealed to me; I've wanted to share it with my companions right away, before God's timing. I've jumped the gun many times. I understand now that God reveals in *part*; the rest is yet to come. Meditate and let God unfold the revelation of the whole – and then it will be time to share. It is all in God's timing.

Revelation is a growing process to be revealed over time, as God would have it. God will let you know when and what to share. Write the revelation down in a journal and pray over it. Talk to God and ask Him if this is what He wants you to share and if there is any more to it. Is it what the Bible is clearly saying? You have to do some digging and search the Scriptures to make sure all related Scriptures have been covered to get the full understanding.

When you only use part of the Scriptures and not the whole *that is* when the revelation is not quite the revelation you thought it was. What God is doing really is leading you to search all the Scriptures.

He brings light on a subject just so you will *"study to show yourself approved unto God, a workman that needeth not to be ashamed, rightly dividing the word of truth."*[19]

That is key: We need not be ashamed if we study the Scriptures. Then we will know the truth, the whole truth, and nothing but the truth – so help us God.

In recent years, God has brought me into some mind-blowing revelations that obviously have been in the Scriptures all along, but I did not have the eyes to see, or the ears to hear. Life experiences have a way of bringing you into the light. (If you travel in the

---

[19] 2 Tim. 2:15

darkness long enough, you will reach the end of the tunnel where the light shines bright.)

You can choose to read and meditate and ask God, "What does that mean?" and wait for His answer, or you can be like Jonah; he went his way, along life's waves, being tossed here and there until, eventually, he ended up on shore and said, "Okay, I've had enough, Lord. Please show me the Way."

Every church has its own message – what God has laid on the pastor's heart to preach and teach. I say that with a disclaimer that the preacher must be a God-fearing, God-loving, open-eyed, open-eared man of God, who seeks and searches after God's heart, and teaches what God is saying to him. Those who are not that way will preach the message of their own heart.

Learn to write out the revelations God is giving you and meditate on them day and night and He will appoint a special time and place for you to reveal them.

### Question:
1. List some ways of dealing with fresh revelation.

## 26. Conquering Pride

*"God resists the proud and gives Grace to the humble." 1Peter 5:5*

It is said that Jesse's youngest son, David, picked up five stones and managed to conquer both Goliath and the Philistines. That is true, but today the Philistines and Israel are still fighting each other. Why?

Although, David slew Goliath, there is always a fight against pride. You may conquer it largely in your life, but pride is always around, trying to raise its ugly head and this can often cause trouble when you receive a high level of revelation and knowledge. *"Knowledge puffs up." 1 Corinthians 8:1.* Too true!

People may have an understanding, or limited understanding of the Bible, but lack practical spiritual maturity. They have knowledge about the Bible, but not in a personal way. This knowledge puffs them up with pride. Revelation can also be like that! You need to incorporate positive and practical outworking of the revelation, so that any built up pride will be diffused!

For four long years, regardless of what time I went to bed at night, I could not get up until three or four in the afternoon the next day. Every day, I would wake up chronically depressed and extremely tired only to take some sleeping tablets to fall asleep again within a few hours. My sleep pattern was totally out of balance. Therefore, I started to stay awake for two days a week to break the cycle and to get myself out of depression.

My own body clock caused an intense form of torture for four years, but it seemed to smash most of the pride out of me. In that period, I busied myself by writing Christian articles on the Internet. In addition, this writing helped to circulate the revelation I was reading in the Bible and other books. Now I am comfortable with myself and I never cease to praise God for natural sleep.

I can assure you, pride is terrible! I found fault with everyone! My closest friends had the same prideful manner and we would gossip together. We wanted to do things better and differently, but no one would give us an opportunity to prove our superior knowledge. The

Bible says in James 4:6 and 1 Peter 5:5 *"GOD RESISTS THE PROUD, BUT GIVES GRACE TO THE HUMBLE."*

Later in James 4:10 *"Humble yourselves in the sight of the Lord, and He will lift you up."* Do not ask God to humble you – we are told to humble ourselves. Believe me, you do not want to be humbled by God, but He can and will do it if necessary, and in some circumstances He will use others to do it for Him.

I suspect that David may have been somewhat prideful – although he truly loved God – because he went through much refining before he was eventually raised as king. It's essential to conquer pride! I know many powerfully anointed men who are incredibly humble – they are servants of everybody! Privately, they do not talk a lot, yet they are marvelous platform speakers full of the wisdom of God. When they mingle with people, they are always asking questions and listening. They have so much humility. Because of my prideful background, my desire would be to be like them one day but I know that any hidden pride in me must first die!

We need to find a positive outlet for frustration because mostly it comes from selfishness which is the root of pride. Determine in your heart not to speak badly about others and speak modestly of yourself and be a servant to all.

## **LAURIE'S REFLECTIONS**

### 26. Conquering Pride

What a topic for me, the Queen of Pride! I would not have believed that of myself, because for a long time I thought I was a very humble person, and I was quite proud of that fact! So prideful was I! And so here is my story and how God handled (and still handles) my pride:

To feed my low self-esteem, I filled my plate up with many deeds for others, being the people-pleaser that I was, running here and there, being the taxi driver wherever anyone needed a ride, providing shelter if they needed a place to live, doing what I could do to fix their situation while my own was a mess. I did not know how to say no.

## 26. CONQUERING PRIDE

In the meantime, my health was deteriorating. I finally went to the doctor and he put me on high blood pressure medicine. I took it for a while, but then became too prideful to take it. I convinced myself I didn't need it.

As time went on, I had headaches that became so severe that I could not lay my head down at night – the pressure was too great. I had nosebleeds for no apparent reason and little perfect circles of blood rose up to just below the surface of my skin on my arms and legs. What finally sent me back to the doctor was when, after a brisk three-mile walk, the lady next to me said, "You are not sweating at all! Look at me! I'm drenched." I looked; she was drenched, but I had not one single drop of sweat -- I was sweat free.

Sweat is needed to regulate your body temperature properly and help rid the body of toxins. Sweating is important to your survival – of course we ladies politely call it perspiring.

Most people know what I am about to tell you: You must drink water if you want to be healthy. You must drink water if you want to live. Well, I did not like the taste of water, so I did not drink it. Oh, my! I was definitely a hot mess! Needless to say, I love water so much now that my body craves it whenever I get slack in drinking it.

There's a real problem when on a hot, sunny, summer morning you have walked three miles at a brisk pace, and yet you have not a drop of sweat.

When I went to see the doctor, he rushed me to the hospital. He said that my blood pressure was at "stroke level." I was put on an I.V. and medicine was administered to me every twenty minutes for two hours! I left the hospital with two prescriptions in hand with orders to go to the doctor within the next week.

Once at the doctor's office, I asked if I could please just take one prescription for one ailment. The doctor looked at me and said that one of those prescriptions was the strongest medicine on the market but it was not strong enough for me, so I had to take a second one. Ouch! Pride just punched me in the stomach… I was a healthy gal! I never got sick! I never had to take medicine, especially the kind that they say once you start taking it you will be on it for the rest of your life!

But that is not the end of my story. Several months later, I was having a phone conversation with my grown son and I did not like the way our discussion was going. He had called me to *question me* about a recent conversation I had with his wife. He was telling me he was choosing to believe his wife over me! What! I carried him for nine months; I gave birth to him and he is telling me I should have "known better" and that he automatically believed her over me?! Well! I never…! And then a wonderful thing happened: I just "let go" and said "okay" and got off the phone.

I relinquished my need to be right! I simply said: "Okay" and ended the conversation. As I hung up, I literally felt the heat leave my body, right up and out of the top of my head. It was a miracle! I checked my blood pressure a few minutes later and indeed my blood pressure was twenty points lower. It was not too long afterwards that I noticed the stronger medication was too strong for me. It took my blood pressure way below the norm and made me extremely dizzy.

I no longer have to take "the strongest medicine on the market" and now I am down to only one pill, not every day, but every other day. I had let go and overcame my prideful self, concerning my child, and realized that he is a grown man and not a momma's boy (thank God) and I wanted him to choose his wife over me and be head of his household as God would have it. I still have this ugly issue of pride to deal with, it seems almost on a daily basis, but now I am able to recognize it and overcome it. *"To him that overcometh will I give to eat of the tree of life, which is in the midst of the paradise of God," Revelation 2:7.*

There is much truth in the saying "Meditation is your medication."[20] I choose to believe that the Lord is shaping me into a vessel He can use, so I "let go and let God,"[21] as much as possible.

---

[20] Master Prophet, Bishop E. Bernard Jordan
[21] Alcoholics Anonymous

## 26. CONQUERING PRIDE

Pride is the love for one's own excellence, thinking too highly of oneself: you think you are really somebody. How shall we overcome this thing called pride? Most assuredly, you must recognize it in yourself. (Many are ignorant of their own condition.) Do you know any prideful people? If so, then most likely you have some pride as well – how else can you look into the mirror of life and see it? How else could you recognize it in others unless it is in you?

Pride is a great obstacle, like a dragon in the path! People will try and call their misnamed pride "Dignity." Pride speaks when respecting itself over others. However, no one can have a sense of worth or dignity, if they have no respect for the equal worth of others. There is no use in building oneself up for one's self-gain. The Word says to build oneself up in the Lord, for the Body of Christ, the Church.

The Biblical story of pride involves a leper's expectation. This particular leper, Naaman, had riches, honor, and power (2 Kings 5) – and ignorance. He thought he would impress Prophet Elisha with all that he could give him, but God does not minister to self-deceiving pride.

The prophet basically ignored him and gave him a process of the cure that was different from what Naaman expected. It was so simple but authoritative. *"Go and wash in the Jordan River seven times."* A child could understand it; a child could do it. It was so simple that only a proud and therefore foolish man would resent and resist it. God never makes His way hard, difficult, obscure, or too involved. His simplicity is our salvation.

Many people are like Naaman; they stagger at the promises of God and walk in disbelief because the way is so light and easy.

Let your pride fall, so you don't have to.

### Questions:
1. What are some ways to overcome pride?
2. Why is it especially dangerous for a prophet to be prideful?

## 27. Dealing with Rejection

*"A prophet is not without honor except in his own country and in his own house." Matthew 13:57*

If being misunderstood or feeling out of place or even being rejected has been a common theme in your life, then the prophetic might just be the life for you.

You may have had a difficult time being part of the "in" crowd and then you came to Christ and became passionate for the things of God! Maybe you started to receive revelation from God, but discovered that people rejected you even more. However, there are good sovereign reasons why God allows a young prophet to suffer rejection – Jesus Christ lived with rejection! Therefore, on the upside, you identify with Jesus, when you have suffered rejection.

It is strange that multitudes came to Jesus from everywhere to hear Him speak, or more often to be healed by Him, but, after His bodily resurrection, we read in the first chapter of the Book of Acts, there were only one hundred and twenty believers in the upper room. These people were praying and fasting with one accord, wondering how they were going to manage without their Lord. Out of the multitudes that flocked to Him, He only had one hundred and twenty loyal followers. Where were the all the others?

Just ponder on the ministry of our Lord. Could it be that He allows you to be rejected and have no friends so you become a closer friend of His? Could it be that He knows how easy it is for others to distract you from the things of God? You have an absolute insatiable desire to stop being lonely, so now you become a closer friend of Jesus and the Father. Could that be actually designed into your life for God's greater purpose?

*"Death and life are in the power of the tongue, and those who love it will eat its fruit," Proverbs 18:21.*

Whenever you say: "Nobody loves me. Everyone rejects me. I have no friends!" you are really speaking curses over yourself! By proclaiming them out loud, you are actually speaking "life" into those curses so that they come to pass as bad fruit in your life.

## 27. DEALING WITH REJECTION

Instead, you are to consciously and habitually speak "life" to yourself and to others, not death! You need to start proclaiming words of affirmation, e.g. "People love me now because *I am lovable*. I'm accepted, just as I am. Life is so good to me!"

This positive fruit needs time to grow, but it WILL manifest. The seed has been planted by your own words and needs constant fertilizing and watering by you. Am I talking craziness? No, we are to continually train our tongue to line up with the Word of God. Every believer who is going to minister in the prophetic must excel in speaking encouragement to others – therefore, practice personal edification, along with edifying others.

When you prophesy over someone, you are speaking through the power of the Holy Spirit. Although you are speaking God's words, you are using your vocal chords, tongue and mouth. The words are not coming from your mind! It may be true that not many people like to be with you, but that can be radically changed by your positive attitude, your character, and what comes out of your mouth about yourself!

As I mellow, people seem to like me more. Also, as I can accept more love into my life – I know more will come. I am encouraged by having friends in my life that love being around me and hardly any of these friends really want to talk about Christ as passionately as I do, but that is okay. I am consciously disciplining myself to talk about other subjects when in their company. It means that I am not always talking about Jesus, but I have more friends in my life and they would still see Christ in me.

You may quietly compare your life to that of leading prophets who are on the world-stage or who have speaking engagements from multiple churches and seem to have an abundance of friends. You may wonder what it takes to get from where you are to where they are. The growth has to start some time from somewhere and you could be the catalyst! If you believe that the whole universe was created by just the spoken Word of God, can you who have been created in the image of God, not speak yourself into a future with friends?

Jesus said: *"A prophet is not without honor except in his own country and in his own house." Matthew 13:57*

These are incredible words from the lips of our Savior. He knew this fact from personal experience. He knew that a prophet of God outside of his own hometown and outside of his own family would receive honor as a prophet, but a prophet's own family and the people of his own town would not give him the honor that was due to him. It was not until after His resurrection that His own brothers finally honored Him.

Jesus was on top of his game, but when He returned to Nazareth, it is recorded that it was nigh impossible for Him to heal anyone because of their unbelief. Could it be in your own church, when around people with whom you are trying to be friends, that they cannot stomach the wine? They cannot endure the revelation that you have because they do not see you as a prophet. Is it not best then, to just keep quiet and talk superficially and leave the deep talk only for those who ask deep questions?

You need to exercise discernment with folk who know you well, whereas a stranger is more likely to readily respond and accept the anointing on your life. They recognize you because of what you have said and not for who you are as a person – because they have no built-up mindsets about you. Could it be that this is the way it is meant to be? This is how it was with Jesus, and what He said was the truth – *"A prophet is not without honor except in his own country and in his own house." Matthew 13:57*

Just rest in God's love and leave your future for Him to work out. Then, in His timing, He will raise you up to the place He has already appointed for you. In the meantime, even when rejection hurts, think back over the prophecies you have received and claim them out loud to yourself. Let hope and faith do their perfect work in your present situation. Make a positive stand against all negativity in your life and particularly in your speech.

Jesus said in Matthew 7:6 *"Do not give what is holy to the dogs; nor cast your pearls before swine."* In other words, do not share your secret and profound revelations with people that you know. We have it from the Master Himself – they will surely not appreciate it. Instead, share your revelations with strangers and with people who are hungry for the things of God. These are just a few tips from me – things that have helped me and I trust will help you too.

## LAURIE'S REFLECTIONS

27. Dealing with Rejection

First pride and then rejection -- Matthew gets right to the heart of things, doesn't he?

Rejection is a necessary thing in the life of a prophet and it has been a major part of my training.

We all feel rejected at some time or another, especially if we have an alcoholic parent, a drug addicted spouse, an unfaithful spouse or all three and then some. Life has a way of dealing out rejection. That's funny – Life deals out rejection as we learn how to deal with it.

I have felt rejected many times in life, mostly it was due to my own insecurities.

God knew who my parents were going to be and He said, Let there be Laurie. God is not surprised by anything. I am not the only person who has dealt with an alcoholic parent or a drug addicted spouse or an unfaithful one – not by a long shot.

Rejection is a tool God uses to grow us up. If we can understand that it is not personal, that God is just trying to get us to see ourselves in the situation or He is trying to get us to lean on him and not man.

Jesus is the chief cornerstone. He was and is still rejected today by many. Jesus was a prophet. Bishop Jordan has taught me that "the greater the rejection, the greater the anointing." God really does use "rejects." I am a reject and God is using me. Have you ever been rejected? Then you are a "reject" and God can use you too.

Joseph was a reject, but he was used by God to feed the people. David was a reject, but still he became king.

Hold fast to the Word, that's how you deal with rejection. If God said it, it is so. Hold fast to your own personal prophecies and hold fast to any prophecies you give out. They will come to pass in due time. It is a prophet's job to change the situation by the Words of their mouth, so it is important not to think about rejection as you are prophesying. If they reject you, they reject God. A prophet is God's spokesperson and always will be.

Have you ever noticed that we usually reject ourselves *before* anyone else has a chance to do it? Out of fear of rejection, we fail to step up to the plate when the call is made – you let everyone else step up, and then, right when you work up the courage, the door is closed. You project rejection on yourself. Remember, God is not going to force you to work for Him, but when you reject yourself, you reject God. You are made in the image and likeness of God. Acceptance is how you deal with rejection. God has already accepted you and everyone else; now you have to.

Accept the prophetic call on your life, but expect rejection because it is just part of the ministry – it is part of the training process. When you accept the rejection as part of the training, there is no rejection; it just fades away into what we call training.

I was so rejected not long ago and it sadden my soul for a couple of days but then I just sighed and said, "God's just dealing with me. I'll be okay."

**Question:**

1. Why is rejection necessary in the life of a prophet?

## 28. Knowing What You Are Called To Do.

*"In his heart a man plans his course but the Lord determines his steps." Proverbs 16:9*

It is a wonderful thing to know your purpose and to start walking towards and in that purpose. I hope that you are beginning to receive more revelation about both who you are and what you are meant to do.

A major part of the work of a prophet is to bind wounds and to help people who are hurting, but a prophet's job is also to inform people about their calling and to mentor them into it. Also, part of a prophet's calling is to correct errors in the body of Christ and to point people toward God, to teach repentance, and to teach them how to live a victorious Christian life, which is a set apart holy life!

Knowing your particular calling brings peace, but floundering in a sea of uncertainty is disturbing and unfruitful. My purpose in writing this book is to give some clarification and understanding about the prophetic life and I hope that you are beginning to believe "Yes, this is what I'm meant to be." Knowing your calling brings great comfort and a sense of excitement as well. You can relax because God knows exactly what He is doing. He has the time and the seasons in his hand and there is a time and a season for everything.

If you are called to be a prophet, there are various dimensions involved: dream interpretation, teaching, and ongoing growth in the prophetic. Over time all will be revealed. Like all God's gifts, when you know your particular calling, an abiding joy and peace manifests in your life.

However, the prophetic office and being a prophet can be hard. It is a calling often associated with tears and suffering. Within this process, you will come to understand the heart and pain of the Father and His concerns for all people, but there is tremendous comfort in being a friend of Almighty God who, at times, shares His heart, His emotions, His plans, and His secrets with you. Therefore, with every negative aspect, there comes a wonderful positive. The more you suffer and are tested, the more you press into God, the more precious and intimate your relationship with Him becomes.

## **LAURIE'S REFLECTIONS**

28. Knowing What You Are Called to Do

To everything there is a season, and you must know your season. You must know what time it is. You must plant (and "bloom where you are planted") and in time you shall have a harvest. It is not called "Seed Time and Harvest" for nothing.

Everyone has an assignment from the Father. It is your responsibility to find out what your assignment is. Whatever you enjoy doing the most is what you are passionate about, and within your passion lays your purpose or your assignment in life. If you are reading this book, most likely you are called to be a prophet or prophetess. *"In his heart a man plans his course but the Lord determines his steps," Proverbs 16:9.*

I have always had a passion to write, but never felt I was good enough to do it. In the beginning, I would just stare at a blank sheet of paper, not knowing what to write, but the Lord has led me to this day, co-writing a book, step-by-step, all the way. It has taken me a while to get here, but God is not in a hurry and we should not be either. Enjoy your journey; everything is in God's timing.

*"To everything there is a season, and a time to every purpose under the heaven: a time to be born, and a time to die; a time to plant, and to pluck up that which is planted; a time to kill, to heal; to break down, and to build up; to weep, to laugh; to mourn, to dance; to cast away stones, to gather stones together; to embrace, to refrain from embracing; to get and to lose; to keep, and to cast away; to rend, to sew; to keep silent, to speak, to love, to hate; a time of war and a time of peace."* (Eccl. 3:1-8.) There's a time for everything! What time is it for you?

I love to teach and first began teaching children in church, when my children were very young. In fact, I have spent about fifteen years teaching young people in church. I love it; I love the way children's

## 28. KNOWING WHAT YOU ARE CALLED TO DO

eyes light up and the way their smile brightens the whole room when they get excited. Teaching is something I do, but mainly I love learning, and then I naturally want to pass it on to others. I have been teaching in some capacity ever since.

God knows and gives us opportunities to obtain the desires of our heart. However, the bigger the dream, the more training (life experience) we will need, and God is a most willing and excellent teacher!

Do not wonder or wander aimlessly throughout life because you do not understand what you are called to do or be in life. God is trying to guide and lead you to your destiny. Pay attention to your interests; they may reveal your assignment. Whatever inspires you is a clue. In the word "inspire" you see "in spirit." Pay attention! It will pay you to attend to your own inspirations. God is trying to guide you in the direction that you should go. Whenever you get excited about some new project or new interest – it is a sure sign that it is God ordained. You don't have to question whether it is what God is calling you to do. The enthusiasm is the call. Wikipedia says the word "enthusiasm" originally meant *inspiration or belief in private revelation, divine favor or communication.*

There are several ways to know your calling. I remember going to my pastor prophet and asking him for an assignment because I kept hearing the word "assignment." Unbeknown to me, at that particular time, he was in the process of handing out assignments to certain people in the church. So you may learn your assignment through a prophet or from your own inner voice – or even God's audible voice!

When you serve to bring forth another man's vision, God will help bring forth your vision. Whom are you serving? It is all about the serving.

### Questions:
1. How important is it to know your calling?
2. What does passion have to do with purpose?
3. What are some ways to discover your assignment in life?

## 29. Dealing with the Book of Revelation

*"Blessed is he that readeth and they that hear the words of this prophecy." Revelation 1:3a*

As you mature with a good understanding of the prophetic voice of God, people may ask your opinion on things written in the Book of Revelation. I believe the intimacy of your relationship with God and the number of hours you have spent in the Old Testament prophets and the words of Jesus will determine how much you understand about the Book of Revelation.

To be honest, this last book in the Bible is not one of my favorite subjects, because I believe that Jesus has commanded us, above all else, to preach the Gospel in order to bring people to salvation. I believe that the enemy may very easily side-track a believer to spend too much time theorizing about this book to the detriment of the Great Commission.

I remember once my parents being excited about a coming series on the Book of Revelation, but our wise and godly Baptist pastor surprised everyone. His series centered on "The LORD," who IS soon coming! (He wisely put God's priority first, as we should all do.) As a result, no one ever did find out his particular stance on pre, mid, or post-tribulation! The series was all about the Lordship of our Lord!

The Book of Revelation is fascinating and very deep, but when I think of what God requires of me, three important verses come to mind:

1. *"Now the purpose of the commandment* (a charge given to you) *is to love from a pure heart* (without blemish, undefiled) *from a good conscience and from sincere faith." 1 Timothy 1:5*
2. *"To do justly; to love mercy, and to walk humbly with your God." Micah 6:8b*
3. *"This is the work of God that you believe in Him whom He sent." John 6:29*

## 29. DEALING WITH THE BOOK OF REVELATION

However, Jesus has never rescinded His final instruction to us – to evangelize. His heart is still for lost sinners, the poor, the widow, and the brokenhearted.

For me, it is not a matter of when the time of the rapture or when future judgments will occur, or who will be the false prophet or the last day antichrist. I am convinced that God wants to see us getting on with the job He has given to us. Therefore, until the Lord tells me otherwise, I want to continue to help people cope now, by bringing them God's solutions for the turmoil in their life today. Probably I will not change from what I am already doing while the Book of Revelation unfolds around me. My mindset is that whatever God has in store for me sits fine with me. He is a good God and I trust in Him.

However, I believe that some pre-tribulation "rapture" believers are not very interested in end time events because they figure they will not be around on earth at that time. I see danger in this attitude, because they may just find themselves totally unprepared for what may unfold around them if their theory does not pan out. In my mind, it would seem best to be prepared for the worst! That way, our faith and focus on God would be much stronger and we would be strengthening ourselves in the Lord and doing our best to help fulfill the Great Commission Jesus gave His church as stated below.

*"Go therefore and make disciples of all the nations, baptizing them in the name of the Father and of the Son and of the Holy Spirit, teaching them to observe all things that I have commanded you; and lo, I am with you always, even to the end of the age. Amen."*
Matthew 28:19-20

Personally, I do not, in any way, feel that just because I am a prophet, I have to have a deep revelation on this difficult book. I believe it is a private book – a personal revelation. Of course, I know that there is a blessing in understanding it: understanding the major players, and how it is all going to go down. You will certainly be a lot better prepared if you know in advance what is going to happen. It is good to try and understand it, but do not feel indebted as a training prophet, or even as a prophet, to make pronouncements and give opinions about the Book of Revelation.

If I am asked a question about something in this very controversial book, I tell people that it is a subject that I do not comment on. I do not like to talk about it because I find that most people are just going on what others have said or have written. Unless the Lord gives me specific information on this subject for a *particular person*, I will continue to answer like that. Actually, I find it quite peculiar that some people feel that writing about the Book of Revelation automatically makes them a prophet!

In the past, I believe that the Holy Spirit has given me some revelations on this book, yet I find that very few people agree with these revelations, but lately I am just beginning to find others who agree with some of the things I know. This is most encouraging because it confirms that I am on the right track with what has been revealed to me by the Holy Spirit.

Sufficient to say, that is all I want to share on the subject. So, please do not write to me about my ideas because I am not sure whether I will be sharing them with you. However, I am sure that you should develop a relationship with the Father, with Jesus, and with the Holy Spirit, and get to know the Bible. That way, you will receive your own revelation on the Book. This would be far, far better than anything I may say.

## **LAURIE'S REFLECTIONS**

29. Dealing with the Book of Revelation

The whole Bible is a revelation, being an unveiling or disclosing of the mind and will of God, which we could not know otherwise, but the Book of Revelation differs in some respects from the other books of Scripture. This particular book is addressed to "His servants."[22] Perhaps that is why most people do not bother with it.

The central message of Revelation is that the Lord God Omnipotent reigns. (19:6) The Book depicts the revelation of the Glory of the victorious and risen Lamb of God.

---

[22] Rev. 1:1

## 29. DEALING WITH THE BOOK OF REVELATION

He is the King of Kings and Lord of Lords, who passed through death, whom God both raised and exalted at His own right hand. It is the revelation of His acquired Glory and how this Glory is to be manifested in connection with the earth. In the Book of Revelation, the Lord Jesus Christ makes the future known to His servants, because His own are partakers with Him in all He received from God.

The Lord has Himself pronounced a blessing upon him who reads the Book of Revelation, and they that hear the words of this prophecy, and keep the things which are written therein; for the time is at hand.

There is no other book that takes us at once into another realm like the Book of Revelation. The world is full of movies with thrilling themes, with grand imagery and such, yet here in the Book of Revelation, as we look into the Kingdom of God, the New Heaven and New Earth, we too have it all – thrilling themes with grand imagery.

The Book of Revelation is like "a panorama of the glory of Christ."

### Questions:
1. Is it important to understand the Book of Revelation?
2. Who is the Book of Revelation addressed to?

## 30. Walking With the Presence and the Peace of God.

*"The Dayspring from on high shall visit us, to shine upon them that sit in darkness and the shadow of death; to guide our feet into the way of peace." Luke 1:78*

I recently saw on YouTube a sixteen year old lad and I was extremely impressed with a particular statement he made: "The peace of God comes in a stronger measure when you're walking in total obedience to Christ."

It was true, but I was amazed at his maturity in the Lord Jesus. He said that even when he is walking in 98% obedience to Christ, the peace of God drops off dramatically. It is only when he is walking in 100% obedience that the peace and the presence of God is powerful in his life. He added: "Walking in the peace and presence of God is an unbelievable feeling. It's just beautiful!" Unless you are totally obedient, you are not going to experience it.

It has only been in the last year that I have felt this in my own life. During that time, I have been consciously aware of obeying everything that He has told me to do – following His and the Holy Spirit's directions in my daily life – so that now I can testify that the life of a prophet is marked by the presence and manifest peace of God, and a prophet is to carry this anointing wherever he goes. Therefore, a prophet is also to be an intimate friend of God.

We know that the Holy Spirit is present in all Christians, but we also need to understand that not all Christians walk in the total manifestation of the Holy Spirit – with the full portion of awareness that God desires. There have been Christians since Christ, who have walked in a very unique anointing.

For example, John G. Lake walked in an anointing of healing that was similar to that of Jesus Christ and that anointing healed many people. In fact, whenever he was working in his healing room in Spokane, Washington, it is said that people who stayed long enough in the city and learned about Christ's healing power, were actually healed! Almost everyone who came to visit him received healing. He received a measure of the Holy Spirit's anointing that is far beyond the normal Christian experience.

Many Christians consciously experience the presence and peace of God when they join in corporate worship at church on Sunday. At that time, the presence, peace, and joy of the Holy Spirit overwhelms them, but that same degree of spiritual awareness may not be with them in their busy everyday life. Up to twelve months ago, I can categorically say that it was not a part of my daily experience either. Therefore, I am not saying this in judgment over other Christians. I do know it was a reality in my life for years that Jesus had been talking to me, and I had been doing my best to obey Him.

However, in recent time, the Holy Spirit's presence has come with more power and of course I know that much more is possible! If you earnestly desire to minister to others in the power of the Holy Spirit, it is obviously best to minister out of the overflow that is in your life, rather than just having enough for yourself. A parable depicting this is the Parable of the Ten Virgins in Matthew 25:1-13, which tells the story of five foolish and five wise virgins.

I believe the five foolish virgins had too much of the lusts of the world in them. They did not have enough of the inspiration, the love, and the presence of the Holy Spirit in their lives because they were too filled with the world's distractions. I believe the oil represents the presence of the Holy Spirit, but when you are full of the world, the Holy Spirit's anointing cannot rest on you.

Actually, the five wise virgins were not all that wise! They had enough oil in their lamps to be saved and taken by the groom to the celebration, but they did not have enough oil to share with the foolish virgins. Therefore, they could have been wiser! By walking in the manifest presence of God, His peace and joy bubbles over so that you have plenty to share with all those who need help. Jesus alluded to this bubbling up experience when He publicly stated on the great day of the Feast of Tabernacles: *"He who believes in Me, as the Scripture has said, out of his heart* (or belly) ***will flow rivers of living water." John 7:38***

The presence of God is to bubble up in you, to create joy and peace and then it is to overflow onto others around you. When you walk in the manifest presence of God with this strong anointing, it gives you something to share with others – to bring hope into their lives. The more you experience first-hand these things, the more you can spark godly hope in others. People desperately need hope today! *"This hope we have is an anchor of the soul, both sure and steadfast, and which enters the Presence behind the veil." Hebrews 6:19*

I had it explained to me once that hope is like a satisfying filling in a sandwich:

Love is the bottom slice of bread because it can endure all things. And Biblical Faith is the top slice of bread that protects and holds strong. For Hope to have its perfect outcome it needs both love that endues and faith to protect and hold strong. A person without hope is wretched and lost!

There is absolutely no way I could ever have spoken the framework of this book without the Holy Spirit guiding my every thought. He first gave me the inspiration and it became a burning desire deep in my spirit. Then I received the actual book title. It was then that I began to write down all the chapter headings. And as I spoke into the video camera, He placed parts of particular verses into my mind. Later on, I had to look up the Scriptures in full and put in their references.

It is important for us to know that, if Bibles were ever taken away by the authorities, it is NOT the references that will hold us, but the actual Word of God. Therefore, it is vital to know the Word of God! (References however, are powerful "evidence" when showing truth to others. I find the concordance at the back of my Bible very helpful when I only just know part of a verse and perhaps the Book it is written in.)

Do you have enough of the Word of God in you to be able to cling to in times of tribulation and to bring others to the saving knowledge of Christ?

## LAURIE'S REFLECTIONS

30. Walking with the Presence and the Peace of God

Peace is usually under-valued by many people as they opt happiness instead. However, happiness is a word never once used by God. It is too thin and flimsy a thing for His children. The words He uses and puts on the lips of His teachers are "blessed" and "peace." Go in peace. Be blessed. There is no state of condition higher in God's scale than Peace.

God's Peace and presence is not just the absence of agitation or some other activity. It is actually the activity of complete harmony where the person is in the full Light and walks in relation to the whole as it is so revealed by God. Peace is a way in which the children of God walk together.

Peace is the result of God's light; it's the adoption of His way of looking at things. In a sense, peace is a gift of God to man, to the individual. Peace is the product of walking in the Light.

*"Glory to God in the highest, and on earth peace among men in whom he is well pleased," Luke 2:14.*

Heaven's peace on earth is God's purpose. *"In whom He is well pleased"* – who is this? God was well pleased in Jesus because He willed all that God willed; He expected all that God expected; He purposed all that God purposed. *"Thou art my beloved Son; in Thee I am well please," Luke 3:22.*

The prophet Isaiah spoke of God's appointed future Servant of the Lord in Isaiah 42:1-9. He also prophesied: *"You will keep him in perfect peace, whose mind is stayed on You. Because he trusts in You," Isaiah 26:3.*

Christ had inner peace, the peace which abided even when everything conspired against it. In God's will, there is peace – that is where a peace of mind can be found.

*"The Lord will bless his people with peace," Psalm 29:10.*

*"Righteousness and peace have kissed each other," Psalm 85:10.*

Righteousness, Peace, and Joy make up the kingdom of God – they travel in the same circle, Romans 14:17. Peace is something that will always have people's attention. Peace is the talk of the nations. Talking of *peace* pulls people in – it is attractive.

*"The Word which He sent unto the children of Israel, preaching good tidings of peace by Jesus Christ," Acts 10:36.*

*"Through Him to reconcile all things unto Himself, having made peace through the blood of the cross," Colossians 1:20.*

When you walk with the presence and the peace of God, the Holy Spirit tells you what to do and what to say and that is what prophesying is all about. Because you walk in the presence and peace of God, you do not have to wonder if you are hearing and seeing for God; you know it is the Word of the Lord.

How can you prophesy to a "name" sent to you through an email or given to you in some other way?

The Word says we are named after Jesus Christ. *"For this cause I bow my knees unto the Father of our Lord Jesus Christ, of whom the whole family in heaven and earth is named," Eph. 3:14-15.* Every being in heaven and earth derives its name from Christ!

When you say a name, the Holy Spirit impresses upon you certain thoughts and feelings concerning that person. Go ahead and speak them out. Trust this process. You will have certain emotions welling up in you, so that you may give encouragement. Just speak it out; you have not just thought it up – no, the Holy Spirit put it in your heart and mind as a blessing for the one that believes. Trust in Him, the Master of masters.

*"Surely the Lord will do nothing that He does not reveal to His prophets. Whatever the Lord God plans to do, He tells His servants, the prophets."*[23]

God has always risen up masters to lead His people. There are many masters – not just in speaking of the prophets. But, for some reason, when the word "master" is attached to anyone in the prophetic or

---

[23] Amos 3:7, KJV and CEV

## 30. WALKING WITH THE PRESENCE AND THE PEACE OF GOD

God's ministry, people get "all freaked out." Yet, there is a master barber, master chef, master mechanic, a Master's degree, and of course in golf there is "The Masters Golf Tournament." In the prophetic, there is a Master Prophet.

Walking in the presence and peace of God gives you the reassurance or blessed assurance that Jesus is Lord. You do not have to question or doubt anything because you know with God on your side, who can be against you?[24] There is nothing like being in the presence and peace of God.

Don't go giving anyone a "piece of your mind." You can't have peace of mind if you are giving it away. Besides, you only have one mind and you need all of it.

### Questions:
1. Where is Peace found?
2. Who travels with Peace?

---

[24] Romans 8:31

**PART 3: Ministering in the Prophetic**

## 30. WALKING WITH THE PRESENCE AND THE PEACE OF GOD

## 31. Prophetic Etiquette in Churches

*"Let all things be done decently and in order," 1 Corinthians 14:40.*

For someone newly growing in the prophetic there are specific rules to adhere to, concerning correct etiquette and behavior, when you are either part of a church or exercising the gift of prophecy within a church.

Some churches, during their praise and worship time or during their prayer time, may open the floor for the sharing of a prophecy, prayer points, or testimony. However, there are not many churches these days that allow open prophecy because it has been much abused in the past.

If it is permissible by the Head Pastor, this open time would be the acceptable time to give a prophetic word to the whole church. However, if you are a regular member or even a visitor, you should first take the time to quietly bring the word God has given you to the pastor's attention well before the service for his approval, before you publicly declare it to the congregation.

Many prophets, young prophets, and prophets in training have specific and varied ideas about God's judgment, His wrath, or His displeasure with the church. Often such a person enters a new church and uses the time in a worship service to launch into a scathing rebuke of the church and its people. This is definitely not proper prophetic etiquette! Even if you really believe that the word you were given came from the Lord God Almighty, you must refrain from doing this, no matter how strong the compulsion is. Why? Because, this type of outburst comes from a wrong spirit!

Scripture confirms that prophecy is to be given to edify or to build up God's people in the love and nurture of Christ and to bring unity to the whole congregation – *"for the equipping of the saints for the work of ministry, for the edifying of the body of Christ," Ephesians 4:12.*

*"But he who prophesies speaks edification and exhortation and comfort to men," 1 Corinthians 14:3. "Even so you, since you are*

*zealous for spiritual gifts, let it be for the edification of the church that you seek to excel," 1 Corinthians 14:12.*

Share your words and intentions with the pastor beforehand. Otherwise, if you are not in a good place personally, you may damage his sheep for they certainly will not understand what has fired you up or what is on your present agenda.

I now want to cover giving personal prophecies for individuals. If you are a visitor just for the day, I believe it is acceptable for you to quietly give a personal prophecy to an individual church member. Nevertheless, it is surely better if you first receive the permission of the pastor, even if you see a person in the church to whom the Lord is directing your eyes and is giving you a prophetic word for them. Ideally, it is best to approach the person, tell them that the Lord has given you a personal prophetic word for them, and could they accompany you to the pastor, as you want him (or her) to witness everything.

There are rules and levels of authority in God's kingdom, just as in the army with a general at the top and levels of command down through the ranks. The kingdom of God is structured orderly and if you do something out of order, it robs you of God's blessing and perhaps those you are trying to help. Within every church, the pastor is God's appointed authority! It is not only etiquette, but is essential for you to obtain the authority and the permission of the pastor to move in the prophetic in any church. *"Recognize those who labor among you, and are over you in the Lord and admonish you, and to esteem them very highly in love for their work's sake. Be at peace among yourselves," 1 Thessalonians 5:12-13.*

Let us just talk for a while about the church that you attend regularly. If you are growing in the prophetic gift, you should share this with your pastor. Then if you have his permission to prophesy, it will be because the Holy Spirit has confirmed that you are trustworthy. He will know that you have a right spirit to give a private prophetic word to his flock.

The pastor at the church I attend wants to hear or see all the prophetic words that I want to give to our church. Originally, in my immaturity, I had a pride issue with this. Over time, I realized that I should simply take this problem up with her privately. (Still, I confess in somewhat of a spirit of rebellion!)

To my relief, my pastor said it is not so much that she does not trust the prophecies that I give, or that she does not believe that I can receive the prophecy from God. It is just that she knows the state of her people. She is aware of their personal development, or the spiritual atmosphere and condition of each of them and she does not want a prophetic word to be so deep, that it may bring misunderstanding to them.

To comply with these wishes, I type out prophetic words that I receive. She can then read them before I pass them on to the person. If there are parts that she thinks might not be clearly understood by the individual, she explains to me what the word could mean to them. Now, because of this, on my prophetic website I tell everybody, that after receiving a prophetic word that we give him or her by e-mail, that they should take it to their own pastor and obtain their approval for that particular word.

If you do not fully approve of your pastor, or if you think that because you have the gift of prophecy you do not need his approval, consider this warning: *you are operating outside the authority of God!* Know that it is not so much the pastor but the office that he holds, that is very precious in the sight of God.

I am very serious – be warned: you are going against the principles of God, and He will not bless you! He will not bless your "going out" or your "coming in." He will not bless the fruit of your hands. If you want to operate in a spirit of rebellion against proper spiritual etiquette, God is going to teach you a correctional lesson somehow, so that you learn to both respect your shepherd and their God-given authority over you.

If you think your church is out of order by not preaching the right material, or you believe that people need to repent, it is not your position to stand in the praise and worship center and reel off a scathing prophetic "thus says the Lord" word in an open rebuke to a church. If you believe the church needs correction through the prophetic word, it is best that you type that prophetic word, give it to your pastor, and ask him if he could read that to the church. Actually, it would be far more God honoring, to humbly fast and pray for your church and to pray for the abundant blessing of God to be released on the pastor and his personal family.

If the shepherd agrees to read your prophecy, then you have done a wonderful job! Moreover, if God is truly speaking and He wants that church to hear that message, He will lay it on the heart of the pastor, who is really the right man for the job, to read that prophecy to the congregation. I hope that has covered some of your concerns.

## **LAURIE'S REFLECTIONS**

31. Prophetic Etiquette in Churches.

"Directing your eyes"...

During a home school conference, the Lord kept directing my eyes to a certain table in the opposite direction of where I was trying to pay attention to a presentation of a certain math program. At the Lord's insistent nudging, I looked and saw nothing; there were many people walking in the aisle and I really could not see anything so I turned my attention back to the presentation.

Well, God was not going to allow me to miss what was at that table across the aisle. Three or four times he had me advert my eyes, until finally it was as if He placed His Hands on both sides of my face and physically turned my head and said, "Go over there and see what I have for you."

"Okay, okay! I'll go over there." I walked across the aisle and stood in front of a plain table, no table cloth, no nothing except a few books on the table. But the books were enough, that's all I needed to get hooked. Here was the Bible-based, Christ-centered curriculum I spoke about in an earlier chapter. It was exactly the type of study program I was looking for.

God is so good. He knows what we are looking for and if we will just listen and obey, He will lead us right to it.

I bought the books and the relationship with that pastor-author blossomed into a ministry that I was involved with for several years. So, when you feel your eyes being directed, pay attention. It is not always that God will press the issue. Make sure you do not let opportunities for His best in your life pass you by.

On the topic of Prophetic Etiquette in Churches – since that is the title of this chapter – you must always be seeking God in your own personal study, and ideally sitting under a leader, pastor, bishop, master, etc. Be like Mary sitting at the feet of Jesus. Find a master-pastor-prophetic teacher and sit at his or her feet.

Once you find your leader, do not try to go ahead of them in your eagerness to "hurry up and learn." Instead, listen and learn from them. Your leader is there to challenge you, to stretch you, not to make things easy for you. You don't gain anything that way.

*"Then rose up Zerubbabel ..., and began to build the house of God which is at Jerusalem;* **and with them were the prophets of God, helping them,"** *Ezra 5:2.*

Help your leader. Whomever God has placed you under, find out what the vision of that house is and do whatever is assigned to you. Don't be a Negative Nancy or Negative Ned! Honor and cover the head – for that is what will keep you covered and protected.

Do not prophesy to someone who does not approve of receiving a prophecy. If you do, you are trying to force the Word of the Lord. You are throwing pearls before swine. That is why I always ask a person if they would *like* to hear a Word that the Lord has given me concerning them.

Just as there must be order in your house and order in the Lord's house, there must be order when giving a prophecy. The head of the church must know and approve before the prophecy is given.

We are all called to submit to someone. *"Let every soul be subject to the higher power," Romans 13:1.* In a prophet's world, this is known as spiritual protocol, as taught to me by Master Prophet Bishop Jordan. The prophets of Old were all subject to their leader, as Jesus Christ was and is to Father God.

## 31. PROPHETIC ETIQUETTE IN CHURCHES

In most churches, order has been established or is being established if it is a new church, and this order should be respected by all, especially the prophets.

*"Let all things be done decently and in order,"* 1 Corinthians 14:40. This means that prophecy is only given after receiving permission by the proper authority.

### Questions:
1. What happens when there is no order?
2. If you have a Word for someone in the congregation, what is the proper protocol?

## 32. Ministering the Prophetic to Christians

*He said, "Listen to My words: When a prophet of the LORD is among you, I reveal Myself to him in visions, I speak to him in dreams." Numbers 12:6*

In the previous chapter, I covered church prophetic etiquette. If your pastor approves of you sharing prophetic words with the congregation, then go ahead and do so. However, if the pastor wants to first check your prophetic words, then abide by this. Do not ignore or try to over-rule the shepherd's God-given authority over you.

What if the Lord gives you a word for someone you meet at a conference – perhaps an acquaintance you know from a former church? The approach I use depends on whether the person is from a Pentecostal church or a main-line conservative church. If from the latter, I would open by saying, "I believe I have a personal message from Jesus for you. Would you like to hear it?" Most people are open to hear the message.

When I start to speak information that I should not ordinarily know, this gets the attention of a non-Pentecostal straightaway. They soon realize that God is supernaturally speaking to them and actually giving them personal direction for their life! Then, they readily agree that the prophecy was authentic. Therefore, I do not often have a problem working prophetically with a Christian who does not come from a Pentecostal background.

With a Pentecostal Christian, I normally start by saying, "The Lord has given me a prophetic word for you, would you like to hear it?" In both cases, it is always best to ask a person whether they would like to hear a prophetic word. We must respect a person's privacy whether or not to listen to "our opinion" of what God wants to tell them. Bear in mind always that God could have made us like robots that are programmed to love Him, but He gave us a free-will. And Jesus paid the ultimate price for our free will!

Often, immature prophets or prophets in training may receive an "authentic" word of God for a person, then barge straight in and deliver the word. This type of attitude comes either from immaturity – lack of knowledge – or from pride as a way of exalting oneself.

Maybe the prophetic word you have can be right on the money, because once God opens your mind to the prophetic messages from His Kingdom, they just begin to flow. Although the message you have is correct, your attitude may not be. Therefore, follow the way of etiquette and always ask for permission first. When the person says yes, which happens in most cases, you can then share the prophetic word with them – and when you share with them, make sure that you move strongly in the word of knowledge.

If God gives you specific information about that person, make sure you mention these words of knowledge because it immediately catches their attention. It makes a person realize that something supernatural is happening – that surely God has revealed this to you because no one else in the world knows these details. Exercise godly boldness and courageously speak these words of knowledge because they will bond to the hearer, just as cement and mortar hold bricks together.

Words of knowledge help the person to hang onto the prophecy even if the fulfillment takes a long time in coming. Even if that person starts to have doubts whether the prophecy is going to come true in their life, they will continue to think, "Yeah, but he knew all those things about me. I have never told anyone those things. It had to be God and God has to be true to His word."

You do people a disservice by not having the faith or the courage to move in the word of knowledge. However, do not expect a big reaction, or even a pat on the back or - "Thank you very much" from a Christian. Most Christians will just say, "I receive that." If they are Pentecostal, perhaps they will say, "Thank you so much. That has blessed me! I'm pleased that you did that." Never try to use the prophetic word to gain advantage for yourself in that person's life or to become a closer friend just because you gave them a prophetic word.

I am saying this because in the past I was guilty of this. I used to move in the prophetic just to have friends and I am imploring you not to try to do that. Just give a person a prophetic word when the Lord tells you to do so. In a later chapter we are going to talk about doing what the Father does – about God's will for moving in the prophetic and what messages He wants you to pass on – and, more important, those messages He wants you to keep to yourself and to just pray for the person.

When you know what God wants you to do, it is possible for you to move in the prophetic in a pure and more wholesome way. You can bless many more people without it being tainted with your will, your emotion, and your desire to be recognized in an attempt to be somebody important in a person's life.

It is all too natural to give a compliment to a person to grow closer and to be liked by the person. Know that a genuine compliment is to be given to edify another person and a prophecy is also to be given for the same reason. In the case of prophecy, all glory belongs to God alone and we are to resist the temptation to accept any advantage or self-glory. Therefore, there is to be no ulterior self-centered motive when working in the prophetic. If there is a continuing problem with this, there may be perhaps, a Jezebel controlling spirit operating. Obviously, this must be dealt with, so that you use the prophetic in a pure and wholesome way.

I still hope that you are learning something here. There is more to come and we have many more topics to cover.

## **LAURIE'S REFLECTIONS**

32. Ministering the Prophetic to Christians

Very recently, I had the opportunity to minister the Word of the Lord to a young Christian man. Afterwards, he said he was so blessed by it because he had not received a Word like that in a long time and it meant so much to him. It was a chance meeting and I have not ever seen him again. There was no personal gain in it for me, except that it was a blessing for the Lord to use me this way. "It is a blessing to be a blessing."

## 32. MINISTERING THE PROPHETIC TO CHRISTIANS

This is the purpose in the prophetic – to give hope, to encourage, to strengthen the people of God. There is no selfish pride in this. I believe it is pure joy to be used in this way.

People have told me that I helped them, even when I was not aware of it; I am just talking to them and listening, making a comment here and there, being a friend. Other prophets tell me I am a pastor and I quickly deny it. Then they say: "You are helping people out, helping them deal with their situation." I agree so they say, "You are pastoring!" I say: "Okay Prophet."

A prophet always speaks life into a situation. Look at the person or the situation and see God in it. See as He sees and you will immediately know what it is that the Lord would have you say.

As a prophet, whenever pride enters into the situation, God will deal with you, so it is very important to stay humble and know that it is not you giving the Word, but it is the Lord. It is not about giving compliments, but sharing what the Lord has for that person.

### Questions:
1. What two things does it take to minister a prophetic word?
2. When you know the Lord is leading you to speak prophetically to someone what should you do? HINT: It is a famous slogan.

## 33. Prophetic Evangelism

*"For the perfecting of the saints in their work of ministry unto the edifying of the body of Christ."* Ephesians 4:12

Prophetic evangelism is the "modern terminology" for something that has been happening since before the church began. It simply refers to evangelism using the prophetic gift that began in the ministry of Jesus in the Gospels.

Jesus had used His prophetic gifting in His conversation with the Samaritan woman at the well. This supernatural knowledge that He had of her so impressed her, that she excitedly told all the people of her town that Jesus was the long awaited Messiah sent by God. He had evangelized her, which in turn enabled the whole town to be evangelized.

At the people's request, Jesus then stayed for a few days teaching them the Word of the Lord. When He finished, they said to the woman: *"Now we believe, not because of what you said, for we ourselves have heard Him and we know that this is indeed the Christ, the Savior of the world," John 4:42.*

Prophetic evangelism is dynamic!

Jesus won people to Himself. He had identified Himself for the very first time as the Jewish Messiah to this outcast Gentile woman, branded as a "nobody" by the Jews. She was also the first Gentile woman converted to the Christian faith. How? Through a prophetic experience! Therefore, prophetic evangelism is essentially using your gift with strangers – impacting people in a non-Christian world.

An excellent insight into this subject can be found in a book called *"Prophetic Evangelism"* by Mark Stibbe, and also in another book called *"Prophetic Fishing."* These books go into detail about this subject. If it is a direction in which you want to move, I urge you to study these books as this short chapter is basically only a brief introduction to the topic.

Often the Holy Spirit says: "I want you to speak to that person." It is as if the person is glowing – their skin seems radiant. To me, they

## 33. PROPHETIC EVANGELISM

are standing out from others, much like a periscope on a submarine! A periscope revolves, it comes across a ship on the water – it stops, goes around again, and comes back to confirm the ship's presence. Well, the Holy Spirit will do that for you, it will select people. Then you check in your spirit: "Is that the person you want me to speak to?" When the Holy Spirit confirms it, then you ask for the message that He has for them. Then you approach that person. Mind you, it takes a great deal of courage to approach a stranger, but it is somewhat exciting. (Rather like a first date, if you know what I mean.)

You are full of trepidation, fear, worry, and anxiety – but it is nevertheless exciting! You have a choice – either you can approach people and give them their message, or not approach them. Because I feel compelled, I mostly approach people, and use the words given to me by the Holy Spirit. Of the thousands of people I have approached, I estimate that only about ten people have rejected my offer. I walk up to them and say, "Excuse me! I have a gift that sometimes gives me the ability to receive a special message for a person. Today I have a message for you, would you like me to share it with you?"

Most of them probably assume that I have clairvoyant tendencies, so they mostly agree. Then I launch into the beginning of the prophetic word. If you have moved in the prophetic, you will know that once you start with the first words, it is like turning on a tap – once the tap is opened, the prophetic words start to flow through you. So, you just need to start with a couple of sentences and the rest will just flow from you.

At the end, you have a choice – you can choose to either say nothing, or like me, depending on what the Holy Spirit has led me to say, conclude with "Now, that might have sounded as if I was a clairvoyant but I'm not. I am a Christian and I have God's Gift of Prophecy. God loves you very much and wanted you to know that message today. Have a wonderful day! God bless you! Bye," Then I simply turn and walk away.

It is important for you to understand that you do not have to convert people – you do not have to win a person to Jesus Christ in a prophetic evangelism encounter. Maybe the word "evangelism" makes you think that you have to win souls, but most evangelists just "leave" people for Christ. I prefer to say that you are a seed planter, and God in His wisdom will water that seed. God places more and more Christians in their path, and one day they will be saved.

You can be sure if God sends you to give a prophetic word to a stranger that He is going to send others into that person's life to water that seed. You are only to do what the Holy Spirit tells you to do. If the Holy Spirit tells you to "lead them into prayer of salvation," then you do that with a joyful heart. However, do not be over-concerned if, like me, you have delivered three or four thousand prophetic words and have only led about fifteen people to the Lord.

I am comforted by knowing that there are now many, many people with major seeds being planted in their life. Moreover, if you have told them that specific things are going to happen in their life – and those things happen – then wonderful things are happening for God. The Holy Spirit can speak even to a non-Christian and remind them: "Remember that Christian prophet who told you that. God arranged that. Is that not amazing?"

I just need to put the thought into their mind and give honor to God – and God will do the reaping of that soul. Prophetic evangelism is so exciting. On my article web site, you can find more writings on prophetic evangelism and other YouTube videos. See if you can get hold of the books I have suggested. These tools are excellent resources!

Prophetic evangelism is one of the most exciting things in my life. I am a seed planter – and it is exciting to be led by the Lord to have a dynamic effect on the life of a total stranger. I encourage you all to step out and ask God to give you Divine encounters so you can practice the gift of prophetic evangelism.

## LAURIE'S REFLECTIONS

33. Prophetic Evangelism.

Prophecy is "a light shining in a dark place." It glimmers faintly at first, like the dim morning twilight, but as it approaches its fulfillment, it becomes brighter, till at length the day dawns, and the future becomes present, and the prophecy is illuminated by the event.

Jesus asked a lot of questions to involve you in the blessings. He asked questions to get people to really think about the Heavenly Father.

- *"Is it not written in your law, I said, Ye are gods?" (John 10:34)*
- *"Don't you know what I have done for you?" (John 13:12)*
- *"Don't you believe Me?" (John 11:26.)*
- *"Didn't I tell you that if you would believe, you will see the glory of God?" (John 11:40)*
- *"Jesus asked: Where have you laid him?" (John 11:34)*

This is just a sample of the questions Jesus asked – even though He knew the answers to them all. As a prophet, you should be asking Jesus questions, and there are also times when you will ask questions to those you are prophesying to, to get them *thinking* on the matter or because you are being led by God in the direction that He would have you go with this person. Sometimes you have to go deep and the way to do that is by asking questions.

God gives seed to the sower and He knows who His sowers are! He gives you the seed to sow into their lives with the word! It is up to you to do the planting. Do not let God's seed go to the wayside! *Plant the seed of the Word; speak those things into existence.*

Prophecy and evangelism as spiritual forces are extremely important and fundamental to the Church. Pastors depend on the energies of evangelism and prophetic leadings of the people. We need prophets today who will speak the prophetic vision and the prophetic message of God. We need a deep yearning for the prophetic, a yearning such as David's.

When I look into my own heart, I pray to be stirred deeper and to be more spiritually passionate. That is my desire.

It is the prophet, stretching himself upon the widow's child, with his face to the child's face and his heart to the child's heart, who brings the child back to life. There is nothing to warm a soul like another soul that is all aglow.

Evangelism really signifies the beginning of life, bringing men from death into life. When you combine the two – the prophetic with the evangelistic – you have a powerful tool – *"for the perfecting of the saints in their work of ministry unto the edifying of the body of Christ." (Ephesians 4:12)*

The Church needs the prophetic gift to go forth evangelistically with inspired men and women of God, representing God as the Living Christ.

**Question:**

1. Why are questions important to ask a person receiving a prophecy?

## 34. Ministering in the Prophetic by E-mail

*"And the Spirit of the Lord will come upon you, and you shall prophesy with them, and shall be turned into another man,"*
*1 Samuel 10:6.*

In our increasingly virtual world, Facebook (among others) has become a way of making new acquaintances and corresponding with old friends. These people would know that you are prophetic and they may ask you for a prophecy – but how do you go about prophesying over someone by e-mail?

I run a prophetic website where between thirty and fifty people write weekly to my e-mail address and ask for a personal prophecy over their lives. About two thirds of the people writing in, tell us of the situation they are in and want some answers for the questions they have. However, the others simply write in and say: "Can I please have a personal prophecy?"

It is a definite challenge for a novice to receive a prophetic word from a total stranger! So how do you even begin? First, you need to be in the anointing of the Holy Spirit! You also then need to be ready and prepared to use any method that has been personally successful in the past.

If you only experience the anointing of God at church on a Sunday, then you need to put on some praise and worship music, some YouTube videos or whatever. You need the words to prayerfully sing along with the music. In addition, praise and worship the Lord until you feel the presence of God resting on you as He does at church. When you are in the anointing and you can feel the presence of God on you then you can ask the Lord, "Lord, give me a word for this person," then sit at your computer and start to type.

When you are giving a face to face prophetic word to someone, it is always much easier because you can see their reactions as you share the words of knowledge. You can see them nodding, or perhaps see their eyes filling with tears – you know that the prophecy has hit its target. This positive feed-back encourages boldness and faith to continue with the prophecy. However, in an e-mail prophecy, you have absolutely no feed-back whatsoever. This situation can lend itself to a personal attack from the enemy.

When you are giving a prophetic word by e-mail, all you can see is a blank screen. While you type, you may begin to get messages in your mind such as, "I'm crazy. There is no way this is real. What if I am wrong? I should just cancel this e-mail. I should tell the person I can't do it." These are all messages of Satan. You think it is your thoughts but that is not so: Satan is attacking you. Just as the Lord IS speaking and giving you a true message for that person, Satan is dropping his negative words into your head to derail the e-mail.

He is trying to interrupt the anointing and destroy the flow of the prophetic. Satan hates the prophetic word because he hates Christians encouraging others. He is the author of intimidation and low self-esteem. He will do anything to stop you. He wants to destroy your faith in God and you as a person. In the flesh, of course, you are afraid of getting it wrong, but God's anointing is with you and He will not get it wrong! You can do all things in Christ.

Submit yourself to God and rebuke the devil in the Name of Jesus Christ. Continue with your message and finish with a paragraph such as, "If there's something in this prophecy you can't understand or if you have any positive or negative feedback please let me know. I'd love to hear how this prophecy has ministered to you." Then, PRESS the "Send" button! By adding that end note, the person has a choice to write back to you and say, "That was spot on. Thank you for this." Or perhaps: "There's one thing I didn't understand; what did God mean when He said…?"

If you write that closing line, then everything is fine. However, you do need to send the message. It is not easy moving in the prophetic by e-mail to a new Facebook friend or to a stranger. Always remember it is very easy for God and you are His spokesperson. That is why this series is called *The Prophetic Supernatural Experience*. You are moving in the supernatural, and what you are actually doing is delivering a message for a stranger – sending a personal message from God by e-mail to another person.

People in Sydney, Australia, where I live, read the psychic or clairvoyant hotlines in the daily newspapers and ring up at $3.00 a minute to receive a message. Imagine if they knew my e-mail address or my prophetic website address, I would be getting thousands of requests a week! If they knew I was doing it free, then everyone would be writing to me.

The only way you can build more faith in your prophetic gift is to walk in the gift successfully. The way to increase your faith and ability and to increase your courage and boldness in this gift is to practice, practice, and practice stepping out in the gift! As ways to prophesy become riskier, the prophesying methods become more difficult, but your faith in your gift and the Giver of the gift grows accordingly – and that is what God desires.

You need to mature in the gift. You need to be confident to prophesy to anyone, at any time, with the Word of the Lord and get it right. Therefore, I am encouraging you to trust God and prophesy by e-mail.

## **LAURIE'S REFLECTIONS**

34. Ministering in the Prophetic by E-mail

Music is just one way to prepare yourself to minister to others.

*"But now bring me a minstrel, and it came to pass when the minstrel played, that the hand of the Lord came upon him,"* 2 Kings 3:15.

The minstrel induces the birth of the Word of the Lord from a prophet.

*"And the Spirit of the Lord will come upon you, and you shall prophesy with them, and shall be turned into another man,"* 1 Samuel 10:6.

*"And the children of Israel arose, and went up to the house of God, and asked counsel of God, and said, which of us shall go up first to the battle against the children of Benjamin? And the Lord said, Judah shall go up first,"* Judges 20:18.

Music prepares the way for you to minister, to prophesy, to pray... The children of Israel asked God who was to be sent first to battle and He replied "Judah." The word, Judah means Praise! Send Praise first. Send your praises first to prepare yourself for the prophetic or for battle. Could that be why most churches begin their services with praise and worship? Prophets of God, prepare yourselves to prophesy. The prophetic is all about "the battlefield of the mind." Prophets are here to set things straight – to win the battle. *"We do not war against flesh and blood but against principalities, against powers, against the rulers of the darkness of this world, against spiritual wickedness in high places," Eph. 6:12.*

Praying in tongues is another way to get into the anointing. I do not know what I am praying, but I know I am receiving what I need from the Lord.

Stepping out, promising a Word from the Lord is sometimes scary for me; it makes me nervous because it is a big responsibility. If you will pray in tongues for just a few minutes before you begin, it will make a big difference in the prophetic flow and in your boldness before the Lord so that you may speak boldly, as you ought to speak. *"Come boldly before the throne of Grace, that we may obtain mercy, and find grace to help in time of need."*[25]

Prophecy is a gift from God. When you let it move in and through you, it is a prophetic supernatural experience.

### Questions:

1. How many ways are there to minister the prophetic Word? Name a couple of different ways.
2. Are all ways just as effective?
3. How do you build more faith in your prophetic gift?

---

[25] Ephes. 6:19-20; Hebrews 4:16

## 35. Ministering in the Prophetic over Facebook

When you work in a church or minister as part of a church body, people soon learn that you are gifted in the prophetic. As they begin to know you, they may approach you and say, "I have a big problem. Can you seek the Lord for a word for me?"

The same happens on Facebook – as you start making and contacting new friends, they soon learn that you are prophetic and have a gift of prophecy. Then they start to ask you on chat or by instant messages: "Can you please prophesy over me?"

First, before you can minister in the prophetic, you have to be in the anointing. In an ideal world, the presence and anointing of the Lord should be on you when someone asks, "Can you prophesy over me?" For me, I am often in the anointing and carrying a strong presence of the Lord from the time I wake until the time I go to sleep. Often, when people ask me for a prophetic word, I am already in the anointing, and I can readily flow with that anointing.

Often the Holy Spirit will have you listening to some Christian music, reading the Bible, praying, or doing something spiritually uplifting when a person asks you to prophesy over them over chat on Facebook. This is not pure coincidence – the Holy Spirit knows in advance that you are going to be asked and the Holy Spirit gets you in a position where you are in the anointing and the presence of God is on you.

Therefore, when they do ask, you can deliver the goods for them. Jesus, the Holy Spirit and God the Father are exceptionally smart like that! Contrary to popular belief, God is wise and makes good decisions. If we want to emulate Him in any way, we must endeavor to obey Him by doing the things He tells us to do.

My point is that often when people ask you to prophesy over chat, the Lord is ready with a prophecy for the person. All you need to do is to say, "Just wait a second, I'll just commit this in prayer," and you spend a minute or two in prayer. You will find that the presence of the Lord will drop on you. You are then in the anointing and you are ready to prophesy!

The Lord wants to encourage His children. If He has you marked as a vessel with the gift of prophecy and the ability to speak life-giving prophetic words into people's lives, He will certainly use you.

In fact, He will give you opportunity after opportunity to minister in your prophetic gifting. If you are an open vessel with a pure heart full of compassion, you do not have to ask the Lord for opportunities to prophesy. The Lord will start bringing them to you because He wants to speak to His people and He wants to use you.

So do not be over-concerned if someone on Facebook suddenly asks you, "Can you prophesy?" Spend a minute or two in prayer with the Lord asking Him for a word and you will probably find that the Lord will give you a word there and then. In fact, you can nearly always receive a prophetic word for a person who asks – it just comes down to your faith, your ability to step out in that faith, and whether you have enough love and compassion for that person.

If you are in a bad mood, tired, or busy and you just cannot be bothered spending the time to give a person a prophetic word, you will probably make the excuse that you are not in the anointing, not prepared, or you cannot hear anything from the Lord. However, just spend those two minutes coming against your feelings, your tiredness, your distractedness or your busyness. Just spend the two minutes counseling your will: "I'll prepare my heart and prepare my spirit so I can prophesy over this person."

It is rare that a person will catch you in a position where you cannot prophesy when someone asks. Do you think a person would ever have approached Jesus where He would not have the answer for the person? In addition, you have the mind of Christ and you are a valued vessel of Jesus Christ! Therefore, what is the use of being baptized in the Holy Spirit and having the gift of prophecy if you cannot operate in it all the time?

I also find that the length of a prophecy, whether spoken, written or a typed prophecy, is dependent on how loving and compassionate you are. I have written a fifteen-page prophecy once – and it took me all of three hours to write that prophecy – and it could have gone on for another fifty pages if I only had the time or the inclination to write that long. The prophetic gift is God speaking to people He loves! Why then would He *not* speak for as long as possible to someone He loves?

However, if you only manage a one-paragraph prophecy for a person, it is not because God does not want to give a full page. Sometimes it has to do with the time that the prophet has available or the faith that they have to receive a short or long word for that person. That is how you can minister to people and prophesy over chat. You take that minute or two to ask the Lord for a word for the person and align your spirit, so that you can prophesy – then go ahead and just do it! That way, you will bless the person and they will most probably give you good feedback as well.

## **LAURIE'S REFLECTIONS**

35. Ministering in the Prophetic over Facebook.

If you truly wish to prophesy and bless people, then God will speak to you concerning them. *"A man's gift makes room for him, and brings him before great men," Prov. 18:16.*

God gave me a Word for someone that said: "I hear something concerning the number eight." A week or so later, this person updated his status to: "I'm delivering eight samples of my new product to sell at several big chain locations." That's how accurate God is. He is perfect. He gets it right every time. Talk about delivering the goods!

I would like to share a recent Facebook prophecy I received from another prophet. God said to me through this prophet:

> *"Biblical Researcher, Scholar and Author ... Next is the Travels to the Holy Land and Beyond ... Eventually a Bible Commentary ... A Legacy of Biblical Documentation and Revelation for Future Generations in order to Preserve the Integrity and Accuracy of the Gospels ..."*

Praise the Lord! The Lord knows the desires of my heart and He knows the desires of your heart. He knows the desires of all hearts –

as there is but one true heart and that is the heart of the Lord. God's heart is the link to all people.

Facebook is an excellent medium to speak out what the Spirit of the Lord is saying to His people -- for prophecies to go forth. The prophecies I received through Facebook have blessed my heart.

The world is at our fingertips – I think God is pleased with this technology, and we should take full advantage of it when prophesying. I just recently received another word regarding a healing ministry via Facebook – a confirmation of a word I received years ago. Use whatever means God has provided – it is all for His Glory.

**Question:**
1. Do you have to be in church to prophesy?

## 36. Doing what the Father does

*"You have the mind of Christ." 1 Corinthians 2:16*

Let me tell you about a book that I read recently by David Herzog about the Glory of God.

David is a pastor, who operates in the anointing of God. He can preach to a few hundred or even a thousand people in a meeting, then have twenty, thirty, or even a hundred people come forward for prayer. With the anointing of God, he can lay hands on the sick and heal them.

David Herzog writes that there is another realm above that, operating in the glory of God. He explains in detail about how it first happened with him – in Africa – with almost ten thousand people at a single meeting and all of them needing prayer – the sick, the suffering, and the demonized. He said that to pray for all these people through the anointing and the laying of hands would take many hours, if not days. It was then for the first time that the Lord told (a surprised and perplexed) David that he would need to operate in the glory of God.

God told David that He was going to send angels to heal and to cast out the spirits. All He needed David to do was to spend a further half hour in worship, and then, "Start to call out when he saw the angels falling. They will be coming to you in the back right corner. They will be coming to you now. Just call out."

When the angels started to appear, he just started to call, and literally hundreds of people fell to the ground. Some were manifesting demons, and he could see two angels over each person taking the demons out of them. Others were on the ground under the Spirit of the Lord and were being healed. That day, many thousands were delivered of demons and healed, and David did not even have to move from the stage.

The angels just dropped all over the stadium and God's work was completed so quickly. David said that after that experience he always wanted to operate in the glory – it was so much easier. He said that when you spend hours praying for people under the anointing, you can return home extremely tired even though you have been operating under supernatural power – it is tiring to stand for six or seven hours praying for people one by one.

However, David writes that a person who operates in this higher gifting needs to learn how to do what he can see the Father doing. What does that mean? Part of it is the visions, and part of it is talking to the Father, asking, "What do you want me to do here?" and receiving instructions from the Father. Jesus operated in this way. Jesus could have performed many more healings, but He was always asking the Father what to do next and then being led by the Holy Spirit and the Father.

I believe that on many occasions Jesus saw what He was going to do in a vision beforehand, then when He arrived at a specific place He performed exactly what the Father had shown Him in the vision. He went about and performed what He had seen. I have now started to operate in a level of the anointing in the prophetic where I can walk out onto a street and I can have a word of knowledge for everyone I see.

Maybe you could call it one hundred percent anointing. Instead of receiving divine assignments to meet one of a hundred people that the Lord has selected for me to speak to, I can actually go to speak with people on a street about a current issue in their lives and with a message from God to address that issue. God started to show me that, although I knew a great deal about these people, He only wanted me to do prophetic evangelism with those people about whom I had asked and to whom I had received His approval to prophesy.

Finding myself at this level of anointing in the prophetic, I receive many prophetic words for people, but God does not want me to share that prophetic word with a specific person. It is as if I am a radio receiver, just receiving messages for people, but God wants me to be conditioned and He wants you to be conditioned, to the point where, despite whether you have a word for a person, He wants you to ask for His permission to share that word. Often I receive a message for a person, but God does not want me to share that word until much later – right now He needs me to pray for that person according to that need.

## 36. DOING WHAT THE FATHER DOES

Originally, when I found that I had this particular anointing, I would have a message for everyone. I was so caught up in "my enthusiasm" that I would approach people without first asking for the Father's approval, but after a time, I discovered that if I did not ask for the Father's approval, then the prophecy I would give lacked somewhat in its effect on the hearer. This is because I had not been directed by the Holy Spirit to step out at that time. God is our Heavenly Father and, as such, He is continually teaching and correcting us.

Sometimes you can have a dream or a vision where the Father shows you what He wants you to do. You have a vision of the future, so when this vision comes to pass, you do exactly what the vision has shown you. On the other hand, you might receive a vision of the future where something goes wrong. I believe you can change future things from happening: you can do something that makes it right before it goes wrong. This is doing what the Father does.

The Father can show you things through a vision or He can tell you by giving personal instructions. The Holy Spirit can direct you by giving commands – we have talked about being directed by the Holy Spirit – essentially, you are taking commands from the Holy Spirit and doing what the Father wants you to do. There is a level of anointing where your anointing is so strong and you are capable of doing so many things that you need to ask permission of God, and discover exactly what "He" is directing you to do.

## **LAURIE'S REFLECTIONS**

36. Doing What the Father Does

When the Father shares information with you, it is not always for you to share that information with others, but sometimes it is just for you to pray over the situation.

Whatever the case may be, the Lord guides gently, so you must always be mindful of God and His purposes. A word given out of season or not in God's timing is not going to be received in the way it was intended. That is why you seek God on when to prophesy.

Prophesying reminds me of the movie: "Back to the Future" where Marty McFly (Michael J. Fox) goes to the future in a time travel machine and changes the events, thereby changing the outcome of people's lives. Prophesying does not use a physical time travel machine – but it does go into the future by way of a spiritual portal – the Holy Spirit.

Lines from Marty McFly, the time traveler: "Yeah, well, history is gonna change!" and "If you put your mind to it, you can accomplish anything." This movie was a huge success. It was the most successful film in 1985. People want to believe in the ability of accomplishing anything they put their mind to.

*"You have the mind of Christ,"*[26] *"...with God all things are possible."*[27]

When a prophet prays, he has the ability to change things around so certain pitfalls can be avoided. You might have a dream about someone and find out they need prayer. Get to praying! A prophet is on the scene to make a change. He speaks a word that changes the future. The future is determined by how you speak now.

Go "back to the future" and rewrite the script. It makes all the difference in the world. Write it out and "make it plain." The future is now.

*"And the Lord answered me, and said, 'Write the vision, and make it plain upon tables, that he may run that readeth it," Habakkuk 2:2.*

### Questions:
1. How does a prophet go into the future?
2. What do you need to rewrite if you want something to be different or if you are making plans for the future?

---

[26] 1 Cor. 2:16
[27] Matt. 19:26; Mark 9:23, 10:27;

## 37. Prophetic Prayer.

*"My people perish for lack of knowledge."  Hosea 4:6*

Prophetic prayer is a combination of the prophetic gifts of prophecy and prayer and it also includes writing in the spirit.

A prayer spoken in "tongues" is a perfect prayer because it comes directly from the Holy Spirit. In 1 Corinthians 14:13 the Apostle Paul instructs us to pray for an interpretation of such a prayer. However, writing a prayer in the Spirit is taking dictation from the Holy Spirit on what to write and say in a prayer. Therefore, when you move in the prophetic, you can ask the Lord to pray a prayer through you, then you just start to say what the Holy Spirit says, and that would be your prayer.

I call this praying in tongues but in English! Such a prayer could be said at a prayer meeting or sent in printed form by e-mail to someone. When you are moving that way, the prayer may contain a dimension of the gift of prophecy flowing with the associated word of knowledge and word of wisdom. (These have been covered in earlier chapters: 6, 8, 9, 10 and 11.) As you can imagine, a prophetic prayer is extremely encouraging. It builds faith in either the hearer of the spoken word, or the receiver of the printed form.

When you are accustomed to ministering in the prophetic, people will respond to such a prayer in a positive way. It really builds up their faith. Prayers should be powerful in the prophetic arena – either for a training prophet or for someone moving in the gifts of prophecy. Prayers are not to come from the flesh or from your own ideas. They should come from the Spirit of God speaking through you as a vessel to accomplish God's will for another person. Of course, you could pray a prophetic prayer for yourself (that would be very edifying) but here I am essentially talking about praying for others.

I would like to pray a prophetic prayer for all my readers, and I will give you an example with a recent prophetic prayer for a friend called Kevin. (Obviously, this is not his real name.)

*Dear Father in Heaven, I pray that you would open the eyes of understanding in Kevin's heart. I pray that you would lead him by your Holy Spirit to open and illuminate each step that he is to take. I pray that you will deal with the insecurities in his heart, and the hurting and the longings in his heart to be loved and truly accepted for the person he is.*

*I pray that you will address the wounds in his life, those wounds of not measuring up to certain people in the past. I pray that through his life, edifying words in the Bible, and through your Holy Spirit, will encourage him and heal those wounds so he can move on as a fully restored sanctified man of God moving on to do your will. I pray specifically that you would equip Kevin with more supernatural wisdom.*

*I pray that wisdom, not only wisdom from you, as a profound insight and direction for his life, but also wisdom coming and bubbling from a spring of his own intellect and knowledge. I pray that Kevin would have an increased ability to remember what he has written; to reprocess and reorganize what he has written and heard, and represent that in what he teaches and what he shares with the students that he works with.*

*I pray that you touch his life with an anointing so strong that when he speaks and when he writes, the people are compelled to listen. I pray that, as he speaks on the things of God, the things in the spiritual dimension, and other practical matters, and shares his heart with the students he is training that their hearts begin to burn within them just as the apostles' hearts burned when listening to Jesus sharing as they walked on the road to Emmaus.*

*I pray that you give Kevin a full insight, a full understanding of his potential that he has in you God. I pray that you open his eyes of understanding to who he really is in you, and to his life purpose and his life potential. I know that you see Kevin, Lord, as someone who could be a seer over a major charity or major organization in any country of the world.*

*I know that you have blessed Kevin with a sharp racing intellect, an understanding character and a loving and compassionate heart, for*

## 37. PROPHETIC PRAYER.

*your purposes. I know Kevin's heart is set on you and on doing the best for you, so I pray that you touch his insecurities and you open them so he is operating in everything he does through a healed life – fully restored through you.*

*Let him remember the wounds and let him remember the hurts, and let him use those in acts of compassion and understanding as he ministers and works with wounded and broken people. Let what has happened to him in his past, and the understanding and the hurts that he has of his past, become regenerated and sanctified so they can be a mighty weapon in his hands against the works of darkness that the enemy brings on the people who live in this world.*

*May you raise him in the eyes of his peers and in the kingdom of God – may you set his feet on high places as a deer running through the mountains of the Lord God Almighty – may you lead him to your holy hill – may you saturate him with your presence – may you increase the anointing in his life and increase his ears of understanding.*

*May you let him apply that wisdom and move in great power, signs, and wonders for the future, and to move supernaturally in your power. Not only in what he says, but also in the practical outworking of his faith, with real signs that even skeptics may believe. I ask all of this in Jesus' name, Amen.*

That is an example of a prophetic prayer containing many words of knowledge. I do not even know Kevin's last name but I am sure he would appreciate receiving that prayer when I send him the link. Moreover, I hope you realize that prayer would also be an edifying prayer for me to have prayed over your personal life.

## **LAURIE'S REFLECTIONS**

37. Prophetic Prayer.

Begin your prayer and let the words flow. That is the only way to pray effectively and prophetically. The prayer may be short or lengthy. Short works well for me, but I know length is what people are looking for. They should understand that it only takes one word from God – just one word.

Each prophet has his own prayer language or method. For instance, when the Lord speaks to me, He may give me a song title, a catchy phrase, a jingle or anything that He knows I have knowledge of. For example, He's given me "Tonight's the Night" (song title by Rod Stewart), "Don't Rock the Boat" (by the Hue Corporation), and other titles. Once I heard these lyrics: Money, money, money, money. That's all I received from the Lord so I sang the words to the tune I heard. Later I found out that it's a line from the song "For the Love of Money" by the O'Jays.

I'm not a music guru, but if the music I do know fits the bill, the Lord speaks to me and I relay the message. The Lord draws on all your knowledge to get the message across.

Your education is very important. He gives you Words from all subjects: science, history, math, music, art, and any special activities such as basketball, hockey, golf etc. He even uses cartoon characters!

Broaden your horizons to give the Lord a broader base to work with. He pulls from your knowledge to fit the person receiving the prophecy. That is why it is so important to read and study – always be about learning *something*. God can and will use your knowledge to be a blessing to others.

I know some powerful prayer warriors. Their words flow out with authority. That is my prayer – to have powerful prophetic prayer flow from my lips to fit whatever situation may arise.

Once the words are spoken, once they have been sent forth, they cannot return void.

### Questions:
1. What helps with the "flow" during a prophetic prayer?
2. How many words should a prophecy contain?

## 38. Getting into the Anointing to Prophesy

*After that thou shalt come to the hill of God, where it is the garrison of the Philistines: and it shall come to pass, when thou art come thither to the city, that thou shalt meet a company of prophets coming down from the high place with a psaltery, and a tambourine, and a pipe, and a harp, before them; and they shall prophesy. And the Spirit of the Lord will come upon thee, and thou shalt prophesy with them, and shalt be turned into another man. And let it be, when these signs are come unto thee, that thou do as occasion serves thee; for God is with thee." 1 Samuel 10:5-7*

If you are like me, it might take some considerable preparation with the Lord, in order to operate in the prophetic gifting. Any Christian, who limits his mind to mortal thoughts throughout his daily routine, cannot move straight into the prophetic. Most times, if you want to move in the gift of prophecy, in a prayer line, or to minister out front in your church, you need a time of preparation so the presence and anointing of God can rest on you.

When a person needs to be ministered to, you need to be in a "state" where you can go outside yourself to receive and deliver God's message to them. You certainly do not want to hamper a prophetic word or to allow flesh words to spoil the flavor of the prophecy for a person. You want to function like a tap that allows fresh, cleansing and invigorating water to be poured out and into a seeker of God's Word. A prophetic person is the pipe that carries God's Word from one place to another.

Every prophetic person has their own unique language, and this is based on the background and intellect of the person delivering the word. This will always be the case, and even when reading the prophets of the Old Testament, you can see several personalities emanating from the prophetic words that they give. Therefore, there are a few ways that I use to put myself in the "right frame of mind" to enter the anointing and deliver a prophetic word.

Most days, I operate in a strong anointing and presence of God all the time, but at times, I use a few "additional" methods that I have spoken of in other chapters. These preparation methods will enable me to enter into the presence and anointing of God.

1. Come before the Lord, and sing praise and worship songs.
2. Spend time with the Lord in prayer.
3. Spend time in the Word of God.

Any, or a combination of these three, for between a half hour and forty-five minutes should prepare you to be receptive to God's voice for someone – you will know yourself that you are closer to God.

Say for example you are going to do a prophecy over me, you would of course want to test your gift of prophecy – in Chapter 55 I share a prayer with you on how you can pray for the gift of prophecy. After preparing yourself with one or all of the methods above, I would suggest that you just sit down at the computer and say, "Lord, please help me with a word for Matthew."

Then open your browser or your e-mail, and start typing, "Matthew, I believe that the Lord has a message for you that says…" As you type the word "says", a new sentence will appear in your mind. You type that sentence and when you have finished, another sentence will appear in your mind, and so it goes on. Often, by about the third or fourth sentence, you might get a thought crossing your mind like: "But this is only me speaking." You ignore that thought because it is coming straight from Satan.

Instead, continue for one or two paragraphs with your prophecy, address it to me, and press, "Send." Anyone who sends me a message like that will receive feedback and I will assure him or her whether that message truly came from God. Getting into the anointing for prophecy is a serious business. If you are not fully prepared and totally immersed in the anointing of God, there is a strong likelihood that you can give a false word or a false prophecy when you speak what you think God wants a person to hear.

If you are not fully prepared in the anointing, you could speak out of your own flesh or even a wrong spirit can speak a message through you to a person. Therefore, it is important for you to place yourself in the anointing. It is not a hard thing to do. Most people feel the presence of God or feel an example of the anointing in their life to a certain extent when they go to church, and sing and worship once a week.

That feeling of peace and joy you feel when worshipping God is the same feeling you want before you start to prophesy. Once you are confident and you have prophesied a few times – and have been right – then just continue to go through the same process each time. It is that easy, folks.

## **LAURIE'S REFLECTIONS**

38. Getting into the Anointing to Prophesy

Music produced a soothing influence on the perplexed spirit of King Saul, who was himself a prophet in some sense, but we are told that whole companies of prophets went in procession with musical instruments before them (1 Sam. 10:5), and Elisha actually sent for a minstrel (a harpist), as if to put himself into a right frame of mind before prophesying (2 Kings 3:15). The habit of prophesying upon a harp, for the purpose of praising God with a musical accompaniment, is referred to in 1 Chronicles 25:1. Music evidently could help prepare for the knowledge of God to come forth.

As a prophet, you should be involved in a prophetic ministry. Ask God to lead you to the right ministry for you, and then "follow the leader." Submit yourself to the leader and be trained under the authority of the head. The anointing flows down, not up.

If you know Prophet Kim Clement, then you know that in order to deliver the Word of the Lord to the nations, he prepares himself through his music.

Others will pray in the Spirit by speaking in tongues, until they feel the release and then they will prophesy. And of course, you must spend time in the Word of God, to deliver a Word from God.

Some people meet God when they raise their hands in praise and worship and thanksgiving. For others, just the simple act of standing when the music starts will bring on the anointing and they will get "caught up in the air and meet Christ there."

I love the use of banners. I love to wave them as I move my arms in praise and worship.

If I listen and sing along with the music long enough, I might "break out" in tongues, or if I start with praying in the Spirit, I might "break out" in song; as the Holy Spirit moves, I might even break out in dance. Watch out now! The Lord has been moving me in the direction of war-like dancing. I feel a kindred spirit with the early worshipers of the One Great Spirit. Sometimes when I dance I can feel my legs getting weaker and I feel as if I might fall to the ground.

I love using the Word of God to bring on the anointing. Sometimes God just wants you to encourage someone with a Scripture. Studying the Word of God can bring such a peace and joy, just like speaking in tongues or singing praises.

All these methods are great ways in which to prepare yourself for a fresh anointing of God.

### Question:

1. How do you prepare yourself to prophesy to others and enter into God's anointing?

## 39. Handling a False Word

*"According to your faith, be it unto you." Matthew 9:29*

Now let us look at what to do when you give a false prophecy to someone. What do you do when you give a prophecy to a person and they say: "There is no way that message came from God because it was all wrong!"?

How then do you cope? What do you do? Do you give up prophesying? I can tell you something for sure – if you are anything like me, you will feel like giving up prophesying right there and then. You will start asking God questions – How could I be wrong Lord?

- "How could you give me a gift of prophecy and let me make a mistake?
- "Don't you know this embarrasses me, God? How can I go on now?"
- "How can I ever be sure that I'm giving a true prophecy to a person?"

These questions will fill your mind with doubt. You will doubt yourself, but even more, you will doubt God's goodness toward you! And is that not what Satan did to Eve in the Garden? Satan wins if he can successfully discredit God in some way! Your ego will want to just walk away from the prophetic office!

If you are going to move in the gift of prophecy and be a prophetic person, there is one thing I can guarantee: you are going to get a prophecy wrong at some time or other. There are many reasons why people deliver a wrong prophecy. I have touched on this in an earlier chapter, but for clarity I am going through it again.

Perhaps you are partly speaking through the flesh – you are not fully in the anointing of God! Therefore, you speak a word that you think God wants to speak but in fact, it is your own idea. You can have a proper prophetic word coming through, but yet you add a sentence or two that you think the person needs to hear.

A wrong or demonic spirit can speak through you and you think it is God. I have had a wrong spirit come on me, and it felt as if I were in an anointing. I felt as if I had the presence of God on me when I prophesied but it came out totally wrong.

You can also be accused of giving a false word even when the word is not false. The person receiving the word fails to properly understand the prophetic word so they dismiss it as being false.

The prophetic word relates to the future: it will manifest later on.

I have given you four reasons and there could possibly be many more. How do you handle it? First, you have to discern your motives that make you want to move in the prophetic office. Are they in line with God's motives? Do you want to encourage people, to build them up, to give them life-affirming messages, to bless people, to do the will of God, to be used by God, to have a gift that can do great things for the people of God? Are you seriously motivated by the joy of helping others and to do your part in advancing God's kingdom purposes on earth?

Alternatively, are you in it for personal advantage in some way? If true, then giving false prophecies will surely damage your ego! You will want to give it all away. In fact, God may make sure that you fail in order for you to search your inner heart. God is not vindictive, but He needs to chastise His children so that they experience repentance. It is only when you have delivered a couple of false prophecies that you begin to realign yourself for the right reasons. If you are in it to bless others, you will quickly get over the fact that you missed it and somehow got one wrong.

Even in basketball, the finest shooters in the world occasionally miss the basket. Do they quit the game? Perhaps a preacher receives a wrong interpretation and preaches this error to his congregation. Do they quit as a pastor? A person who does not understand the Bible as clearly as you do, might write a book on a certain aspect that is wrong. Just because he does not fully understand the subject, does he cancel the book? You miss it with one prophecy and get it wrong. Do you quit prophesying?

People have a nasty habit of holding on to Old Testament laws by saying that a prophet must be right all the time. However, I will tell you something for free: if I were right all the time, I would be having a serious problem with pride. As with any other occupation, as a prophet matures, the accuracy level of the prophecy improves. Also, as a prophet matures, the depth of his prophecies will grow.

The flesh becomes less involved and the person begins to distinguish when they are in or not in the anointing of God. Also they will discern when they have a counterfeit word given through them. How do you handle delivering a false word? You get over it! You apologize to the person then you get on with more prophecies. With ongoing positive feedback from correct prophecies, your confidence will grow again!

You are going to be attacked by Satan, and he is going to try to discourage you in all sorts of ways when you move in the prophetic. One of his best ways of knocking people out of the race is having them deliver false prophecies so they begin to mistrust themselves or become embarrassed. They then lament "Oh, I can never be trusted anymore. I've just ruined my name."

Are you in it for your own glory? Are you in it for your own name? On the other hand, are you in it to serve God and to serve the people of God? Were you called by God to prophesy or is it something that you thought you might try because it is trendy? If you are prophesying for the right reasons, no false prophecy will stop you! I hope I have encouraged you just a little more!

## **LAURIE'S REFLECTIONS**

39. Handling a False Word

I prophesy and moved on to the next prophecy without thoughts as to whether the one receiving it believes it to be true or not. I believe the words to be from God – how could I think them up? I won't lie. Thoughts do try to enter in, but I cut them off before they have a chance to finish one complete sentence. Be gone! I always say.

God plants thoughts, but if you think it to be false, it will be false. *"According to your faith, be it unto you,"* Matthew 9:29.

Sometimes, people will say, "Well, you got that one wrong," and you can say, "Well, okay, if you say so." It is up to the receiver to receive. Your job is to deliver and leave the rest up to God. If you are a true prophet, the Word of the Lord will not fail. It may take a while for things to line up for that Word to come to pass, but it is not up to you to line things up and it does not make you a false prophet.

Do not be moved by people's faces. They will look at you as if to say, "What does that mean? Give me another Word; I don't like that one. You don't know what you are talking about. This is all a fake!" Do not be moved. Continue doing what you know God has called you to do – PROPHESY!

Maybe God is dealing with you and your pride, so He throws you a curve ball in the form of a disbelieving look. If you know that you know that a Word is coming from God, be humble of course, but do not worry yourself over it. God is just helping you become strong in Him.

Thank God for the gift of prophecy. It is a great gift that is used for edification (a lifting up), exhortation (to encourage), and to comfort others. If you keep these three "reasons for prophecy" in mind, you cannot go wrong. God is true to His Word. God cannot lie.

When you are prophesying, it is not about you. If you give a false word, it might be because you are prophesying to someone who believes a lie! If he is expecting a lie, he will indeed receive a lie! That is hard to understand, but God honors our expectations. If you expect a true word, you will receive a true word and that is the truth of it.

There is a fine line in the spirit realm that would be wise for you not to cross; it is so fine that it is best not to get near it. It is the line that divides a truth from a lie. God is the author and finisher of my faith, (Heb. 12:2.) Anything outside of that is a lie from the pit of hell.

God has allowed me to go take a "look-see" at the dark side of the matter. It is not a good place. I did not go very deep, but it was deep enough for it to "mess with my mind" for a little bit – until I decided that I never want to go back there again!

While I was in this place of "discovering" for myself this thing called "prophecy," I was in training (I am always in training, I just mean that I was in the first stages of training) and standing before the prophets with my family, everyone received a prophecy except me.

During this "dark" time in my life, I knew it was because the prophets felt the presence of an evil spirit upon me so they left me alone for my own good. I am very thankful to them for that. I remember one time in particular standing before a very seasoned prophet; when he looked upon me, I saw the look that said, "What's wrong with you? Why are you at the place that you are at?" I was defiant at that moment and embarrassed the next.

Needless to say, I left that dark place soon with the knowing that I know: that Christ is the ONLY WAY. It is hard for me to even say that because, of course, He is; I have always believed that, but when you start learning some of the mysteries of God, you need to keep the right perspective or you may find yourself somewhere where you do not want to be.

As you mature in the Lord, let Him lead and guide you in your prophetic walk.

### Questions:
1. Why would a person receive a false word?
2. Why would a prophet give a false word?

## 40. Handling Satan's Attacks

*"All things work together for good for those who love God and are called according to His purpose." Romans 8:28*

All prophetic people come under extreme assault by Satan; his primary purpose and plan of attack is to make you give up! He does this by causing you to doubt yourself, and worse still, to doubt God Himself!

Imagine bombs start exploding all around an advancing battalion of soldiers, what would be their instant response? If they had not been properly trained, terror would cause them to just run! This is the reaction of an untrained person. Therefore, all soldiers need to be trained to advance regardless of what kind of attack they are under, and often today, these people are trained under real battle conditions – flying bullets and all. They are put through professional training and monotonous drills in order to be taught the discipline of every soldier needs. They are trained to handle fear and how to instantly take commands from their superiors without question!

Many people who move in the prophetic have not really been given due warning by the Holy Spirit (or one of his earthly helpers) that Satan is going to attack them in a fierce way. I had been operating in the prophetic for several years when one day Jesus woke me from my sleep. While I was talking to Him, He suddenly said, "I want you to start a prophetic web site," and of course, I replied, "How?"

He said, "Just write a web site and put it up online." I already knew how to write certain words on the front-page of a web site so it could be quickly found by the search engines, and placed on the first pages of Yahoo and MSN (I think they call it Bing now). Anyway, my web page reached number one and two on MSN and Yahoo, and suddenly I was busy taking requests for prophecy.

All my life, it seems, I have been in a Christian battle, with what seemed like spiritual bullets flying past me all the time. However, as soon as I started the prophetic web site, it was no longer just bullets flying past me – it was now more like bombs, mortars, shells (and a few intergalactic ballistic missiles thrown in) were going off all

## 41. Hearing Jesus Speak

around me. It was dangerous. It was frightening – and all I had done was to start a web site offering prophecy for Christians. I had no idea of how much Satan hated me doing that.

Therefore, we need to establish spiritual warfare strategies for victory. There are several things you need to do.

- You have to be established in the Word of God.
- You have to know who God is.
- You have to know what your spiritual rights are, as a Christian.
- You have to know the promises of God.
- You have to understand that everything happens for a reason. Memorize and claim Romans 8:28, *"All things work together for good for those who love God and are called according to His purpose."*

If you have been called to be a prophet or to operate in the prophetic, that is God's purpose in your life – that is God's calling! Therefore, no matter how bad things get or what happens to you, when you enter the prophetic or while ever you are operating in the prophetic, all things will work out together for good. You have to know that – Romans 8:28! You have to know that the Holy Spirit is far more powerful than Satan is. *"He who is in you, is greater than he who is in the world."* I John 4:4a

You have to understand that no matter how rough the waters become (even if it seems as though your boat will not weather the storm and is likely to sink), you still have a Jesus who is yesterday, today and forever the same! He can still say 'Peace' to the storm and solve the problem. You still have a Jesus that walks on water. You still have a Jesus whose hand you can grab and walk with Him right out of the stormy sea until there is land.

You have to understand that God the Father loves you and you will only receive a certain number of attacks – attacks on which to build your faith, your courage, and who you are. You have to understand that God never allows us to suffer more than we can endure. You have to know there is no temptation in which God has not provided an escape route for you. (1 Corinthians 10:13) You have to understand all that!

Another way of handling Satan's attack is to have people who love you, to start praying for you and holding you up in prayer to give you a covering. The most important thing for you to do is to have your prophetic lifestyle and prophetic ministry supported and covered by your pastor. You need to approach your pastor and say that you have been called by God to start ministering in the prophetic – find out from the pastor what you need to do to become accepted and authenticated to move in the prophetic at church, and whether you have your pastor's approval.

If you are moving in ministry or joining a prophetic group who ministers in the prophetic, you need your pastor to give approval for that as well, because if you move in the prophetic and your pastor is not covering you by giving approval to what you are doing, you are outside the protection of God and you are wide open to be attacked by Satan; he has legal right to attack you because you have stepped outside of God's set down guidelines.

It does not matter if a prophetic group says that they will cover you. You need to be covered by your local pastor. If you go ahead and join such a group without your pastor's approval, then you are setting yourself up as a prime target! You will need to either find a church and a pastor that approves of your move or dismiss the group idea all together!

The last thing you want is to allow pride, rebellion and disobedience to rob you of God's blessings. In that condition, you are no benefit to anyone. A verse comes to mind: *"You are the salt of the earth; but if the salt loses its flavor, how shall it be seasoned? It is then good for nothing but to be thrown out and trampled underfoot by men." Matthew 5:13* – Satan's trampling would be far worse! A favorite preacher of mine says: "Satan will eat your lunch and pop the bag!"

Based on my own experience and my own understanding, all the following is true! With people praying for you, with a proper understanding of the Word of God, with prayer in your own life, with time and intimacy with God, and with your pastor's covering,

## 41. Hearing Jesus Speak

you will be just fine. You will weather the attacks, you will grow in God, and that is how you handle Satan's attacks – and win.

## LAURIE'S REFLECTIONS

40. Handling Satan's Attacks

I recently heard Pastor Ron Carpenter teach a sermon called "Staying in the Area of Blessings"; if you do that, then Satan cannot reach you, but if you move yourself out of the area of blessings, watch out! Satan can and will attack. He said that there are three areas of blessings based on Scripture, and in summary, those areas are: the family, your church, and your tithes.

1. The Family: Your family must be in order, starting with the head and helper, and then the children. When your house is out of order, it gives the enemy ground for a foothold.

2. Your church: If your church is not in order, then the whole house is out of order. Look at your leadership and the families that make up the church. Is everything in order?

3. Your tithes: If you are not tithing, you have no personal spiritual covering.

Being in the prophetic brings double attack, so it is of the utmost importance that you have things in order and stay covered through tithes and offerings and keep yourself under your covering, be it your mentor, pastor, husband, or parents.

Bishop Charlie Berrian's teachings on the adversity helped me understand and accept certain "weather conditions" (storms.) They are based on the Scripture found in Isaiah:

> *"And though **the Lord** gives you the bread [food] of adversity [trouble], and the water [drink] of affliction [sorrow], yet **shall not** thy teachers [the Lord has appointed the adversity to be your teacher] be removed into a corner anymore, but your eyes shall see your teachers. And your ears shall hear a word behind you, saying: "This is the way,*

*walk you in it, when you turn to the right hand, and when you turn to the left," Isaiah 30:20-21.*

When you know God, you will know that the adversary is your teacher.

*And the Lord stirred up an <u>adversary</u> unto Solomon[28]...And God stirred him up another <u>adversary</u>, Rezon...thus said the Lord God; An <u>adversary</u> there shall be...*

The Lord sends the adversary to you as your teacher. It is hard at times, but as you walk through the process, God is by your side. As you control your emotions and believe that God will take you through the fire and bring you out without the smell of smoke, you can be comforted in knowing that God has your back; He is behind you, in front of you, beneath you, holding you up. He is on all sides protecting you from the fiery darts of hell. *"No weapon formed against you shall prosper," Isaiah 54:17.*

### Questions:
1. Who gives you the bread of adversity and the water of affliction?
2. Who is your teacher?
3. How do you handle certain attacks?

---

[28] 1 Kings 11:14; 11:23; Amos 3:11

## 41. Hearing Jesus Speak

**PART 4: The Supernatural Experience**

## 41. Hearing Jesus Speak

*"My sheep hear my voice, and I know them, and they follow me." John 10:27*

I was saved at the age of eight. At church we sung various choruses from a book called "Scripture in Song", which was almost word-for-word Scriptures set to music. I know that it was at that time that Jesus first began speaking to me. When I was feeling down or I needed an answer, one of these choruses would begin to play in my head – I just knew it was Jesus ministering to me. Soon, I would be reassured and happy again. Also, I began to feel increasingly reassured with every new Scripture verse I learned.

My mother was a Sunday-School teacher. Her method of having us memorizing Scripture verses paid off! She would not give us our weekly pocket money until we could memorize a Bible verse that was placed on the bathroom mirror each week. As we brushed our teeth or had a morning shower, we had to read the verse, so that by the end of the week, we would have to recite it and its reference to her. Then we were paid our pocket money. (Bribery for children works very well!)

Therefore, over the years, I retained a fair percentage of memorized verses. I might be walking down the street feeling sad or worried or even talking to Jesus when a scripture verse would just pop into my mind, and that is how Jesus began speaking to me – first through choruses and Bible verses, and then slowly He began to speak in a voice with clear sentences just for me. This has continually progressed. Now I can have a two-way conversation with Jesus where He can speak a sentence to me, and I will reply with a sentence for Him. Today, I sit at my computer and take dictation from Him – He can speak to me or speak to others through me. What I am saying is that it all came from a planted seed that was fertilized and nurtured.

The longest prophecy I have ever given is fifteen pages – three hours' worth of flat-out typing. This prophecy blessed the person who received it for many years. Hearing from Jesus is something extremely exciting! Not just the voice of the Holy Spirit – although

## 41. HEARING JESUS SPEAK

the Holy Spirit acts as a telephone cord to bring the voice of Jesus. This is Jesus, the Messiah, the Son of God who died on the cross – Jesus talking to He and me wants to do the same for all His siblings.

However, I have come to realize that this is unusual to most Christians, but I am so glad it has happened to me! Many talk about receiving impressions or ideas from God or the Holy Spirit, but it is rare for them to say they have heard a clear sentence being spoken. In John 10, Jesus said He is the Good Shepherd and His sheep hear His voice, so they will not be deceived by a false shepherd. Therefore, I wonder why more Christians do not regularly hear Jesus speak to them. I think it is out of ignorance, mostly.

When someone is preaching, often they move from flesh into the Holy Spirit, and they begin speaking the words of the Holy Spirit. If you are in touch with the Holy Spirit and the voice of Jesus, you know exactly when this shift occurs. You know His voice just as you know the unique voice of each of your siblings. So it is with God the Father and Jesus when they speak to me – I know their voices for I can distinguish the different resonance.

This ability may be a gift or a developed talent, but I know how I sound when I talk to myself and I have learned the sound of my Savior's voice. I live alone and Jesus is my best friend. I talk about everything with Him! Got instance, when a famous singer was in trouble, I asked Jesus: "Did he really do that, or was he just foolish sleeping with a young child?" Jesus replied, "He is just foolish. He is like a child himself." Many fans turned away because of that controversy, but with one simple question to Jesus, everything was settled in my mind.

It is one thing to know about Jesus, but it is another thing to hear Him speak – to discuss Scriptures with Him, to discuss books, people, situations, and world events with Him. To walk and talk... as in the old song, *"and He walks with me and He talks with me, and He tells me I am His own."* (This is from an old hymn: maybe called: *"In The Garden."*) That too, was a wonderful seed planted in my early days! I have always wanted to walk and talk with Jesus, just He and I all alone!

## LAURIE'S REFLECTIONS

41. Hearing Jesus Speak

Jesus speaks to me through His Word, yes, but I also hear Him at other times; He tells us all what is on His mind, and the Father commands us to hear Him. *"Hear ye Him," Matthew 17:5.* He speaks to us on a variety of subjects; He instructs, exhorts, warns, directs, and comforts. He always speaks in love. Every word is intended to do us good.

Train yourself to listen and hear His voice. It takes time to build up your spirit. Most people think they do not have time. Make the time. Do an inventory of your time. Where has your time gone? We all have the same amount of time – twenty-four hours in each day. What we call "spare" time is not spare time at all; it is the time when you should be listening to what the Spirit of the Lord is saying to you. It is time given to you to study His Word.

Jesus speaks in many ways. I have already mentioned that He speaks to me through songs, and movies but other times it could be a street sign or through what someone else has said. Sometimes it is through my children.

If you listen carefully, you can hear His voice when others speak. When you listen to a pastor or teacher, you can hear the Lord Jesus speaking directly to you through them.

We hear His voice speaking to us in our own hearts. We hear for ourselves, not for other people. God is speaking to you about you, not about your spouse or your neighbor – it's all about you. THEN – when you get that; when you go through the process of the purification – you can hear on behalf of others, but still God is talking to you, about you.

This is the hearing of the inner voice of God.

**Question:**

1. How does Jesus usually speak to you?

## 42. Hearing the Father Speak

*"Faith comes by hearing and hearing the Word of God."*
*Romans 10:17*

For years, my father had a serious anger problem. He has mellowed out now, but when we were kids and teenagers, he used to lose his temper over "anything" and I was constantly afraid of him – nowadays many would say that my two brothers and I suffered an abusive relationship with him. Even by his own admission, he would punish us boys in anger. I never saw him act this way with my elder sister though. His outbursts of anger caused emotional damage in my life, but worse, it caused spiritual damage because, for most of my life I was afraid to address God the Father because I had the idea that He would be angry with me too.

Jesus was my friend; He was safe; He is God, but like a brother. He was my friend or mate (as we Aussies say), but the concept of God the Father just filled me with fear. Fear is debilitating: it robs you and the devil loves it!

It took many years of talking and growing close to Jesus before I was even willing to speak to God the Father or I was able to hear Him speak. Maybe, like me, you found that you were more comfortable having a relationship with Jesus – talking and praying to Jesus – but I am a living testimony that these wounds can be healed and you can forgive, and you can come to the point where you are comfortable talking to God the Father *and your own father*.

When I was ready, the Father began to speak to me. I could hear Him and I was comfortable with Him. Many people say that the difference with the Father is the quiet and gentle voice as mentioned in 1 Kings 19:12. Here, Elijah, the prophet describes God's voice as a *still small voice*. All I can say is that when the Father speaks to me there is more authority in His voice – because it is serious business! To me, it suggests seriousness in the resonance and the frequency of His voice. There also seems to be more power and authority in His voice. Moreover, if I am in any doubt as to who is speaking to me, I will just ask, "Is that you, Father?" I will get a Yes or a No answer. If it is a No, I will hear: "It is Jesus."

Now I know all three members of the Trinity. Many think the Father knows more than the Son does. The Son was promoted to sit on the right side of the Father in the seat of authority in heaven. People quote Jesus and say that He does not know the day or the hour that He is going to return, and because of that, He knows less than the Father does. (I believe that Jesus humbled Himself to live a subordinate role on earth, in order to identify with man, but as Lord of Heaven He would now know the date of His return.) Because of the Cross, Jesus is the designated Judge of the whole earth. He will personally take down Satan and rule here on earth for one thousand years.

Therefore, the idea of the Father knowing more, to my mind, is stretching things somewhat. The Triune God is God having three unique roles to play. They are all on the same page! As I said, I think Jesus may be well aware of the day of His return, but I could be wrong. Scripturally, you may want to take issue with me on this point, but what does that have to do with the Father? All I am saying is that Jesus and the Father are on the same page! Therefore, if you are like me and have developed a friendship with Jesus, then it is not much of a step to have a relationship with the Father.

If you go through counseling to develop inner healing and forgiveness in your relationships with men, you can reach a stage where you realize that the Father is not going to be angry with you. If you have experienced Jesus talking to you, then it is going to be no different with the Father. However, the Father is not going to speak to you against your will – He is a perfect gentleman and He is not going to intrude or push Himself on you. It took many years – more than twenty years – before the Father began to speak to me.

Jesus says, *"I'm the Way, the Truth, and the Life. No one comes to the Father except through Me,"* John 14:6.

I can vouch for the truth of this in my life as I only come to know the Father through His son, Jesus Christ. It took me a long time as a Christian to reach that stage, and a few more years before I was ready to talk, pray, and converse with the Father. Therefore, I can understand if you have trepidation or concern in this area. Once I had a vision of going to heaven, but I feared meeting the Father because I was in a particular sin at the time and I believed that on meeting the Father, I would be struck dead.

To the reader, my theology may be rather strange. I have never gone to Bible College because God has never led me that way. This book is the result of my walk with God, Bible study, and experiences that God has allowed me to go through. This book has blessed me and I hope it is blessing you as well.

## LAURIE'S REFLECTIONS

42 Hearing the Father Speak

Have I mentioned that my father is an alcoholic, and that when I was a young girl he became an absentee father? He left, not to be heard from again – until twenty years later. By that time I was all grown up with children of my own.

Father God *"shall never leave you nor forsake you."* But that is not what happened in my family. It is no wonder that I had pictured God somewhere way over there, high in the sky, absent from my life.

As a mother, I wanted to take my children to church. We attended the same church for many years – up until I felt the Lord leading me deeper into His Word and into a deeper walk with Him. Each church has been beneficial in my spiritual growth and I would not change that walk. I can see how, in the past fifteen or twenty years, each place of worship has brought me closer to God and has opened up my mind to receive the Truth.

I believe just as recently as this week (in 2011) that I have learned the difference in the sound of the Son and the Father, because Scripture says, *"I and my father are one,"* John 10:30, so I just assumed they sounded the same, but the other day when I audibly heard a voice that was loud and clear, I knew it was my Heavenly Father – it was so authoritative!

There is one particular prophet that sounds like a father when he prophesies to me, and I know that Father God is speaking to me – it's so authoritative! He is even called "Father" in the ministry.

My God loves me and wants only the best for me, so I know that when he is correcting me or needs to give me a stern word, it comes through this prophet, Father ------. It does not necessarily have to be stern anymore because the Lord has made it clear that hearing this particular prophet is like hearing the Father speak.

The principal of a school I taught at years ago said: Don't smile until after Christmas. This gives the class time enough to understand that you mean business! Once back from the Christmas break, the class pretty much understands the rules. It is no longer necessary to be so stern and the kids are happy when the teacher finally smiles.

I was dreaming one night that I woke up and saw three men sitting outside my bedroom in straight-back chairs lined up against the hall wall. They were not smiling; but had sober looks on their faces and were sitting up straight and tall at attention, looking straight ahead – at me, watching me. Then I woke up.

I realized these men in my dream represent the Father, the Son, and the Holy Spirit – One Almighty God working as three separate entities – all watching over me while I sleep. And that is no laughing matter. It is serious business watching over me. God wanted to let me know that He takes care of me and watches over me, so he sent me a dream.

Jesus said only what His Father said. The red letters in the red-letter Bibles are the words that Jesus spoke, repeating the Father's Words. When you hear the red-letter words, you know you are hearing the Father speak.

**Question:**
1. Does the Father sound the same as the Son?

## 43. Hearing the Holy Spirit Speak

*"And I will pray the Father, and He will give you another Comforter that He may abide with you forever - the Spirit of truth, whom the world cannot receive, because it neither sees Him nor knows Him; but you know Him, for he dwells with you and will be in you." John 14:16-17*

It is a somewhat strange situation – after all my experiences in hearing the voice of Jesus and later the voice of the Father, it is only recently, that I have been speaking to the Holy Spirit and beginning to hear the clear voice of the Holy Spirit directing me.

The Holy Spirit can direct you by giving impressions or leadings, such as giving you the feeling that you should call a certain person or to visit them or pray for them. If you follow this prompting, you will discover that it was the exact thing that was needed. The Holy Spirit does lead us through impressions in our mind, but having several sentences spoken to you directly as a thought by the Holy Spirit is a higher level of communication that was new to me. For many years, I have been taking directions from Jesus, but now the Holy Spirit has also been giving me directions. I know it is the Holy Spirit, because we are beginning to have conversations with each other.

I can now enjoy two-way dialogues with the Holy Spirit, but earlier I likened Him to being a "telephone wire," the conduit that brought the voice of Jesus and the Father to me. The Holy Spirit is a wonderful secretary – even a personal assistant. He can manage your day – wake you at a specific time in the morning – order your day – fill you with His presence when you are walking in obedience. He covers you with His peace, joy, and love. By this He actually manifests Himself to you – leads you – gives you inspiration – directs your day – shares His heart with you. He leads you into adoration of Jesus and of the Father. He inspires you to seek answers and dialogs with Jesus. He is such a happy camper and a constant companion wherever you go!

As told in Chapter One, someone gave me a prophecy, and I later had a dream. I wanted an interpretation of the dream, and I asked a prophetic person on my website to do that for me – the interpretation of the dream was that I had to write a book. Then, two days later, another person wrote a prophecy over my life saying, "God wants you to write a book about the supernatural and the prophetic." Things were starting to become clearer for me. One night about 8:30pm, the Holy Spirit inspired me to grab a pen and write down all the chapter headings to this book.

As I have said before, the videos are totally unedited, so making them into a book needed a lot of work, but without the Holy Spirit inspiring me to make a start with the videos, the book would never have been written. I was used to taking dictation from the Holy Spirit, so receiving the titles of the chapters was such a big help to know even how to begin. The whole fifty-five chapters were then recorded onto my video camera within forty-eight hours of the Holy Spirit giving the first instruction. I knew straight away that I had the basis for a book to preach from. After producing the videos, I was talking to the Holy Spirit and He told me that He is proud of me and He knows that the book will be even better!

This is a comprehensive book for people new to the prophetic and eager to know more about it. It is something that I wish I could have read when I was a young prophet. I was talking to the Holy Spirit and He said, "It makes a difference, doesn't it? For a few years, you have always wanted a special theme and a title for a book, and now everything is coming together for you."

I knew that this book was ordained and commissioned by God even before it was typed. When the Holy Spirit was talking to me, I had already preached thirty of the chapters into video; I was happy with what I had achieved, and I knew in my mind what was required for the other chapters. Who would have thought that you could produce a first draft of a book directly to a video camera within forty-eight hours? Who can do that? Answer: only someone who is inspired by and moving in the Holy Spirit.

To hear the Holy Spirit giving you directions and to be able to talk and have a relationship with Him is supernatural! It is part of the supernatural experience – to hear Jesus speak, to hear the Father speak, and to hear the Holy Spirit speak – and to know the difference between them. Even to know when they are speaking to you is itself a gift from God! It is a wonderful joy to live and walk in that realm where you have a relationship with the whole Trinity. I encourage you to begin to know each of them!

## **LAURIE'S REFLECTIONS**

43. Hearing the Holy Spirit Speak

Go back and read the verse at the beginning of this chapter. The word "Comforter" here, in Greek, means *counselor, helper, intercessor, advocate, strengthener,* and *standby*. Jesus is the first "Comforter" and the Holy Spirit is "another" Comforter. We have two Comforters, two Counselors, two Helpers, two Intercessors, two Advocates, two Strengtheners, and two Stand-bys.

Both Christ and the Holy Spirit are in you and with you. Wherever you go, they go, just like your shadow – sometimes you see them, sometimes you don't, but they are always there forever waiting on your questions. You ask the Holy Spirit, "What should I do next?" The Holy Spirit asks Jesus, Jesus tells the Holy Spirit and the Holy Spirit comes back and directs, guides, and leads you in the "way that you should go" through impressions, leadings, or feelings – through a voice, through a song, through a sign – all in the matter of a split second.

It is the same when you ask the Holy Spirit something on behalf of someone else. As a prophet or prophetess, you are being trained to hear and see what the Lord has for others and is saying to others. It is our job to pass the information on to them – unless you feel the Lord leading you to pray and intercede on their behalf instead.

When the Holy Spirit speaks to me, it is ever so gently. If I am not fully aware, I will miss it. I must pay attention to the leading. When I am paying attention, my day goes very smoothly; things happen at just the right time and place; I may get reminded of something I needed to know just in the nick of time; I get that nudge ever so gently that leads me in the right direction.

I purchased a certain book, not really knowing why, but I began reading it and then I received an e-mail from someone that had a question concerning the same topic as that book. The Holy Spirit knew I would need that information in preparation for the later conversation.

I am driving down the road and cannot decide: should I turn or go straight? I ask, "Which way?" Turns out, Spirit was correct. It pays to listen to the Holy Spirit.

You hear the Holy Spirit by quieting your own mind. It is from the Holy Spirit, not you because you have quieted your mind. Now the Mind of Christ can take over and speak through you. You are not thinking; you are not wondering – you are just speaking for the Lord. A prophet is never at a "loss for words" if they are in the anointing.

Do not try to analyze what you hear. It is not from you or to you. It is from the Lord to the person you are prophesying to. How are you going to analyze that? I have a very analytical mind and have to tell myself not to analyze my own prophecies. I give that up to the Lord. It is not for me to know the details of how, when, or why.

For the sake of our own personal prophecies, we need to know that the Holy Spirit is giving us a message to rest in and to give praise for. My advice is to rest in the goodness of the Lord while you do what you know to do and let God do the rest.

**Questions:**
1. The Holy Spirit directs you with _____ or by _____.

2. Is it possible to hear the Holy Spirit and yourself talking at the same time?

## 44. Making the Bible Come Alive

*"And the Word was made flesh, and dwelt among us, and we behold his glory, the glory as of the only begotten of the Father; full of grace and truth," John 1:14.*

How can you make the Bible come alive? Many people say that the Bible is dry and boring. What can we do to move the Bible from being dry and boring – to make it come alive and begin to speak to you?

There are several things you can do. First, you can spend time – twenty minutes to half an hour, in prayer or worship, to come into the presence of the Lord, before you open the Bible. When the presence of the Holy Spirit starts to manifest in your life then the Holy Spirit will help you to read in such a way that the Bible comes alive to you. If you begin to obey the commands of Jesus, you will demonstrate your love for Him and that you want to become His friend. In response and as part of His love for you, He will draw close to you: *"Draw near to God and He will draw near to you," James 4:8.*

In saying this, I am not teaching salvation by works! But, as you spend time obeying the commands of Jesus, you are showing your commitment to Him and He will have the Holy Spirit draw closer to you. Then too, the Bible will start to come alive to you. The more you obey it, the more active you become in your faith and the more the Bible makes sense. When this happens, you will begin to discover meanings in the Bible that you would not ordinarily see.

The more you walk in the revelation that you have received, the more revelation you will receive. However, if you are choosing to live a life in disobedience, then the Bible will most certainly be dead and dry to you. Even sermons at church will seem dull and boring if your mind-set and behavior do not reflect the guidance you have received from the Holy Spirit. Sadly, I have been there many times. It is far better to be able to read and work through passages and ideas in the Bible, and to grow in spiritual understanding.

If you are walking in obedience with the Lord, it is amazing how often the pastor or teacher will illuminate a subject that you have been thinking about. The Holy Spirit may even change the pastor's original sermon because you are dealing with a particular topic on that specific day. If you have a relationship with Jesus, then it is as He says: *"He who has My commandments and keeps them, it is he who loves Me. And he who loves Me will be loved by My Father, and I will love him and manifest Myself to him," John 14:21.*

The word "manifest" might mean that He will turn up in a vision or that He might show you more of His character. However, in John 1:1-3 we read: *"In the beginning was the Word, and the Word was with God, and the Word was God. He was in the beginning with God. All things were made through Him, and without Him nothing was made that was made."*

Before the Cross, Jesus spent time with His Father talking about His people and future believers. He said to His Father: *"Sanctify them by Your truth. Your word is truth," John 17:17.* We know that, in John 14:6, Jesus told us that He is the Truth! Therefore, the Word of God and Jesus are the same. The "Word of God" created the Universe and everything in it.

If you allow Jesus to rule in your life, so that you do the things He wants you to do, we have His Word that He WILL reveal to you more of His heart and nature and you will understand what the Word of God is saying. I hope you understand, for there is no other way for the Bible to come alive to you. Begin to say "No" to sin. This starts an upward spiral to the image of Christ.

- Obedience brings prayer, thanksgiving, and praise.
- Prayer, thanksgiving, and praise bring intimacy with Jesus.
- Intimacy with the Word (Jesus) brings new Bible revelation.
- Bible revelation brings repentance.
- Repentance brings change of behavior.
- Changed behavior over time will transform you into the image of Christ

Similarly, when you fall away and stop obeying, the cycle spirals downward.

- Disobedience hinders prayer, thanksgiving, and praise.
- Lack of prayer, thanksgiving, and praise hinders intimacy with Jesus.
- Lack of intimacy with the Word (Jesus) stifles new Bible revelation.
- Lack of Bible revelation stifles repentance.
- Lack of Repentance cannot change fleshly behavior.
- Fleshly behavior over time will stifle God's best for you.

An unsaved person has no interest in the Bible. A casual glance confirms to them that it is dry and dull. It literally sends them to sleep. I know that the Holy Spirit used this information to bring someone to the Lord. Let me explain:

A preacher friend invited a Christian wife (with a Muslim husband) around for dinner one evening, and while they were eating, the husband shared that he was having trouble in getting to sleep. Surprisingly, He asked the pastor to pray for him. The pastor replied, "Hey, look, I'll pray for you, but what I suggest is that you get your wife's Bible and when you want to go to sleep, just start reading it and that will send you to sleep in no time. Her Bible will just make you tired."

The Muslim listened to the words and began reading his wife's Bible – and, yes, it was like a sleeping pill – it just knocked him right out. This impressed the Muslim so much that he carried on with his Bible reading every night and within a short while it led to his conversion to Christ.

Satan hates the Bible and he will do anything to prevent you from reading it. He will have you read anything – he will have you watching every single program on television – he will even have you working every spare minute at church – anything to stop you from reading the Bible. Of course, another thing Satan loves to do is to stop you from praying.

Maybe hundreds of books have been written on prayer, and millions of dollars may have been spent on publishing these books – yet most Christians struggle in this area and resist praying! There are also many books that teach on the importance of regular Bible reading, yet many Christians only read it on Sundays at church. However, if you obey and trust Jesus, the Bible will come alive for you. When the Bible comes alive, it is a supernatural feeling – and a feeling a prophet needs to continually experience.

## **LAURIE'S REFLECTIONS**

44. Making the Bible Come Alive

Years ago, a dear friend told me to personalize the Bible when I read the It by placing my own name in the verses. When you do that, the Bible comes alive. You begin to see yourself in the Scriptures and know that God's Word is very relevant to your life. Do not let anyone tell you that the Bible is not relevant for today, that they or you need a "now" Word. Every Word in the Bible is a "now" Word, that is why the Bible is called the Living Word.

Dr. Mike Murdock says to kiss and hug your Bible, because the words in it are precious. When you are living the life of God's Promises, you cannot help to come alive with excitement. The words themselves must be alive because how can something dead make you alive? When the Bible is alive to you, you are spiritually alive! If the Bible seems dead, it is because you are spiritually dead – like those who fall asleep the minute they hit the pew!

It is hard to praise if you are not raised, but the very act of praise will raise you up. Raise yourself up with the rays of the Son! How do you do that? Ask God to reveal the deeper meaning of His Word and when He does, it will cause the dry bones to come alive.

Let God take you where you have never been before – the Bible is a Living Word and was made flesh. *"For the Logos of God is a living thing, active and more cutting than any sword with double edge, penetrating to the very division of soul and spirit, joint and marrow – scrutinizing the very thoughts and ideas of the heart."*

The Word comes alive when we act upon it. Do not be a hearer only! Instead get up and be a doer of the Word, for that activates the power within the Word!

## 44. MAKING THE BIBLE COME ALIVE

I felt led to study under a ministry on television that read each verse in each chapter – verse by verse, and then chapter by chapter. It gave me the jump-start I needed to become a life-time student of the Word.

There are commentaries that can help you make the Word come alive. Just be committed to the project of learning the Word, making it meaningful for you on a personal level. The Lord knows your heart. He will send teachers and helpers your way.

I know someone who, as a child, acted out all the stories in the Bible and then acted them out in reverse. She learned the Bible "inside out." The Word of God just flows out of her mouth like a rushing, mighty river, because the whole word of God connects for her, from Genesis to Revelation. That prophetess is definitely not at a loss for words. Life and death are in the power of the tongue. When you speak out the Word of God, you make it come alive.

**Question:**

1. What are some ways of making the Bible come alive to you?

## 45. My Visions of Heaven

*"He giveth to his beloved in sleep." Psalm 127:2*

Physical death is the absence of the human soul and spirit, leaving behind an empty body to be disposed of. Hebrews 9:27, says that we will all die once and after that the judgment comes. Psalm 78:39, says that we are a breath that passes away and does not come again.

At times, in my visions of heaven, I have seen my body on the bed and then just passed through the ceiling to another place. Obviously, I was not dead, but my spirit *or* my soul temporarily left my body. I am aware that Satan is the master counterfeiter and he counterfeits the legitimate things of God. He also gives a similar false version, called something like astral-travelling. *But Satan never brings a person closer to the Biblical God!*

Also, I have been in heaven and on earth at the same time! The first time this happened was while I was explaining heaven to a girl in an e-mail prophecy. I went into a room in heaven with a big wall, and at the same time, I was explaining everything to the girl in my prophetic word.

This vision really impacted me. The wall was hundreds of feet high and just as long, but it was covered in a smoky mist so I could not see the top or the end – it just seemed to go on forever. Jesus told me to put my hand in the wall, and I pulled out a big ball-shaped object – it was a huge diamond! Jesus said to me, "Can you see all the other diamonds?" Even though the wall went on forever, I could only say "Yeah!" I was stunned speechless.

Then God the Father explained: "Matthew, that diamond you have in your hand – you realize that it is just one diamond out of the millions that are here. That single diamond in your hand is absolutely exquisite. If it were sold on earth, the money would run the United States government for two hundred years! That is how much it is worth." Then He added: "Now you can see what money means to us up here."

## 45. MY VISIONS OF HEAVEN

I have told this story to many people. That single diamond would make you the richest person in the world. Yet, heaven has millions of them because money is meaningless! It is the diamond's inner beauty and not its monetary value that is so precious to God. In heaven, there is an incomprehensible over-abundance of precious jewels and metals *everywhere*. They are in fact, common building materials because of their startling eternal beauty.

It did not cost God a single cent to mine those beautiful things! (I guess, even if all the precious commodities on earth were mined by man, God would still have plenty of other planets for His angels to mine.) No! Just kidding – God just speaks things into existence as He did in Genesis One and Two.

That was my first vision of heaven.

Another far more memorable vision occurred when I was in prayer-counseling one day. The counselor said, "You are going to see a picture in your mind. I want you to tell me what you see." To his astonishment, I told him that I was in heaven.

He said, "Really? And who else is there?"

I replied: "Jesus." With that, Jesus took off His crown and placed it on my head. He took off His signet ring and put it on my finger, and He took off His robe and put it around me. He then led me into the Throne Room and, as I walked through a sea of people, I fell over more than eight times on the way up to the throne. Jesus continually picked me up as I made my way to the front.

Then God the Father said to me: *"Come and sit on My right side, on my Son's throne."* (I had the authority and permission to sit on the throne?) Jesus left me there and I walked up and sat on God's right side on Jesus' throne. I was totally in awe and felt incredibly conspicuous. Much later on, I read the Scripture: *"To him who overcomes I will grant to sit with Me on My throne, as I also overcame and sat with My Father on His throne."* Revelation 3:21

I certainly did not feel an over-comer at that stage, but in reflection, I think God was saying to me that He saw me as an over-comer because of the covering of the blood of His Son on me and one day I really would be an over-comer.

It was as if God was just a big ball of light – I could not see His face or body. He was just speaking out of this light – I knew it was His voice because I had been speaking to Him for years. Then He opened the roof of the Throne Room and I could clearly see all the galaxies and all the planets moving around heaven just as if they were only a few miles away. He said to me, "See Matthew, I can control all of this. I could drop just one of those planets on earth and, if I did, then that is the end of earth." I was just astonished! Then He said, "If I can control all of that, don't you think I can control your life? Let me do that for you."

That had a profound effect on me. Then Jesus picked up a microphone (we only see what we know on earth so I imagined He picked up a microphone) and began to sing – a love song – a song to me! He dedicated it to me and sang it to the whole Throne Room, "This song's for Matthew. *I could sing of your love forever,"* That is what He said about me in heaven.

I was in tears, as many Old Testament prophets came and appeared before me. They introduced themselves, waved at me, and walked off. The last one to appear was Joseph and he waved at me, but he stayed and said: "What color is the robe that Jesus gave you?"

I thought it was a white one, but he said: "I don't think it's white. Look down."

I looked and it was a coat of many colors that I was wearing – the same as the coat that Jacob had given to Joseph. Then Jesus said to me, "I have given you the robe of many colors. This robe of many colors is your robe of righteousness from now on, Matthew."

I knew Joseph was the dreamer, so this was like a 'dreamer's coat' to me. If you have been watching the complete series, you may be wondering why I have been wearing the same shirt all the time. This shirt is multicolored – I wanted to be in the Joseph anointing, because I too am somewhat a dreamer.

That was my second vision of heaven.

Now, I want to say something that will *really shock you!* At the time of these two visions, I was in deep sin – I was in a twenty year-long sexual addiction! Yet, I was taken into the Throne Room of God! They crucified our Lord for the supposed sin of blasphemy and treason, yet this supernatural event happened to me of all people! My only explanation as I see it now is that it was a supernatural and striking testimony of God's incredible saving Grace! There is simply no other explanation!

At the time of my vision, I did not know much about God's grace because I was extremely legalistic in my interpretation of the Bible. I knew that, under Old Testament Jewish Law, I would have been stoned to death for my behavior over that twenty-year period. Yet, in that disgusting state, I was taken into Heaven to meet God, and to sit on Jesus' throne – as a filthy sinner! I know that this will mess with your theology and you may even throw this book out with contempt and I would not blame you in the slightest.

But, in hindsight, that profound experience personally demonstrated to me God's boundless grace! As a young prophet, all you can see is judgment for personal sin, errors in the church, errors in people's doctrine, and the certainty of God's impending judgment on sinners, particularly on those who claim to be Christians. (Now, praise the Lord I know that He has already judged our sin. We as believers can boldly testify of that, but back then, I was ignorant.)

Then, out of the blue, God treats you with so much grace and mercy and love! It certainly messes with your theology, but it gives you the courage to overcome your addiction and to walk free from it – and I have remained free from it for over four years. Praise God. May He bless you as well, and I will share another vision with you shortly.

## **LAURIE'S REFLECTIONS**

45. My Visions of Heaven

Read the passage of Scripture in Acts 10:10-16. In this passage, Peter saw a vision, not once, not twice but three times! This vision ultimately opened Peter's spiritual eyes to a new revelation concerning God's love for the Gentiles. (God's Grace is manifested through the living "bread" of Truth.)

Natural sleep is a mild trance state; a dream is a vision seen in sleep. More than a fourth of our life is lived in the world of sleep and dreams. When darkness and silence falls upon us, an inner world of imagination, a picture show of sights and sounds appears – to go into a deep sleep is to dream.

Robert Louis Stevenson says that the plots or even whole chapters of stories were given to him in his dreams. They were given to him by what he called "the Brownies," (little people). He wrote essays on dream creativity because of the visitors in his dreams (Brownies) that helped him to compose. He was sickly as a child and had what he called at that time, night terrors or nightmares, but he later discovered that his dreams were just adventures that he learned to welcome as he travelled to far-away places. He read stories in his dreams and when he woke, he transcribed them. What a wonderful way for God to communicate to someone!

Most people have heard of *Dr. Jekyll and Mr. Hyde* – that story came directly from Mr. Stevenson's dreams. His dreams were very profitable for him.

*"Thus says the LORD, thy Redeemer, the Holy One of Israel; I am the LORD thy God which teaches you to profit, which leads you by the way that you should go," Isaiah 48:17.*

The answers to many problems can be a gift of a dreaming mind.

You say, "I haven't dreamed in a long time." I say: Are you using your imagination during the day, are you daydreaming? Start dreaming intentionally or consciously and see if that does not help your "night life" or your subconscious mind open up. Open up to the many possibilities for "life and life more abundantly."

One of my sons, Kenan Hicks, wrote a book called Just Dream. It is a great little read on the topic of allowing your self to dream big and then living the dream as it comes into fruition.

## 45. MY VISIONS OF HEAVEN

There was a time when my dreams "escaped" me, and I would wake up with a blank – could not remember one single dream. Then I read a book by Bishop Jordan about dreams and visions. He teaches that dreams are like "mail from God." I thought, mail? Well, I wasn't opening any of my mail at that point because it was all from creditors. Who wants to open letters from the creditors? I let them pile up until I eventually threw them in the trash, unopened. I was not receiving any mail whatsoever during the day or night (dreams are like mail from God – that was news to me!)

What if I was receiving a "debt cancellation" notice? What if I had been asked to attend to a special meeting of opportunity? I was throwing all my dreams in the trash!

I immediately started opening up every piece of mail addressed to me, and what do you know? I started receiving mail at night as well. It was wonderful to be opening up to my nightlife – my dreams -- my nighttime mail – to see visions of heaven. Do not be closed-minded! Open your mind to receive at night through your dream-state and be willing to venture out into the unknown.

Into the unknown – that is deep. And, to be honest, I am still waiting for *that* vision of heaven, but I can tell you how God was taking me there once, but I got scared and God is not in the business of scaring people. He waits until people are ready, and then He is there to take them to the next level.

One afternoon while I was taking a nap, I knew God was taking me somewhere I had never been before, kind of like in Star Trek when Captain Kirk says, "Warp speed ahead," only I was traveling through space without a starship. There was no "Enterprise." It was as if I personally went through a spiritual portal and was traveling leisurely through space – kind of floating, yet it was on a clear path to "Somewhere." It was a very dark, very black space. I did not see anyone with me, but their presence was known and I did not feel alone – I was not scared at that point, but a second later I started seeing little lights in the atmosphere, like stars from a distance and knew we were in space without an aircraft. As we progressed, the lights became brighter. There was one source where the lights were as rays from the sun or Son. It was becoming brighter and brighter.

(Seeing the bright light means you have died and gone to heaven, right? The dying part is a little intimidating for me right now. I'm not quite ready for that.)

I suddenly knew I was going somewhere new and foreign to me. It scared me (I need to work on that) because I have always been scared to travel to foreign or unknown places and now in the Spirit, it was happening. I jerked, just a little in my sleep, and poof! The opportunity was gone and I was awake. I was instantly saddened by my own fear of the unknown, but that was then – this is now – I eagerly await a second opportunity to visit God's universe in the way that He would take me – in a heavenly vision.

This was a prophetic moment that will come around again. Years before that day, I had been riding in the car with my husband, looking out the window when God told me that I would "go places I've never gone before." This made me think of Star Trek and places where "man has never been before" – man has not, but Spirit has, my spirit shall go where man has never been before. I was excited way back then and I am excited now. God is a God of second chances and next time I will be ready to see the journey through!

### Questions:
1. Who would write a book from a first draft produced in only two days?
2. Share any "out of this world" experiences or heavenly visions you have had.

## 46. My Visions of Heaven – Part Two

*"Our Father who is in heaven, hallowed be your name. Your kingdom come, your will be done, on earth as it is in heaven."*
Luke 11:2

This is another memorable vision I had of heaven. I was just walking around, and suddenly in my mind I saw a picture of heaven. It was as if I was in a large amusement park – about the size of two Australian football fields (roughly the size of four American football fields) put together – full of swings, carousels, and rides, and thousands of children playing. The children were just having so much fun. But as I watched them all playing, I realized there was not an adult to be seen anywhere. Not one adult! I knew I was in heaven but there were no adults, and I started to become somewhat fearful for the children.

However, straightaway I heard Jesus speak to me, "There are no sexual predators up here, Matthew. The children are safe. And don't you think children play so much better together when they are not being supervised?"

For a moment, I thought that children are liable to do some crazy things when adults are not looking, but then I realized that nobody is going to break their arm in heaven. With all those angels nearby, no child innocently playing in heaven is going to fall off the high horse or the monkey bars and break their arm, right? It was wonderful to watch all these children playing, because it was more than six years since I had seen my son, who would have been about thirteen or fourteen at the time.

Suddenly, a thirteen-year old girl came up and said: "Hello Matthew."

I replied: "Hello, but how do you know my name?"

She said: "Of course I know you. I can see you from heaven. Your son often comes to play with me when he is sleeping."

I asked, "How do you know my son?"

She replied, "Sometimes when he goes to sleep he dreams of me and we play in this park, and I tell him all about you and about everything that is happening to you."

I was so emotional that I began crying - *here on earth*. Since my ex-wife remarried, she would not allow me to see my son anymore. It was the most distressing thing that has ever happened to me and it was the cause of much grief and suffering in my life. Then amazingly, my vision continued.

She was saying: "Can I take you to my favorite place?" No sooner had I agreed – we were there! SNAP, just like that!

I have read in books about visions of heaven and apparently, there is no travelling time! As soon as you have decided where you want to go, then you are there – and that is what happened to me. Immediately we were near a fence running over a hill – an incline that went for about a mile, covered with deep beautiful lush green grass. Grass in heaven is such a *bright* green!

She said, "Look down there," and my eyes followed her pointing finger – there were hundreds of wooden buildings. "That's where they stable all the horses." I instantly remembered a song about a girl riding on the horses in heaven. I asked her whether she had ridden any of them. She said, "Yes, I've ridden by myself and I've ridden with angels."

I asked if she had ever met Michael the Archangel. She said, "Yes! And I've ridden a horse with him. It was great fun – way cool! I just love coming here and riding the horses."

If you grew up in a country town as I did, you would know that girls living on a property with some acreage love to have their own horse. Therefore, it must be heavenly for a thirteen-year old girl just to pop down from the park, and go for a ride on a horse whenever she wants.

It was a tremendous vision for me to see all those children enjoying themselves in the heavenly park. They have schools – and they have foster parents. (These children have died while still young). They even have grandfathers up there to build toys for them: men who had enjoyed woodworking on earth and died at a ripe old age, and who love their new grandchildren. They have lathes, woodworking equipment, and metal working equipment up there so they can make toys, train sets, race cars, and all kinds of things for the children.

Heaven is not only about God's Throne Room and worshiping God. Everyone has a job to do! There are coffee shops with cakes and fruit, so you can go out for a cuppa! On the other hand, you can invite some of your friends around for dinner, a banquet, or just to sit on the porch and watch people go by.

Heaven is like earth in many ways, only a hundred times better! There are dimensions, levels, glories, and there is so much treasure in heaven. As Jesus often tells us, the more treasure that you build up on earth, the bigger the reward in heaven. If you invest all your money in advancing the kingdom of God on earth, or in giving to others less fortunate, you are going to be rewarded for that. There is reward for all the poor people and all the people who have denied themselves on earth.

There are levels of opportunities and experiences in heaven for everyone. I must confess that I would quickly become bored if all I did was to sing hymns and choruses all day every day. I need to get involved in doing things. I would certainly love to get involved in delving into the Book of Isaiah for at least ten years, and to have Jesus or perhaps even Isaiah teach me things he recorded in the Bible. I trust this vision has given you some further insight into heaven!

## **LAURIE'S REFLECTIONS**

Chapter 46. My Visions of Heaven, Part Two

In the spirit, as soon as you know where you are going, you are there.

*"And when they were come up out of the water, the Spirit of the Lord caught away Phillip, that the eunuch saw him no more* [poof! Phillip was gone] *..." Acts 8:39.*

This is why, in an instant, your dreams change from one minute to the next when at first you are riding a bike then you are driving a car, because there is no time, nor space in the heavenly realm.

*"God has raised us up together, and made us sit together in heavenly places in Christ Jesus." Eph. 2:6*

As we are in Christ, so we are in heavenly places.

There are actually many other Scriptures where angels and men just appear and disappear. When you are there in mind, you are there, and when you are not, you are not, instantly in the twinkling of an eye. That is why so much happens in one night's worth of dreams. One moment you are playing golf and the next you are climbing a mountain all in the same dream. We still call it "time travel" but it is not, it is just travel, instant travel because "time" and "space" are earthly elements.

*"Our Father who is in heaven, hallowed be Your name. Your kingdom come; Your will be done, on earth as it is in heaven."*[29]

Why should it be hard to believe that heaven is the way Matthew has described it, with gold and diamonds, and horses and toys? We have all these things here on earth.

*"Neither shall they say, 'Lo here! Or, lo there! For, behold, the kingdom of God is within you,'" Luke 17:21.*

*Heaven is within you!* This and everything else is revealed to you in the Scriptures. Read them carefully. We are to rejoice! We are to have no fear. Fear is the cloud that dimmed my spiritual vision just before I jerked myself awake.

### Questions:

1. What two earth elements are not needed in heaven or the spiritual realm?
2. Where is heaven?

---

[29] Matthew 6:9-10

## 47. Meeting Jesus on Earth in Visions

*"But whoever drinks of the water that I will give him will never thirst again;" John 4:14*

Although I have met Jesus many times in visions, I have met Him here on earth, as well – in the form of a homeless person. Jesus had told me that I was going to meet Him soon, and I did. Strangely enough, I actually met Him in the flesh, before I met Him in a vision.

Jesus performed some supernatural signs and wonders at the time that I met Him to prove to me, beyond doubt, that I was really meeting Him. One of the signs was that He disappeared before my eyes – from his flesh body to nothing! To me that was pretty convincing! I turned my head away for less than a second and He was gone – He could not have gone two feet in that fleeting moment even if He was running flat out, but He was nowhere to be seen. Angels too, that I have met in the flesh would often disappear into thin air, but not when you are looking at them. Then, when you look back they have just disappeared.

However, I have read in a book, *Angels on Assignment* by Roland Buck, of someone who has seen angels walking in the flesh and then disappear into thin air right in front of his eyes.

On three occasions, I have met Jesus in the form of a real homeless person, as someone I have known and to whom I have actually given money or a drink. On these three occasions, these homeless people have gone into a trance-like state then Jesus began speaking to me through them. Sometimes, the conversations have lasted up to twenty-five minutes with me questioning and Jesus answering through a real live person only they were not even aware that Jesus was doing the talking.

Perhaps, right now, you are thinking – you would need to be out of your mind to think that could happen!

However, there have been many occasions when I have been the conduit, but I have been aware that Jesus is talking through me to another person. It brings a tremendous blessing to people you are with, but not as much as the blessing of having a two-way conversation with Jesus in the flesh. Often, Jesus will draw alongside of me, especially when I am really sad or disheartened. I will be casually walking along the street when I suddenly feel a presence next to me, and I will ask, "Is that you, Jesus?"

Once, Jesus was walking side by side with me down the road and we were talking together. I recalled an old chorus I used to sing as a child in the Baptist church: *'and He walks with me and He talks with me, and He tells me I am His own..."* It was such a wonderful feeling!

I often remember the words of the song, *"Come to the waters; stand by my side. I know you are thirsty, you won't be denied. I felt every teardrop when in darkness you cried and I strove to remind you that for those tears, I died."* (Marsh and Russ Stevens created the words and music.) I have been down to the water and Jesus has come down to the water with me.

I have even met Jesus once at McDonalds. I was with a couple of friends when Jesus came to me. One friend could tell Jesus was there, but the other friend was skeptical and said, "No, it's not Jesus. It's a demon and he's mad and you're crazy!" Then I saw a tear come out of Jesus' eye and run down his cheek. I saw Him crying! I asked Him why He was crying, and He replied: "You can only take certain people so far." Our friend was so full of unbelief and fear that he made Jesus cry! Believe me, it was an extremely emotional experience to see Jesus Christ cry that day.

Once I also saw Jesus in a vision, when I was at church. He appeared with a blood-red face and blood all his over his clothes. He had on a white robe but the robe was so covered in blood that only a few speckles of white remained. He turned around and showed me what His back looked like after the whipping He received before He was hung on the cross.

Not even modern medicine, with all its technology, could have saved Jesus from being dead. You could see the organs – you could see the bones in His flesh – they just ripped His flesh apart. *"The Passion of The Christ"* does not even give a ten percent impression of what

Jesus looked like. What I saw that day, was the most graphic vision I have of Jesus.

When He walked into that church, He said, "I want you to really look at me today." Although I have seen Jesus in visions many times, I have not really focused my eyes, my spiritual eyes, because I did not want to see Him shining in His glory – because I did not think I would be able to handle it.

Most of my life, I have been depressed and once, suicidal. When I saw Him smiling and so full of love, I wanted to be with Him for all eternity. Although I have met Him on many occasions, I had never really focused in properly, but on that day, in that church, He told me to focus in. That is how I saw the crucified Christ – and, as I shared earlier, you do NOT ever forget it!

Just as when I sat on the Throne and spoke to God and He showed me the planets and all the signs in Heaven, there are some things that you just never forget! But especially when you see the crucified Jesus Christ, you cannot forget. He was standing on the stage and the worship team was singing: "Thank You Jesus for dying on the Cross and saving me from my sin."

He stood with His arms outstretched in the form of a cross and He said, "Are they singing about this, Matthew? To whom are they singing? Why are they singing? I am right here. I am standing on the worship stage. Why have they not stopped singing? Why are they not talking to me? Are you the only one in this building who knows I am here?"

It gives you somewhat of a wake-up call. So many times, I have been at a church when Jesus comes and sits by me, to join in the worship or to talk to me. He just turns up, but people ask me, how I know He is there? Can you feel Him? Often angels come and join in the worship, but do you know they are there? Can you see them? Jesus is wonderful, because when you are a prophet or called to the prophetic office, you become a friend of His and He begins to visit you in visions. I hope that my stories are blessing you.

## **LAURIE'S REFLECTIONS**

## 47. Meeting Jesus on Earth in Visions

I have also seen what looked like an ordinary person on the street and I turned to look back because something caught my attention, but he or she was gone, poof! Just like Philip (Acts 8:39,) gone in an instant. We have already established that this must be a spiritual being.

My mother passed away in 2004, but I still see her sometimes in others – until I get up close. I know it is not my mother, but I get closer anyway to get a better look-see and then, the looks change, but for that brief moment, God allowed me to see my mother.

It is so peaceful when you sense the presence of the Lord with you during a trying time, just sitting with you until you feel better. Who else actually does that without looking at their watch? Jesus is never too busy for you. He always has time for you.

Reading Matthew's book humbles me. To be in the presence of someone who has experienced all that he has with the triune of God is very humbling. When I read his words, it brings me into the presence of the same anointing. This chapter has truly blessed me. Thank you, Matthew.

**Question:**

1. Have you ever seen Jesus or anyone else who has already passed on to the "other side"?

## 48. Meeting Angels on Earth in Visions

*"Be not forgetful to entertain strangers: for thereby some have entertained angels unawares."*
*Hebrews 13:2*

Meeting angels is also a wonderful experience. I have been privileged to meet many angels. Angels seem to love me and I love them to visit me and walk with me. I have had the privilege of meeting with Michael the Archangel on many occasions. Many people might scoff and say, "That's crazy – it's a hallucination – he is having delusions! Who is he to say that he has met one of the most important angels in Heaven?" Sorry to burst their bubble, but it has happened, and I have met Gabriel on at least five occasions. I really am used to meeting angels.

One of my favorite experiences with angels happened at my church. I knew that my friend had brought someone new, so I knew who the stranger was, but he had no idea about who I was. Jesus once said: *"A prophet is not without honor, except in his own country and in his own house,"* Matthew 13:57. This means that a true prophet has honor everywhere, except around people who know him. Those who know him do not recognize his gift, but strangers can recognize it and they love him.

Later, the visitor and I began talking. He said: "I wish I could see angels like you do." Many times, I have opened people's spiritual eyes and pointed out angels to them. So I said "Are you serious, do you really want to see an angel?"

"Ah, I would just *love* to see them," he responded.

I said, "Okay, let's do an exercise - just pretend there are ten Roman soldiers standing to the left of you. They are all about six-foot seven-inches tall and are just standing there. What color are they dressed in?"

He said, "They're in brown, and there's some red."

I then asked, "Okay, now what have they got on their feet?"

He replied, "Sandals and they're laced up, too." He was beginning to see a vision. I said, "They're all angels. Now look at their backs, see their wings, how they sprout from their backs." He could see them, and he said, "That's amazing man! How did you do that?"

I replied, "Well actually, you did it! Now, watch this. They're going to levitate off the ground and they're going to spin in a circle." The ten angels then spun and did tumble turns. Then I said, "Can you see a big angel coming down the middle of them? Does it seem as though he has plenty of authority?"

He replied, "Yeah. He seems very powerful!"

I said, "That's Michael the Archangel." He came and shook my hand, and greeted my new friend. Then the angels shot up into the air, and did all sorts of things that made my friend laugh. He was just blown away and so was I. I was astonished that the angels would do all this to demonstrate that if you walked in supernatural faith, the Lord will command His angels, so as to increase your faith! They show you that they are His servants and they will help a saint to believe. It was wonderful! I took this man home and we had something to eat. Then he asked me to prophesy over him. I told him that I was really very tired, but he insisted.

"Please. Please, I really feel you should!" The prophecy took a full twenty-five minutes. He told me that he had received about a hundred prophecies in his life, but that twenty-five minute prophecy seemed to summarize all of them. He thanked me and was amazed that everything had been confirmed to him.

Meeting angels builds your faith in the supernatural. As a prophet, you will not only be prophetic, but you may also see angels, and even converse with them. However, many people say that fascination with the angelic realm is a form of worship that breaks the first commandment. That is not true for me; I worship God alone!

I hope that, as you read this book, you will realize that I love Jesus Christ, and I glorify Jesus and God the Father. I worship them – I do not worship angels. Many angels are allowed to appear and show you things, but usually they are not allowed to talk to you. You can ask them, but they will not answer. Occasionally, they may come and say something to you, but it is rare. Therefore, in no way am I endorsing the worship of angels or saying that you should seek angels. Angels just turn up. I have never sought them out! They just turn up at times.

I believe that a true prophet can distinguish the voices of God. Also, because the Bible is so alive to them, many prophets have visions of heaven and meet angels. They may talk to Jesus in their sleep, have prophetic dreams, and have interpretations of dreams. That is all part of the prophetic lifestyle, and angels form just one portion of that lifestyle.

In the Book of Hebrews, Chapter One, God the Father is elevating God the Son and it says in verses 13-14, *"But to which of the angels has He ever said: 'Sit at My right hand, till I make your enemies your footstool.' Are they not all ministering spirits sent forth to minister for those who will inherit salvation?"*

So we have it, angels are ministering spirits or God's heavenly assistants, sent to minister to the elect of God and to all those who are yet to come into God's kingdom. They are sent to advance God's kingdom on earth and to bring glory to the Savior of the world, the Lord Jesus Christ. I hope that what I have shared with you in this chapter has encouraged you to go deeper in the Lord.

## **LAURIE'S REFLECTIONS**

48. Meeting Angels on Earth in Visions.

It is best to go ahead and entertain strangers,[30] because as Scripture tells us, you never know when the stranger is an angel in disguise.

We earthlings "entertain" the idea of angels all the time. There is talk about angels everywhere – in books, movies and songs.

In the music industry, just to name a few: "Earth Angel," (The Penguins, 1954, Johnny Tillotson, 1961, Marvin Berry & the Starlighters, 1985) "Angel Eyes," (Willie Nelson, 1984; Duke

---

[30] Hebrews 13:2

Pearson, 1968; ABBA; Matt Dennis, 1946; The Jeff Healey Band, 1988) "Johnny Angel," (Shelley Fabares, 1962) "Guardian Angel" (The Judds) "Angel" (Madonna) and "the beat goes on" with many more angel songs – too many to list.

The movie industry gives us: *It's a Wonderful Life* (1946), *Angels in the Outfield* (1951 and 1994), *The Preacher's Wife* (1990,) *Michael* (1990) *City of Angels* (1998), *Angels in the Infield* (2000) and many more -- too many to list.

We've had television shows about angels, such as *Highway to Heaven* and *Touched by an Angel* and many books have been written on the subject of angels. An angel book I am currently reading is *"Ask Your Angels"* written by Alma Daniel, Timothy Wyllie, and Andrew Ramer (1992). It really stimulated an interest in guardian angels, to the point where I asked God to confirm the name of my personal guardian angel, which He did. This led me to further ask Him to please let me see an angel – which He did.

Open yourself up to meeting your personal angel (a messenger who brings a message from God.) We usually refer to angels as our guardian angels, but after a while, they become our companions who guide rather than guard us, because as we grow in light and love, the act of guarding us is needed less and the act of gently guiding is needed more.[31]

*"He shall give His angels charge over you, to keep you in all your ways. They shall bear you up in their hands, lest you dash your foot against a stone."*[32]

Indeed, angels are around to minister to us. *"Write the vision, and make it plain, that he may run that reads it. For the vision is set for an appointed time; but in the end – it shall speak, and it shall not lie. No matter how long it takes, wait for it, because it will surely come to pass – it will not tarry."* Habakkuk 2:2

Write your plans down because your angels are waiting on their assignment from you. Ask God to let you see an angel.

---

[31] Ask Your Angels, by Daniel, Wyllie and Ramer, 1992
[32] Ps. 91:11,12 and Matt. 4:6

## 48. MEETING ANGELS ON EARTH IN VISIONS

My angel looked directly at me as I looked directly into his eyes. They were piercing. I don't think I've ever seen piercing eyes before, but this angel was in the disguise of a man who had run out of gas; he had piercing eyes – not scary like you read in a mystery novel or see in a movie, no these were deep eyes – the eyes of an angel.

This was during a women's Bible study group, and when he left there were at least two other women that confirmed him as an angel but none of them noticed his piercing eyes. I do believe this angel was sent to me because I had asked to see an angel. *"Ask and you shall receive."*

The message he gave before he left was this: Thank you for the money you gave me for gas. The amount you gave doesn't matter!

It's the same message God gave to me through a prophecy I received from Matthew! The amount you give doesn't matter, it's your heart that matters.

Write your plan and envision your angels setting things about for them to come to pass, just like the Scripture says.

Angels minister on a personal level:

- Three angels appeared to Abraham, and one of them spoke as God, and was addressed as God;
- Later, two went to Sodom, to the house of Lot (Gen. 18:19.)
- When Hagar, with her son Ishmael, was dismissed from Abraham's tents, an angel saved her from despair, and her child from death (Gen. 21:17.)
- The Lord sent an angel before the Israelites in their wanderings.
- Stephen declared that they received the law by the ministration of angels (Acts 7:53.)

A good simple way to receive communication from your angel during your quiet time is to sit quietly with pen and paper. Close your eyes and when you feel and hear a word coming up from deep down in your heart – open your eyes and write it down on your paper. Close your eyes again and wait for the next word.

If you are asking for a word on the behalf of someone else, write their name down and wait for God to give you a word for them. Then, open your eyes and write it down. When the time is right, give them the Word of the Lord.

John Milton (1608-1674), who wrote the poem *Paradise Lost,* said that he received inspiration from a vision, a muse who dictated to him his "unpremeditated song."

While Mozart was composing his "Requiem," he had a vision of a man dressed in black rose who urged him to complete the composition without delay. When the requiem (funeral hymn) was finished, the vision ceased to appear. Mozart died shortly afterwards. He was being urged on by an angel to complete his work before his death.

There is no right way or wrong way to meet your angel – so do not get hung up in expecting a certain "thing" to happen. Just open yourself up to it and it will happen when the time is right. No two angel encounters are exactly the same, so *"Be not forgetful to entertain strangers: for thereby some have entertained angels unawares."*

### Questions:

1. Angels bring us a _____, that's why they are called messengers.

## 49. Having Visions and Talking to Jesus in Your Sleep

*"And it shall come to pass in the last days, says God, that I will pour out of My spirit on all flesh; your sons and your daughters shall prophesy, your young men shall see visions, your old men shall dream dreams."* Joel 2:28, Acts 2:17

A vision is a supernatural experience where you see something, even if you are asleep. Therefore, you can be having a dream and see Jesus walk into your house, comfort your baby by putting His hands around your child, and then walk out of your house. When you wake in the morning, you find your sick baby is now well and sitting up in its cot happy. Then you realize that last night when you were dreaming, you saw a vision of Jesus. It was not a dream; you actually saw Jesus come into your house and heal your baby.

About eight years ago, Jesus said to me: "Matthew, you need to ask me for something, you're always talking to me but you never ask for anything for yourself. You don't pray to me for personal things, but this time I want you to ask me something."

I said, "How long do I have to think about it?"

Jesus replied, "Well, just think of something now and ask me."

I realized afterward that The Holy Spirit put into my mind these words: *"... your young men shall see visions, your old men shall dream dreams."* This is part of a prophecy in Joel 2:28, and quoted again in Acts 2:17. Then I said to Jesus, "I would really like you to give me prophetic dreams and visions."

Since that night, I began to see visions of Jesus, of angels, and visions of Bible saints. I had a vision in a dream and talked to Jesus in my sleep and you can do the same. Jesus has answered that prayer more than I could have imagined. There is a Biblical precedent; I can honestly say, never did I once go looking for them. Not only angels of God, but Old Testament Bible saints have just come down with Jesus so I could meet them. You too can have dreams and visions in your sleep and see things in the future.

What people often describe as a dream can in fact be a vision. This is not a dream of the future, but it is a vision they are actually seeing, while they are asleep. They are seeing the future unfold and many people experience a feeling of *déjà vu*. And when the future arrives, it is exactly the same as in the vision. People call it the natural experience of *déjà vu*, but Jesus uses visions in your sleep to direct your course so you are prepared for events before they arrive. This may become a regular experience for you as a prophet!

One thing I need to add here: once I was asleep and Satan spoke to me – I recognized his voice, and I said, "You have no authority to speak to me." He replied, "That pornography in your cupboard gives me all the authority I need to speak to you." He was right – it did. If you have pornography on your computer's hard drive, in a hidden drawer, or on a DVD anywhere in your home, it gives Satan free access to your house because you are walking out of covenant with the Lord. The same applies to having anything of the occult in your home that you have not yet destroyed.

It came as a big shock to me, and I trashed all the pornography in the bin first thing the following day. Just a warning that even Satan can speak to you in your sleep – not just Jesus. I hope you have a wonderful day and that you continue with the teachings.

## LAURIE'S REFLECTIONS

49. Having Visions and Talking to Jesus in Your Sleep

When you have dreams and visions in your sleep you see things in the future, but your dream state is now, making the future right now. That is why faith is "now faith" (Heb. 11:1). The future is brought into the present (pre-sent) by your dreams and visions and you can have faith right now for those things. Once you see it in your mind, you can believe it, thereby prepare for it, expect it, declare it, and have it!

*Déjà vu* is common in my household. We are always saying, "I've done this before! This exact same thing – I've been here, done that!"

*Déjà vu* was the 9/11 experience I wrote about in a previous chapter.

## 49. HAVING VISIONS AND TALKING TO JESUS IN YOUR SLEEP

My son had a *déjà vu* experience one day and his little eyes were all wide and bright as he told me "I've seen these books before!" when the delivery truck brought the first printing of my new books. They had never been produced before so it was not possible for him to see them before that day – except in a vision. God is so good! He was really excited. It blessed him and me to know that God's hand was in our lives and had orchestrated the whole thing – and told this young boy about what was to come!

My 14 year old son had a *déjà vu* just the other day; it was only the two of us doing home school together. He had envisioned that setting, and us saying the same words *before* that day. That let him know that he was at the right place at the right time – right where he was supposed to be – right where God wanted him. God is good like that. He lets us know through our dreams and visions and then later in our *déjà vu* moments, that our steps are truly ordered.

We are experiencing *déjà vu* all day long – when we remember the dream or vision of it.

Jesus Christ, God, is always talking to people in their dreams.

In Genesis 20:3-7, God had a whole conversation with Abimelech during a dream he was having. God was warning him not to touch another man's wife (Abraham's wife, Sarah,) and He went to him "in a dream by night."

Jacob's dream of the angels ascending and descending the ladder[33] and then when he wrestled with God[34] are both two very famous dreams. People are still talking about those dreams today!

Angels visited Joseph and Mary, as well as the Magi – to give divine knowledge, instruction, and warnings. Peter, Paul, John and do not forget about Daniel, all had dreams and visions.

Angels are God's messengers delivering God's message and Jesus Christ's message. Many people talk to Jesus in their sleep. If you want to talk to Jesus in your dreams, you should simply ask Him to come and talk with you. That's what I did.

---

[33] Gen. 28:10-19
[34] Gen. 32:22-31

In a recent dream, Jesus came down to me in a great cloud with his arms stretched out, just like the pictures depict. I think He is preparing me gently to be able to speak with Him face-to-face with out me completely freaking out. Even in the dream I was getting very excited, saying, "Oh my God, there He is! There He is!" He was getting closer and closer to me -- and then the dream ended.

A face-to-face meeting is something I am working up to – but in the meantime I am speaking to Jesus in the more usual ways like the quiet voice or someone in the flesh, but with a different face, and in my dreams as well.

It seems my emotions need to be toned down a bit. I'm either too scared or too excited! Balance is what I need. I get caught up in the emotion of the experience, which puts me outside of it, instead of letting myself rest in the experience so I can be a part of it.

Soon.


Questions:

1. The future is _____.
2. *Déjà vu* is really just _____ what you have already seen.
3. What do you need to do to talk with Jesus in your sleep?

## 50. Dreams and Interpretation

*"In a dream, in a vision of the night, when deep sleep falls upon men, while slumbering on their beds, then He opens the ears, and seals their instructions."* Job 33:15-16

To me, this is something new that I have been avidly exploring recently. I have come to realize that there are classic symbols in the Bible that have distinct meanings in dreams. Now I feel the Lord has directed me to train myself to be able to interpret dreams. God instructs us in our dreams and in our night sleep because He wants to teach us and to show us things. His prophets in the Bible were often used for the purpose of dream interpretation.

I had already asked the Lord to give me visions and dreams, He has done that, but as yet, I do not know how to interpret them. What I thought were prophetic dreams, were in fact visions of things yet to come to pass. A prophetic dream is like a normal dream but needs to be shared with a dream interpreter who has been trained in this area so as to pass on God's instruction to the dreamer.

As stated elsewhere, this book is the result of a dream I had and an interpreter's explanation. Previously, I had already known that God wanted me to write another book, but I was stuck in the creative process. This dream I had, was a part of unlocking God's specific will for me. Then, just two days later, I received a prophecy, which said, "God wants you to write a book on the prophetic and on the supernatural dimensions of the prophetic."

I consulted with a dream interpreter on my prophetic web site and she said that, while there are many books on prophecy, not many are practical enough to teach the fundamentals of the prophetic lifestyle. She felt that I could write a good book on the subject and suggested that I should call it *The Prophetic Supernatural Experience.*

I had the title and I had some experience in the subject, so starting at 8:30 in the evening, I began to write the titles of the various parts – Part One, *All About Prophecy*, Part Two, *The Prophetic Person*, Part Three, *Ministering in The Prophetic*, Part Four, *The Supernatural Experience* and Part Five, *The Well-Known Secrets of The Anointing.*

The interpretation of that dream finally resulted in the book you are now reading. I encourage you to avail yourself of the services of a Christian dream interpreter whenever you suspect that a dream you have had is God trying to tell you something important. There is so much to be learned. It is the same as receiving a prophecy. If you can write down your dream, then send it in to get an interpretation of it. It is part of the supernatural experience to have prophetic dreams and to have those dreams interpreted.

It is certainly scriptural that a good prophet should be able to interpret the dreams of others. Daniel interpreted the dreams of Nebuchadnezzar and Joseph interpreted the dreams of the Pharaoh. Both led to senior leadership positions in the government of the day because of their prophetic ability. Sorcerers and people involved in the dark arts had failed to interpret these dreams, but on both occasions, the men of God succeeded.

Even in today's world, with its many psychics and clairvoyants, the users of the dark arts can only use a host of strange words. They cannot interpret the real meanings of dreams. The true prophets, such as Daniel or Joseph, knew the secret of correct dream interpretations. They both adamantly claimed that God alone was their interpreter.

Part of the prophetic supernatural experience is – *"young men shall see visions, your old men shall dream dreams," Joel 2:28.* The verse is talking about spiritual maturity, not age in years. Therefore, both the old and the young can see visions and dream dreams.

When you are spiritually young in the prophetic, you will have visions. You may see angels and you will experience other visions. However, it takes spiritual maturity to visualize, to interpret and to thereby understand the significance of a dream. A dream is like a night parable that needs maturity and the wisdom of God to interpret. As you mature in your prophetic anointing, you will be able to interpret dreams. You will both have dreams and interpret them. You will be like an older man, even though you may only be twenty-two.

## LAURIE'S REFLECTIONS
50. Dreams and Interpretation

## 50. DREAMS AND INTERPRETATION

A car is coming down the road: "Is that the police?" We moved to the side of the road and he looked down so I asked, "Have you done something?" With a sad look upon his face, he spoke, in a low tone, "Yes." – Then I woke up!

I called this person in my dream and told him about it. I guess he dismissed it, because a couple of days later, I found out that he received a ticket for driving with an expired tag. They took him to jail. He was impressed that I had dreamed about his "trouble with the law." In my spirit, I feel that this person knows the Lord is dealing with him and also that the Lord has him marked for the ministry.

Another time, I had a dream that we had three dogs. At the time we only had one and she died not long after that. So, of course, I thought I was supposed to go out and get three dogs. It does not actually work that way. Be careful with your interpretation and application – it might not be what God is saying. I went out and found a couple of cute puppies, but it turned out that we could not keep them. It was so sad to bond with them and then to have to find homes for them a little later.

But sure enough, in God's timing, we have three dogs! It is a long story how we came to have them, but just know that the details are in God's hands, not ours. He knows the end from the beginning. A lot of times we think we know it all! When God has given you a Word in part, let Him guide you to and through that Word. God works everything out. He is just letting us know things in advance, so there can be no doubt that God is in control.

My heart still yearns for those cute little puppies I had to give up. If I had just trusted in the Lord, I would have realized that He was letting me know that "one day" there would come a time when we would have three dogs, and I was to know that it was God ordained -- but Lord, three dogs! Really? Yes, says the Lord.

Pay attention to your dreams. Write them down and you will begin to see a pattern of how God speaks to you. You can learn to interpret your own dreams. God is so good that He has designed a special way of speaking to you – in your dreams – because most times, we are talking too much in our awake state, to hear anything He has to say, so He waits until we are "knocked out," unconscious, in a deep sleep.

God lets us know that He knows where our mind is at! Sometimes you might have a dream involving something you are not proud of. God is telling you to be aware of your thoughts and where they might take you.

Or He might be trying to get you to deal with a deep seeded issue – something that you are hiding deep within your soul. God wants to bring it up now so you can let it go.

To interpret a dream means to find out its inner and often hidden meaning, to be aware of the thoughts or mental processes which have produced the dream. Dreams make abundant use of symbolism to disguise the underlying thoughts producing the dream, and these symbols have basically the same general meaning in all dreams because they belong to the unconscious thinking of the human brain. Occasionally, there will be different meanings for different people – according to what they believe, or their upbringing or culture.

Here is my interpretation of three separate dreams – all involving rats. I call them "my rat dreams."

> Dream # 1: Rats were scurrying around the house, chatting with one another. I got scared – I don't like rodents of any kind – and I tried to get away from them, but instead of them coming towards me, they went in the opposite direction. My kitty-cat was nearby but she did not go after the rats.

My interpretation of this dream:

Since my cat did not go after the rats, the rats were symbolic and not literal. Symbolically, rats can mean betrayal, or "ratting on someone." God was letting me know that there was betrayal going on in my life.

I started feeling quite ashamed. Who am I betraying? I questioned myself until I asked a close friend about it and she told me, "Not you. You are not the betrayer, but you are being betrayed.

Then I asked myself, "Who are the rats?" I instantly understood. I was having some houseguests soon. I should be on my P's and Q's because I would soon have some rats in the house! The rats at this point symbolized people gossiping – chatting with one another about me, behind my back.

<u>Dream # 2:</u> There was an extra-large mouse entrance. Even though it was large, I still had to bend down to see in. I looked inside; it was all lit up, not dark and dingy like you would expect. To my surprise, my two faithful, and obviously loyal cats were standing guard right inside the large mouse entrance! My cats were protecting me from the rats – I woke up and thought: who are my faithful and loyal cats?

My interpretation:

At the time, I had a very good friend who was aware of my situation and was praying for me – she was one of my cats. She was keeping the rats at bay! Thank you, God, for my cats. The other cat? My guardian angel!

The large lit up rat hole was symbolic of a human living space and not an actual rat hole.

God is making these rat dreams very clear to me.

<u>Dream # 3:</u> My third and final rat dream was very short and to the point. I was walking down the street and saw some dead rats on the side of the road. The rats in my home and life were gone – the betrayal was over! Praise God!

Dreams are very important, do not disregard them. God is trying to get a message to you through your dreams.

**Questions:**
1. Dreams are God's way of getting a _____ to us.
2. The language of dreams is _____.

**Part 5 - Well-known Secrets to the Anointing**

## 51. Being a Friend of God

*"A man that has friends must show himself friendly: and there is a friend that sticks closer than a brother."* Proverbs 18:24

The Bible tells us that Abram was a friend of God. During his lifetime he desired to please God. One day, God called him to leave his hometown and to go by faith to an unknown land and to make his home there. (Later, God changed his name to Abraham, so from now on I will use his new name.)

Abraham received great and mighty promises from God. He also promised him a son. His wife was named Sarai, but God later changed her name to Sarah. At seventy five she was *still barren* and now she was way past childbearing age. The news that they were going to produce a son of their own seemed in the natural to be impossible but we read in Romans 4:17-21 the following words:

*"And not being weak in faith, he (Abraham) did not consider his own body, already dead (since he was about a hundred years old) and the deadness of Sarah's womb. He did not waver at the promise of God through unbelief, but was strengthened in faith, giving glory to God, and being fully convinced that what He had promised He was also able to perform. And therefore it was accounted to him for righteousness."*

So salvation is not just a New Testament miracle. Abraham received salvation because of his faith in God's word, just like we do today. Abraham, in fact, is called: "The Father of Faith." From his descendants came the Muslim faith, the Jewish faith and the Christian faith. For twenty-five years, Abraham had hung on to God's promise that he and his wife would produce a son and that their descendants would be more than the stars in the sky, just as God said.

He did for a brief moment weaken to his wife's suggestion to have a child to her maid Hagar. Probably to settle his wife, He had a boy to Hagar and named him Ishmael. Today, the descendants of Ishmael make up a large percentage of the Muslim persuasion. Many of them are in fact hostile enemies of Israel. When we do things our way instead of God's way, we can expect negative results.

Eventually, his wife miraculously gave birth to Isaac, God's promised son! Then, when the boy was just a young teenager, God told Abraham to place the lad on an altar as a sacrifice to Him. The next morning, Abraham takes his precious son to carry out God's will, but as he was about to push the knife into the boy's heart, God stopped him and provided a lamb as a suitable sacrifice.

To be a friend of God, you must be prepared to make personal sacrifices. You must humbly take God at His Word and be obedient to His will. This proves that you surrender to His ultimate goodness and His sovereignty over you.

Some people will say that God is Sovereign because He is the Supreme Being of the universe, but they have no trouble in running their own lives as they see fit. That is not faith! It is self-promotion! As a result, most people, even in the church, at times only give lip service to God, by indulging in feeding their own appetites, regardless of whether it is opposed to God's Word.

I include myself here, as I too am guilty of indulging myself and disregarding God's plans for me. We all take on the position of avenger when others fail to treat us as we think we deserve. It is called sin. When we disobey God we are actually seeing ourselves *higher* than God!

In the Gospels, Jesus said, *"Why do you call Me 'Lord, Lord' and not do the things which I say!" Luke 6:46.* A person doing that is building their life on a wrong foundation, which will result in calamity. The word "Lord" means "Master!" In olden times in England, a Lord used to own the land, and everyone was subservient to them. Today, there are relatively few Christians who are truly subservient to Christ.

Also, to be a friend of God means you must first become a friend of Jesus, His Son. For example: to be a friend of Rupert Murdoch, you would also need to befriend his son. No father is going to respect a person who disrespects his son.

## 51. BEING A FRIEND OF GOD

To obey Jesus is one of the best-known secrets of the anointing! When either the Father or Jesus says: "Jump" just say "How high God?" Do not use fleshly logic or wisdom. Be like Abraham and just obey, because God always has a very good reason why He acts the way He does.

Isaac had asked his father: "Where is the sacrifice?" And Abraham replied: "God will provide." In his heart, his father knew that all would go well, even if it meant God having to raise his boy from the dead. Abraham had God's prophecy that he would be the father of many nations, so there was no way that his son could stay dead. He had confidently told his waiting servants: *"Stay here with the donkey; the lad and I will go yonder and worship, and we will come back to you." Genesis 22:5*

Abraham saw this whole episode as an act of worship to his Lord. God was not only prepared to sacrifice His Own Son, He actually carried it off! However, Jesus knew what His "sin-rescue-mission" entailed: He and His Father had planned it all! But in Abraham's case, obedience and faith were put to the ultimate test.

Truly Abraham was indeed a true friend of God! When I understood this story, it was a turning point in my life. I was about fourteen at that time and I remember kneeling by my bed and crying out to Jesus: "I want to be a friend of Yours God, just like Abraham was." It had dawned on me that to be known as a "friend" of God, meant first and foremost, that I would have to be willing to do everything He said. Although my track record in the past was not good, this revelation has remained with me just as strong today, as it was back then. I try hard to live up to it, but, like everyone else, I fail because only Jesus is perfectly obedient and we need to put our trust in His finished work that was accomplished for us.

People rarely shake nations enough to qualify as a friend of God. I certainly do not. I have prophetic gifts, but I have only been used by God three times in healing someone. Nevertheless, it is not my works, but my heart's attitude and motive that will cause me to become a friend of God.

I do however see myself as a growing friend, because God alone knows the desires of my heart. A friend is someone you want to talk to; to meet with; to do things together; to share deep heart things with; to spend quality time in their company and to please and to make happy. If a friend is hurt or treated badly by others, it really hurts and upsets you!

One of the secrets of being a friend of God is having the right motive for wanting to be His friend. Your motive must come from a pure heart of compassion for others. As Christians we have been told that we have the mind of Christ but we must seek the obedience of Christ.

It is wonderful to draw close to Jesus and to know God's calling for your life. You need to be a friend of God because all true prophets are His friends.

## **LAURIE'S REFLECTIONS**
51. Being a Friend of God.

You are not a true friend unless you can be trusted. Who can you really trust? Can *you* be trusted all the time? If you are going to have just one friend, let it be God: He always keeps His promises and He most assuredly can be trusted.

You can't really say that about anyone else because at different times there always seems to be *something* that comes up and now they can't keep their promise or even they failed in the trust department. Whether it is intentionally or unintentionally, it is still a broken promise or unfriendly gesture. This is because we are only hu-man (who? man?) God, on the other hand, always keeps His Word. We may say: "If there's any possible way, I'll keep my word." With God, it is just "Way." He is the Way. He is the Way the Word is always kept – only with God.

I had to work through a lot of junk before I understood that my heavenly Father loves me -- I am in Him and He is in me. As Matthew stated in Chapter 42, your relationship with your heavenly Father can be hindered by a poor relationship with an earthly father.

Healing for me probably began when I was pregnant with my third child. My father used to be a very skilled carpenter, and when I became pregnant, I asked him if he would build a crib for the baby. He said yes, and set about doing it. I cried. My father was doing something special for me. The last thing he had done for me was leave me – maybe that was a blessing in disguise? He was, after all, an actively drinking alcoholic. But he did care. He cared enough to take the time to do something nice and meaningful for me. It was the beginning of the healing process between my father and I.

Many years later, he told me he was sorry for not being in my life when I was younger, for missing out on so much. It was part of the healing process for us both. All is well.

I know Father God has my back on every situation and that nothing will ever come between that. There will never be "something came up and I couldn't be there for you" from God because *"I am a friend of God; He calls me friend."* (song by Clint Brown)

**Questions:**
1. All true prophets are _____ of God.

## 52. Developing Intimacy with God

*"Seek ye first the kingdom of God and His righteousness..."*
Matthew 6:33

When I think of the word "intimacy" – sexual intimacy in a marriage comes to mind, but it is only a very small component of human intimacy because true intimacy is far more than physical love. It is as if the wife is about to say something at a dinner table and the husband knows exactly how her mind is thinking and lovingly finishes her sentence.

Intimacy is to sit in the same room with a loved one; to be very comfortable in each other's presence, without any other form of distraction in the room. Intimacy happens when you are both eating dinner and having five-minute's silence but the love still flows between you like arched lightning between two lightning rods. Intimacy is to know the deep longings of your soul-mate and wanting to help them fulfill their personal desires.

There is so much to human intimacy. However, do you have intimacy with God? When you want to walk in the strong anointing and power of God, you need to know Him, not just know about Him. To only know a lot about God will actually hinder intimacy, because human pride feeds on knowledge! Such people will confidently tell you the solutions for all types of problems. They read their Bible, so that they can answer people's questions about God. They know everything about the Bible, but lack true intimacy with Him because that has not been their motive in studying God's Word.

A person who has the gift of teaching may in fact be robbed of God's best for them. They may study the Bible with the mindset of wanting to teach it to others and that is a good thing, but it is not God's prime reason for raising you up as a teacher. His reason for you to read His Word is to establish intimacy with Him. He wants you to take on His characteristics, His desires, and His love for people, so that you are "complete" and have no lack in your life. That peace and security will witness to others far more effectively than anything you teach in words!

When I want to know something, I ask God, both in my secular life and my spiritual life. He has all the right answers about everything! His presence floods me when I wake up each day, so that I feel His peace and joy in my soul. His Holy Spirit gives me directions for my day. God is just one breath away! Jesus and the Father want to hear my words – "What should I do, God?"

This builds an intimacy with God because He knows that you mean what you say – that you want to do only what He wants that day.

When we compare our Heavenly Father to our earthly father, we may have negative responses, as was my case before I was emotionally healed. Many Christians have similar deep pain. This type of emotional damage left unattended will certainly hinder true intimacy with God the Father. You need to be willing to allow God to do a work of healing in your life, so that you become "willing" to forgive your father, then God will be free to perform His miraculous healing into your heart. You will then be able to genuinely love and honor your father as He has commanded you to do.

God should be your best friend. Jesus should be your best friend. In fact, if you are called to be a prophet, they both need to be your best friends, as there can be a lot of rejection and misunderstanding in a prophet's life. God allows this so that a prophet will draw closer to Him. He needs a prophet to bring change, repentance, correction, and to dispel lies and mistruths in His church.

He wants someone who is honorable and will always see things from His perspective. He uses a person who is not persuaded by money, riches, or lusts of the world, and is not a respecter of persons. You may be extremely wealthy or have a tremendous television ministry that reaches a world-wide audience, but you have to know that it was God that set everything up to be that way. Make sure that you give Him all the glory! None of it happened without His intervention in your life. The incarnate Jesus was the epitome of humility!

God wants *you* to be His friend. He does not *need* your friendship, but He desires it! God is complete in Himself, but He delights in sharing His completeness in you: to make you complete! Friendship that entails intimacy requires both trust and faithfulness between both parties. God never fails in His part! On our part, intimacy does not just happen: it is purposely established over time in prayer, obedience, worshipping, reading the Bible, and mixing with other like-minded people. Seek these people out to be your close friends.

It is not easy to find people who delight in talking about the goodness of God, people who are action-people, not just content to remain passive about everything. No, mix with those who want to live crucified lives of self-denial in order to build up God's kingdom on earth. People who are in tune with God's voice and want only to do and say the things He directs them to.

Just as an intimate couple can complete each other's sentences, a child of God needs to be able to be God's spokesperson to others. To do so, they must first have an intimate relationship with the Triune God and have ongoing personal revelation of the Word of God.

A prophetic person may go to an important meeting and have a question burning in their mind and ask God: "Do you want me to say this Lord?" And the Holy Spirit may reply: "No, someone else is going to share this for you." You are not the only one whom God uses. There may be other prophetic people that God has in the meeting. They too are in tune with God's agenda! They too have an intimacy with God.

Like anything, a good relationship comes through the sacrifice of personal time. Take time to get closer to God. Draw near to Him today and pray that He will lead you into a closer relationship with Him. To be a true prophet of God, this is absolutely necessary.

## **LAURIE'S REFLECTIONS**

52. Developing Intimacy with God

Surface study makes for a surface relationship – nothing deep and revealing, nothing that will sustain you through hard times.

Intimacy with God takes place in God's bedchamber. His Bedchamber is His Word. Crawl into bed with God and let His Word seduce you. He is the great seed producer and His seed (word) is available to those who will allow the planting of that seed. You then

## 52. DEVELOPING INTIMACY WITH GOD

have to take the time to develop it. You have to water the seed by the renewing of your mind, daily. You have to meditate on the Word and talk to God. An intimate relationship with Him is the result of all that -- and then the fruit is produced.

Everyone likes being "sought after." This includes God. He says: *"Seek ye first the kingdom of God and His righteousness...,"* Matthew 6:33.

Marriage to God is everlasting. Others may forsake you - especially after intimacy but God has promised that: *"He will never leave you nor forsake you."* With God, you are free to be you and still, He will never leave you. God is willing and able to marry us – our mind to His Will – and the two shall become one – being the Mind of Christ and walking in His Spirit. Digging deep into His Word is the very act of intercourse (communication) and intimacy with God – which excites God. This causes Him to produce Seed which is planted in us. The Seed of God grows in us and allows us to help give birth to the souls that need to be "born-again."

As you develop an intimate relationship with God, there is a sense that I am God's and He is mine. Just let yourself go, so you can feel free to flow in a passionate love affair from within. This connects us to God in such a way that we simply cannot live without **it** – and God is *It*.

When someone is speaking intimately to you, they usually use a quiet voice. God speaks very intimately by means of the still small voice from within. He is whispering in your ear. Can you hear Him?

Read a few words of this song. It is called, "The Martyr Song" by Rick Pino:

> They overcame by the blood of the Lamb
> And by the words of their testimonies
> They loved not their lives even unto death
> Raise up an army of laid down lovers

Do we not all love the Lord? Yes, we all love the Lord, but some of us have laid down and fallen asleep – while still awake. Raise up an army of laid down lovers. Develop intimacy with God; it will raise up a laid down lover.

Questions:
1. List some ways in which you can develop or expand your intimacy with God.
2. What does it take most of all to develop anything?

## 53. Humility

*"I am crucified with Christ: nevertheless I live; yet not I, but Christ liveth in me: and the life which I now live in the flesh I live by the faith of the Son of God, who loved me, and gave Himself for me."*
*Galatians 2:20*

Humility is the KEY to the gifts.

Due to the fact that unrepentant sin in my life had held me captive, I constantly felt the associated guilt and condemnation from the devil. Consequently, I deliberately stayed away from church for many years, but one day I actually felt like going to church. So, I went to the morning service at a lively Pentecostal church nearby. It was a good church, doing great outreach work with the homeless and assisting the poor in the red-light district of Brisbane, Australia.

It was as if I was meant to listen to the message that day. The pastor said: "You know that people look for the power of God and His anointed gifts of healing, miracles, signs, and wonders. They expect that these gifts are related to the elevated places a person has in the world: the higher they are in the world's eyes the higher anointing they will receive in doing mighty works for God. People assume it is a level of height that a person attains to, but the reverse is true. It is the level of lowness that opens the door for the power of God to be released." The Pastor had *hugely* attracted my attention.

In one of the poorest places in the world, a missionary called Heidi Baker has helped plant ten thousand churches in Mozambique. Every morning, she spends three to five hours on her face before the Lord. She says that even when she is so low to the ground, she does not feel low enough to meet with her awesome God. It makes me wonder about the people in the Throne Room of God – are they praising God on their feet, with their hands raised in the air, or are they laying prostrate on the floor, weeping in adoration?

Heidi Baker knows that whenever she goes to any church, in whatever denomination, there will be a trickle of the Holy Spirit's anointing presence in the church. She can always feel the presence of the Lord and is always blessed. She knows that without humility in her life, she will never reach the higher levels in God.

I have to confess, that the finest individuals I have met in my Christian life have been tremendously humble servants of the Lord. I met a man once who made me feel as if I was in the presence of Jesus. His Bible was marked heavily on every single page. You could spend ten minutes on each page just reading all his scrawled notes in trying to understand the knowledge and wisdom that had been revealed to him. Yet, this humble man just quietly sat with me for hours on end, listening intently to me for the entire time. He was the one with all the knowledge, but in wisdom and love, he just sat and listened to me rave on!

I asked him heaps and heaps of questions, but what I was really doing was venting my opinions that others vehemently opposed. He just patiently listened. For a person with the authority and power, together with godly knowledge, he should have been the one speaking, not listening. In hindsight, I felt that he should have told me, "Just be quiet, Matthew, I need to say something!" But he never did. He just listened because Jesus was making me lowly that day.

I have learnt that without humility, you will not be able to reach the higher levels of anointing, because unless you are humble, you are not capable of unrestrained obedience. If you think you know it all, you cannot truly be directed and fashioned by the Lord. Therefore, when the Lord disciplines you, chastises you, or puts you through a series of trials, and you are not humbled, you become bitter and angry and seriously rebel against God.

The Lord allows persecution, trials and storms in life to temper our character and our humility. When we can genuinely praise Him even in the storm, then we know that we have progressed in our faith. Personally, I still have a long way to go to conquer pride, for I can still be somewhat boastful. Although I am still working on my new identity in Christ and the inheritance of my adoption by the Father, I am beginning to realize that I do not need to boast to anyone, because God knows exactly who I am, and He loves me as I am.

## 53. HUMILITY

One day, when we were sharing during a group study, an assistant pastor at my church said she had received a word for me, but she would share it on the way home. Later, she told me what the Lord had said: "Matthew's my silent prophet." I was so encouraged by that, because I always feel that I talk too much and also, that He saw me as a prophet, which really uplifted me.

I am relatively quiet in church when it comes to showing my knowledge of God. But ordinarily, I feel that I am far from silent. I feel that the Lord wants me to be quiet around people who love me, people from my own hometown or from my own church. Now I only open my mouth on the deeper things of God around people who have a real hunger for these things. In general, I do not often go around boasting as I once did. The Bible says: humble yourself!

*"Humble yourself under the mighty hand of God, that He may exalt you in due time."* And: *"Humble yourselves in the sight of the Lord, and He will lift you up."* 1 Peter 5:6 and James 4:10

The Lord is telling us to humble ourselves. Obviously, it is far less painful that way. Before you can become a mature and powerful prophet of God, you must learn the way of humility.

## **LAURIE'S REFLECTIONS**

### 53. Humility

Being humble is a sign that you know, understand, and are in agreement that -- someone <u>else</u> is in charge. Humility is a quality that speaks volumes regarding a person's character and is a required trait for every prophet. But not to worry, if you are not there yet, you will be; God will see to that, but it is a work in progress – it is a process.

Is it possible for a man to be alive on earth with God *not* working in Him? No, we walk before the Lord humbly, yes, but there, still within us, lay deep seeded (seated) roots that need digging up.

There is a fine line between humility and pride. You cannot "see" either one necessarily – only by taking a closer look. It is good to be proud of your work, committed and dedicated, but when you become prideful and haughty like: "It's all about me, yeah! It's because I'm so good!" then look out because *"Pride comes before the fall,"* so, again, let your pride fall so you don't have to.

Before you get filled with pride, give God all the glory for your success, your children's success, and your grandchildren's success. Always point the glory back to God: strive to show God's Handiwork and He will make sure you get all the credit.

Humility is a wonderful way to walk. Walking in humility takes all the burdens off your shoulders because you know that everything is being worked out. Taking credit and being prideful leads to so much more than you are called to carry.

The Lord wants to mold you and shape you into a vessel fit for the Master's use and it starts with learning humility. What that really means is you have to get your emotions out of the way – completely out of the picture – because being humble is not just about pride; it is also about any other negative emotion, especially anger! Gain control of your anger! This is sometimes hard for a prophet to do.

I am so speaking to myself right now. I work and I work and I work on my anger. Just when I think I have been doing a good job with not blowing up – bam! I explode! God tests me. I do not always pass. We prophets have to learn how to control our emotions – positive and negative – we do not need to be unbalanced on either side of the equation. And if we just understand that it is all God, we would take in a deep breath of His Breath, inhaling deeply – holding it in as long as possible. Then breathe God's breath out onto the situation. Just let it all go through you – not to you and stop there – but all the way *through* you! Then you will be walking in true humility, knowing that God is God because He is All in all.

If you need a lesson in humility, just go stay at your in-law's house for a while. Be determined to be a servant to them. The way up is through servant-hood. Learn to serve and you will learn to be humble. If moving in with your in-laws is out of the question, find someone you can be a true servant to – maybe your pastor or mentor or even maybe your spouse! People generally have a hard time serving others on a true servant-hood level. They think: Who are you? But I am telling you, it is a very humbling experience to serve with an attitude of gratitude – with the intent that you are there to serve and nothing else.

Andrew Murray said that humility is the beauty of holiness – with you understanding that holiness is fleeing to Jesus and hiding yourself in Him until you are clothed with His humility. An old saying is: "I would rather have defeat with humility than conquest with boasting."

The key to the prophetic is humility and the key of humility is servant-hood. The command to be humble comes from the Throne of God: *Humble yourself.* Here are a few additional tips for learning to be humble:

- Self-denial – accept every humiliation as a means of grace to humble yourself. Look at every person who tries or troubles you as a needed experience in your walk of humility. (Read and study 2 Sam. 16:5-12.)
- Stop complaining – James 5:9 says, *"Grudge not one against another, brethren, lest you be condemned: behold, the judge stands before the door."*
- Resist taking the credit – James 4:6 says, *"God resists the proud, but gives grace to the humble."*
- Judge not – Read James 4:11 and 12. Criticism of others is one of the ways pride gets revealed through our speech. It is an offense both to the person and to God. Do not hate the person criticizing you as you stand there criticizing others.

When a person is truly humble, he is truly empty of himself; he is a vessel to God, overflowing with God's Grace. He is the son of all the beatitudes – poor in spirit, meek of heart, hungering and thirsting after righteousness.

Just when I think I am making a little headway in humility – news flash – I have to take another lesson in it. I love the outcome; it is just that at that moment when I am humbling myself, I have to use all the humility I have gained up to that point – or lose it.

In ministry, pride is especially running amuck. Remember, everything is for the sake of spreading the Gospel. We are not in competition with one another – we do not need to compare gifts. Big, fat, ugly pride would want us to do that. Pride wants you focused on you prophesying better, praying better, or singing better than anyone else – that is not the way of Jesus.

Jesus was the epitome of humility – humility in its purest form – no pride was in the mix, no religious traditions of men, no additives could be found. Anything in its purest form is in its best possible form.

What is true in the physical is true in the spirit. Look at the food we eat with all its additives and processes it goes through. Not a pretty sight! Raw or fresh produce is always the best. And humility in its purest form is Christ's humility.

If you will take on Christ's humility, you will find rest and grace to do the "greater works" that Jesus spoke about. All labor is in vain if it is without humility. Choose humility (humble yourselves) or be humiliated! It is just the way It works. It is much easier to humble yourself. Search your heart and see the pride – repent and move on.

Humility has one of the greatest benefits. Check out Zephaniah 2:3 – "..., _seek humility. It may be that you will be hidden in the day of the Lord's anger._

Humility brings divine protection! Humility brings on the anointing. Humility brings greatness (Matt. 20:25-28.) Not humiliation, but humility. There's a difference. It's okay not to be right all the time and it's okay when you are right but no one knows it but God and yourself. He protects you when you just humble yourself and let others think what they will. He anoints you and appoints you as you walk in humility and accept and admit that you are not the Know-It-All. God is God and you are god.[35] At least you are kin to the Know-It-All. There can be only one know-it-all and that's God; God is the only One that gets things right all the time, that's why His Word tells us to "..._seek righteousness,"_ Zeph. 2:3.

---

[35] Ps. 82:6; John 10:34

## 53. HUMILITY

Jesus instructed His disciples to lead by example and not by control. When you develop true humility and servant-hood, others will follow and submit, even though you are not asking for their submission, nor seeking it – It is a Divine Law.

The key to the true and hidden interpretation of the Scriptures is humility, an implicit reliance on the spirit of God to reveal revelation to you – an ever increasing and fervent desire for light, for increasing knowledge to be shown. Had the wise men not possessed a child-like, humble spirit, they would not have fallen down and worshipped Him.

As I have said, one of my biggest obstacles in prophesying is my pride. I remember someone telling me once that I might not speak much, but when I did – It was powerful. Well, that is because I weighed my words carefully and did not speak unless I was sure beyond a shadow of a doubt, but that just caused more pride! Instead of giving all the glory to God because God is It – I got prideful. Silly me.

I have learned to trust that it is God speaking through me. It's all God. The Word is going to challenge them; it is going to provoke some thinking; it is going to inspire them – making it all good.

Humble yourself and trust God.

The word "shy" means "introverted, withdrawn, timid, bashful, uncomfortable with others, cautious, reluctant, short of something, not reproducing easily…" I can be all of those at times. I do believe it has something to do with my pride, or am I really just shy? Pride relates more to our opinion of ourselves; vanity relates to what we would have others think of us. Maybe I am just plain vain – I need to get over myself and understand that God wants to use me if I will but let him do so.

Humility *is* the key to the gifts.

**Questions:**
1. What is there a lot of in a prophet's life?
2. Who does the real power of God come to?

3. What is the key to the gifts?
4. What is the key to humility?

## 54. Obedience to God

> *"He who has My commandments and keeps them, it is he who loves Me. And he who loves Me will be loved by My Father, and I will love him and manifest Myself to him." John 14:21*

When a word or phrase was repeated by the people, in the time of Jesus, it was deliberately done as a way of saying "Listen, this is very important for you to understand." If the same word or phrase was said three times in quick succession you had best make sure you got the message! People did not just carelessly repeat themselves!

Jesus often said the words, "Truly, truly, I say unto you." Or perhaps, "Verily, verily, I say unto you." The duplication of a word signified the importance of what He was about to say. At other times, He would give a command, two or three times within a short space of time.

But we note that, when Jesus spoke on the necessity of "obedience to God," He took this repetition formula to new heights! In a short space of time, Jesus stressed not twice, not three times, not four times, *but five times* that obedience was to be the outward evidence of true heart commitment.

1. John 14:15 *"If you love Me keep My commandments."*

2. John 14:21 *"He who has My commandments and keeps them, it is he who loves Me. And he who loves Me will be loved by My Father, and I will love him and manifest Myself to him."*

3. John 14:23 *"If anyone loves Me he will keep My word, and My Father will love him, and We will come to him and make Our home with him."*

4. John 15:10 *"If you keep My commandments, you will abide in My love, just as I have kept My Father's commandments and abide in His love."*

5. *John 15:14 "You are My friends if you do whatever I command you."*

Jesus has definitely made His point to us. Did He think His audience was slow in their comprehension ability? NO! He was pointing out that genuine love of God should automatically result in willing obedience! If Jesus is our Lord – and He only ever did the things that pleased His Father – should we not do the things that please the Father as well?

At the Mount of Transfiguration, the Father's voice boomed out: *"This is My beloved Son, in whom I am well pleased. Hear Him!" Matthew 17:5b*

This command by God, the Father, was witnessed by Peter, James, and John – together with Moses, Elijah and Jesus Himself. Representatives of both the Old and New Testament heard these words. (An Old Testament principle was that you had to have two or three reliable witnesses in a Court of Law.)

Legally, we have no other recourse but to obey the Lord Jesus Christ, if we profess to be His disciples. Jesus was not being manipulative or condemning; He was merely pointing out that our words and our actions must agree.

I can vividly remember my mother pointing this out to us kids. As a young child, I would desperately want her approval but I stubbornly refused to do some of the simple things she told me to. You do not have to be an Einstein to figure this principle out! If your heart is full of genuine love for someone, nothing will stop you from doing the things that will please them. In fact, you will go out of your way to do *everything* in your power to please them.

True faith in God means that confession and expression go hand in hand. This principle applies to salvation as well. Paul said: *"If you **confess with your mouth** the Lord Jesus and **believe in your heart** that God has raised Him from the dead, you will be saved. For with the heart one believes unto righteousness, and with the mouth confession is made unto salvation."*

## 54. OBEDIENCE TO GOD

At Gethsemane, the loyal and bold Simon-Peter had boasted that he would never deny the Lord, even if everyone else deserted him. Jesus, prophesied that indeed Peter would deny Him three times before the early morning crowing of the rooster. Jesus knew that, soon, overwhelming grief and fear would cause the prophetic word to come to pass and it did that very night.

Intense shame caused Peter to return to his former occupation as a local fisherman. Then, after the resurrection, when Jesus singled him out and pointedly asked THREE TIMES if he loved Him, this truly broke Peter's heart because, as a Jew, repeating yourself made the words seem harsher and harsher! But, each time Peter said "Yes" he was told to care for Jesus' sheep or lambs.

Was Jesus just trying to rub in the fact that he had been such a rotten coward?

No, of course not; Jesus is merciful and full of grace. Jesus was saying: Peter, I understand. Do you not realize that I know how hard it is to be a human like you? It really is okay! I love you and I honestly trust you with my precious sheep! You were weak, but believe Me: you will be strong! Feed My lambs: Tend to my sheep; Feed my sheep for Me. (See story in John 21:15-17.)

For many years, my pet hobby-horse was "obedience to the commands of Jesus" and if you know me well, you will discover that this is still my hobby-horse! But the way I formerly expressed the need for obedience was tied to my past legalistic ways. Since then, I have discovered that there is a better way and that is to imitate the mercy, love, and grace of Jesus to ALL people and they will then SEE Jesus! I have to constantly fight against tendencies to judge Christians in this area. God has given me great compassion for "selective people" and these are hurting people of the world. I do my very best to be Jesus to them, but I tend not to be as compassionate to my brothers and sisters in the Lord. I have to keep telling myself that Jesus is their judge, not Matthew.

We all have God's three-time promise! He WILL finish the work He has started in each of us! (Philippians 1:6, 1 Corinthians 1:8 and 2 Timothy 4:18.) **Three times!** – that is very interesting!

If you are God's friend, you need to lay down your life for Him; Jesus said: *"Whoever desires to come after Me, let him deny himself, and take up his cross, and follow Me. Mark 8:34.* Being obedient means commitment to a sacrificial life of self-denial. If you want to walk in a strong anointing with God and reach your full potential as a prophet, live only to do the will of God and Jesus. As a prophet, you will know the will of God for your life; you will know your purpose and destiny and the Holy Spirit will direct your steps.

Many people desire to perform signs and wonders and walk in a strong anointing of God, but they are not prepared to do the groundwork for that anointing. Therefore, the choice is yours; God is calling you. He wants to use you as a *tractor*, not just as a horse and plow.

Many are called to the office of prophet, but will not submit to the time and training that it takes. A life of obedience will put you in an ideal place to progress to your prophetic destiny. Everything else that I was going to say in this chapter has been said in former chapters. So I will leave you in the hands of the Holy Spirit to work out your particular "obedience" details.

## **LAURIE'S REFLECTIONS**

54. Obedience to God

Are you inclined to act too fast or too slow when God gives you an instruction? We want to obey, but like learning anything, until we have perfected it, our timing may be a little off. When we learn to be sensitive to the Spirit, we will line up with God and the "two shall become one," and the manifestation of God in our lives will be apparent to everyone.

Obedience is the door to the Kingdom. There is no doubt that Jesus' fellowship with His Father was developed and perfected through his absolute surrender of his will to God. *"Not my will but Thine be done,"* was his daily prayer.

Jesus did the will of God against the will of all his friends and relatives. When Peter tried to hold him back from the cross: from

## 54. OBEDIENCE TO GOD

obedience to God, Jesus instantly rebuked him as one who tempted him; *"Get you behind me, Satan."* Even when his mother was in his way of obedience to God, Jesus rebuked and disowned her at the time. Jesus regarded anyone who tried to bind or blind him from the will of God, as His greatest foe.

Obedience to God is the only logical way to genuine fellowship with God, and it is fruitless to seek any other way. Follow Jesus' Way. Jesus had an instinct for God, like a child has for its mother, like a bee has for the honey. He felt the presence of God's spirit knocking at the door of His being and calling Him to fellowship – He felt the larger love knocking at the door of His heart; He felt the larger righteousness knocking at the door of His conscience; He felt the larger truth knocking at the door of His mind. Spirit was speaking to spirit.

When your mind aligns with God's Spirit-in-you, then you will be walking in the Spirit and your life will be a life of "obedience to God" – with all the blessings and benefits thereof.

A word on disobedience: Disobedience leads to having to repeat the same cycle one more time. In life we are suppose to be going up in a spiral motion according to our consciousness level. But disobedience keeps us at the same level year after year.

Having the mind of Christ keeps us going up, up, up and over the top!

### Questions:

1. How complete was the surrender of Christ's will to his Father?
2. How do you walk through the door to the Kingdom?

## 55. Impartation of Mantles and Gifts

*"Stir up the gift of God which is in you through the laying on of my hands." 1Timothy 1:6*

One of the ways to walk in a stronger anointing is for another prophet to impart his mantle, or his anointing to you, just as Moses passed on his mantle to Joshua or as Elijah passed on a double anointing to Elisha. Scripture confirms that Elijah performed seven miracles and Elisha went on to perform fourteen.

Today, Heidi Baker has literally performed thousands of miracles! You may recall that I have spoken of her a few times, as she is one of my heroes of the faith. You can do a Google search on her, or Iris Ministries and you will discover for yourself the reason for my high praise.

1Timothy 1:6 - *"Stir up the gift of God which is in you through the laying on of my hands."* The Apostle Paul said this to young Timothy, as Timothy had received the impartation of the gifts of the Holy Spirit. If you are walking strong in the gift of prophecy, you can impart that gift to another believer – unless the other believer is in rebellion or deep sin, and God does not want that gift to rest upon them, but if the believer has a good heart, the gift will be imparted. So you see that you too, can impart a mantle on a fellow believer.

Sometimes, the mantle that I carry is a strong one even though I am not a well-known prophet at the present time. However, those who have a higher anointing can recognize it on me. Therefore, passing on my mantle to you could be quite beneficial to your ministry in the Lord.

Recently, I was reading the biography of Reinhard Bonnke, the famous European evangelist. One day he went to a friend's house and asked, "Is he here?" The woman at the door said he was, but he was not to be disturbed. Straight away came another voice, "No, let him come in!" Reinhard entered the room and said to the old evangelist sitting on a lounge: "Can you please pray for me?"

This well-known revivalist evangelist immediately fell to his knees and started praying in the spirit. Even though the older man could hardly walk anymore, the power and the presence of God on Him was so strong! It was not long after this meeting that the old gentleman died, but Reinhard had received his mantle and had also received a prophecy from him that he would save more than a million people within the space of five days, when he went on his campaigns in Africa. He received a massive anointing and Reinhard went on to fulfill that prophecy.

All I have is the gift and the ability to walk in prophecy, but I also have a mantle of a typical prophet. However, I want to pray for you to receive the gifts of prophecy and a mantle higher than my own. I want to use either the video or this book to pray for that now. If you say 'Amen' at the close of this prayer and believe in faith, then write to me at my website and give me a personal prophecy to prove to you that you indeed have received the gift.

*"Dear Heavenly Father, the Apostle Paul urged us to covet the gift of prophecy for it is the best gift! As a child of God, I want to walk in this gift. I want to walk in the prophetic with its associated gifts of the Word of Knowledge and the Word of Wisdom. I truly want to bless and encourage people through these gifts. I ask that You will impart these gifts to me through Matthew and through this prayer. I ask for Your perfect will to be done concerning these things. I ask that You will cause me to love others as You love them and I will practice these gifts, as often as You lead me to, from this time on. I sincerely thank You for hearing my prayer and for imparting these gifts to me. I ask these things in the precious name of Jesus, Amen."*

Dear Heavenly Father, I pray for everyone within the sound of my voice on the video or those who have read this book from beginning to end and have absorbed this information. I am specifically praying for all those who sincerely want to walk in the prophetic office and this is my prayer for you:

"Father, You know those with pure, sincere and contrite hearts. You know those who do not lie against their neighbors, who keep themselves from sin and do not practice evil and desire always to walk in Your presence. You know the believers who genuinely love

You and who want to walk in Your anointing of the prophetic, so that they will have a profound and positive impact on earth.

I pray for those devoted and hungry believers who want to walk in the office of prophet or the gifts of the prophetic anointing. I ask You now to pass my mantle onto their shoulders today and that this mantle will start to manifest in their life with an explosion of gifts and anointing in multiple dimensions in their life.

May both their natural words and their prophetic words increasingly grow more powerful as they submit themselves to Your teaching. May they feel the presence of the Holy Spirit bubble up in joy and the anointing presence of God increase in their daily life! May there be many tangible signs that this mantle has been imparted to them. May at least three of their associates testify to the great change that has occurred in their life and to give glory to You. May it be also confirmed in both their own spirit and in their heart, that they have indeed received this mantle from this prayer!

I also ask that You will raise up three witnesses with spiritual authority to further validate this mantle on them, as a firm confirmation to their step of faith. You already know those you want to receive such a mantle. I freely pass it on and pray that you bless these people and they even go on and exceed the position that you have called me to and to go to the world and exceed the place that you are calling me to.

Dear Father, in Jesus' name and as a servant of Yours, please pass on this mantle and a mantle of anything higher or lower according to Your will for the particular person and their destiny. I ask that You would double the authority and anointing on every contrite and pure, sincere believer who is listening or reading this book today. I humbly ask and thank you in Jesus' name for doing Your will and for achieving Your purposes in this book. I thank You for giving me the dream, the prophecy, the insight, the revelation, the enthusiasm and tenacity to complete this book. In Jesus' name I pray. Amen."

# APPENDIX

## Answers to Chapter Questions

### Chapter 2: Some Definitions Used in the Prophetic

1. **What do we learn from Exodus 7:1 as to the meaning of the word "prophet"?** A prophet is the spokesperson for God.
2. **Define the difference between wisdom and words of wisdom.** Wisdom is natural human wisdom that smart people use in their everyday living, but a word of wisdom is wisdom from God imparted by the Holy Spirit that is beyond any natural wisdom and is only available as the Holy Spirit reveals.

### Chapter 3: Choosing the Prophetic Experience

1. **Why does Satan hate the prophetic?** Satan hates the prophetic because he is a liar and therefore hates the truth. He hates the positive. Satan hates, period.
2. **Will you choose to answer the call that God has placed on your life?**

### Chapter 4: Can All Christians Be Prophetic?

1. **Can all Christians be prophetic?** Yes they can. Numbers 11:29, and 1 Cor. 14:31.
2. **Do you need to be baptized in the Holy Spirit to prophesy?** No.

### Chapter 5: If All Christians Can Be Prophetic, Why Not You?

1. **Is there anything that could keep you from receiving the gift of prophecy?** Yes, unbelief.
2. "Surely the Lord God will do nothing but he revealeth his **SECRETS** unto his servants the **PROPHETS**." Amos 3:7

### Chapter 6: The Gift of Prophecy – What Is It?

1. **What is prophecy?** A process in which a message from the heart and mind of God is communicated to a prophet and then communicated to others.
2. **What are the three elements of prophecy?** 1. Words of knowledge; 2. Words of wisdom; 3. And everything in between.
3. **What are some ways in which God has been preparing you for the prophetic ministry?** When things do not go right, no matter what you do, you are being prepared for the prophetic ministry! When everyone seems to be against you, you are being prepared for the prophetic ministry! When you are having marriage problems, you are being prepared for the prophetic ministry! When you are being despised and rejected by men, when you have been acquainted with grief, you are being prepared for the prophetic ministry! All this while, God is just trying to get your attention – using the words of "Uncle Sam": He wants you!

## Chapter 7: Using Prophecy

1. **Give two good reasons why we should all prophesy.**
    - Prophecy can be medicine to someone who is suffering hardship or confusion; it can be a healing balm to the human spirit.
    - Prophecy can be a tool of encouragement to live a victorious life.
    - Prophecy can give positive hope and vision for a person's future by giving them an understanding of their destiny and purpose.

2. **Who is prophecy for?** Everyone – believers and non-believers. It will make a believer out of them. It is also for the prophets. Prophets need prophets in their life as well.

## Chapter 8: The Gift of the Word of Knowledge – What Is It?

1. **What is the difference between a Word of Knowledge and a Word of Wisdom?** A word of knowledge is certain supernatural information or knowledge that you would not

have any way of knowing except that the Lord has revealed it to you and a word of wisdom is information as to what to do concerning a certain situation. A word of wisdom is the practical application of the word of knowledge.
2. **How does the Word of the Lord come to you?** Spontaneously, suddenly, without you thinking about "what to say."
3. **Why is the gift of the Word of Knowledge a valuable gift?** It impresses people to believe. It confirms that you are truly receiving your knowledge from the Lord. It is the evidence people need to believe and be strengthened by the prophecy.

## Chapter 9: Using the Word of Knowledge – A Risky Gift

1. **Why is the Word of Knowledge a "risky gift"?** Risky because we do not understand the word and so we get in the way of God, but well worth the risk if you have been trained and understand that you just need to give the Word as it is given to you and trust God to reveal the meaning to the individual.
2. **How often do you need to renew your mind with the Word of God?** Daily

## Chapter 10: The Gift of the Word of Wisdom – What Is It?

1. **What is the difference between wisdom and a Word of Wisdom?** "Wisdom" is general knowledge that can be obtained somehow in the natural. However, a "Word of Wisdom" comes supernaturally from God at a crucial moment.

## Chapter 11: Using Words of Wisdom

1. **What can cripple your spiritual life?** Not following the commands of words of wisdom because you lose hope when you do not follow God's directional guidance.
2. **What is the purpose of Words of Wisdom?** To give you direction.

## Chapter 12: Can Prophecies Contain the Flesh?

1. **What can take the flesh out of prophesying?** Discipline and renewing the mind.
2. The Lord God does not make leaders; He makes **SERVANTS** who become leaders. –Bishop E. Bernard Jordan

## Chapter 13: Are There Reasons Why Prophecies Do Not Come True?

1. **What are some reasons why a prophecy might not come true?**

   - Words were spoken partly by the flesh.
   - A wrong spirit may have influenced the prophecy.
   - Words of wisdom in the prophecy were not obeyed.
   - Personal character traits may first need to be developed before God allows the prophecy to come to pass.
   - Everything is not lined up.

2. **What is the difference between the psychic network and the prophetic ministry?** The psychic network is there to impress for their own personal glory and some are there to pull you into the dark side of things, while the prophetic ministry is all for the glory of the Lord and for the lifting up of the saints.

## Chapter 14: Why Some Prophecies You Think Are False Are Not

1. **Is it possible to think you have a false prophecy, but you do not?** Yes, you may just not fully understand the prophecy or maybe the prophecy has not come to pass YET.
2. **How long does it take for a prophecy to come to pass?** As long as it takes for everything to line up. God only knows.

## Chapter 15: The Gift of Encouragement

1. **What other gift goes well with the Gift of Encouragement?** The gift of prophecy because most prophecies are an encouragement.

2. **What do you need for both the Gift of Prophecy and the Gift of Encouragement?** An unconditional love for people.

## Chapter 16: My First Experiences with Prophecy

1. **Are all experiences the same?** No, rarely are two experiences the same.
2. **Do you have to be an expert to start prophesying?** Of course not!

## Chapter 17: My Call to Be Prophetic

1. **When you are called by God, are you automatically a prophet?** No, you have to answer the call.
2. **When does training begin? When does it end?** Training begins when you are born and it never ends. It is an ongoing process.
3. **Is it okay to have the gift of prophecy and not be a prophet?** Yes.
4. **Quote 2 Chronicles 20:20.** *"Believe in the Lord our God, so shall ye be established; believe His prophets, so shall you prosper."*

## Chapter 18: Being a Strange Fish and a Fool for Christ

1. **Do prophets "fit in" usually?** No.
2. **What does 1 Peter 2:9 say that we are?** We are a chosen generation, a royal priesthood, a holy nation, and a peculiar or strange people.

## Chapter 19: Learning Obedience

1. **What constitutes real obedience?** Personal choice.
2. **How did Jesus learn obedience?** By the things which He suffered. By doing only the things His Father said to do.
3. **Can you be lazy and still do God's work?** No.

## Chapter 20: Developing a Deep Relationship with Jesus

1. **How can you begin and continue to develop a deep relationship with Jesus?** We can only develop a deep

relationship with Him by self-denial and following in His footsteps. You can develop a deep relationship with Jesus by obeying Him, by reading about Him, and by talking with Him. It comes from being in His Word, by leaning on Him, by believing in His Word. Willing obedience leads to an intimate relationship with Jesus.
2. **Can you be a truly effective prophetic person without that deep personal relationship?** To be an effective prophetic person, you need to develop a deep relationship with Jesus.

## Chapter 21: Getting to Know the Father

1. **Why do people constantly look to the world for pleasure, for recognition, for love and acceptance, for knowledge or satisfaction in life?** People do not know what they do not know. When they know different they will do differently. Until then, people are just people. They do what they think is right for them; they look to the world for pleasure, recognition and acceptance. They look for love in all the wrong places.

## Chapter 22: Getting to Know the Holy Spirit

1. **What do you need to be able to say with all sincerity in order to receive the Holy Spirit?** Jesus is Lord.

## Chapter 23: Getting to Know the Bible

1. **How many things *work together for the good to those who are called according to His purpose?*** ALL THINGS
2. **How many things is God aware of?** ALL THINGS
3. **Is there anything missing from the Word?** NO. The Word covers everything.

## Chapter 24: Being a Prophet in Training

1. **If everything a prophet does or says must be 100% perfectly said and done, how are prophets to be trained?** Practice makes perfect. Practice, practice, practice. You must use it or lose it! Use your prophetic gift or you will lose

it. Do not go to the grave never having used or passed on your gift. In other words, don't take your gift with you when you go --- you won't need it then. Share it while you can.

## Chapter 25: Learning to Deal with Revelation

1. **List some ways of dealing with fresh revelation.** You can write it down in a journal, do a YouTube video, write articles and books, mediate on it etc.

## Chapter 26: Conquering Pride

1. **What are some ways to overcome pride?** Be honest with yourself; know yourself. Know that you are not any better than the next person. God is not a respecter of persons. We are all the same in His eyes.
2. **Why is it dangerous for a prophet to be prideful?** Pride can stop you from hearing from God. Pride comes before a fall. You really should let the pride fall away, so you do not have to.

## Chapter 27: Dealing with Rejection

1. **Why is rejection necessary in the life of a prophet?** It is part of the training process.

## Chapter 28: Knowing What You Are Called To Do

1. **How important is it to know your calling?** Very. You could spend a lot of years wandering aimlessly unless you understand the path on which God is trying to take you down.
2. **What does passion have to do with purpose?** Your passion is a clue to your purpose. What is it that you love to do? What would you do in your spare time and not get paid for it? That is something you are passionate about and where you will find your purpose. What inspires you? In the word "inspire" you see the words "in spirit."
3. **What are some ways to discover your assignment in life?** Through a prophet, through your own inner voice, God's audible voice, maybe through a dream or even some incident that happens to bring your attention to something you had

never considered before. Pay attention! God will show you what your assignment is. What are you enthusiastic about? The word "enthusiastic" in the Greek language means having "god within," the word is equivalent to the "en" plus "thous" or "theos, god-possessing. So in (en) having god-possessing enthusiasm or extreme interest about something is a God ordained thing.

## Chapter 29: Dealing with the Book of Revelation

1. **Is it important to understand the Book of Revelation?** Yes, as the Lord reveals it to you.
2. **Who is the Book of Revelation addressed to?** To His servants.

## Chapter 30: Walking With the Presence and the Peace of God

1. **Where is Peace found?** In God's will. Stay in God's will.
2. **Who travels with Peace?** Righteousness and Joy.

## Chapter 31: Prophetic Etiquette in Churches

1. **What happens when there is no order?** There is chaos. The Father brings order.
2. **If you have a Word for someone in the congregation, what is the proper protocol?** Approval from the leader should be obtained. If you know that a certain church approves of prophetic words being spoken to others in the congregation, or if you have already been given permission, then go ahead, but, in most cases, you should ask first and then give the prophecy if, permission is granted by the individual person. Ask them if they would like to receive a Word from the Lord.

## Chapter 32: Ministering the Prophetic to Christians

1. **What two things does it take to minister a prophetic word?** Faith and Courage – Godly boldness.

2. **When you know the Lord is leading you to speak prophetically to someone what should you do? HINT: It is a famous slogan.** Just Do It!

### Chapter 33: Prophetic Evangelism

1. **Why are questions important to ask a person receiving a prophecy?** It causes the person to think about things. Questions can lead things into another direction. Jesus asked questions to involve you in the blessings – to make you aware.

### Chapter 34: Ministering in the Prophetic by E-mail

1. **How many ways are there to minister the prophetic Word?** There are a number of ways: in person, tongues and interpretation, via chat, via email.
2. **Are all ways just as effective?** Yes, but not for all. You must find what works best for you.
3. **How do you build more faith in your prophetic gift?** The only way is to walk in the gift successfully and the only way to do that is by stepping out in faith and JUST DO IT! Practice, practice and more practice makes perfect.

### Chapter 35: Ministering in the Prophetic over Facebook

1. **Do you have to be in church to prophesy?** No, you can be in the comfort of your home, in a hotel room, doing video or mp3 prophecies, or written Facebook or email prophecies from anywhere around the world.

### Chapter 36: Doing What the Father Does

1. **How does a prophet "go into the future"?** By way of Spirit.
2. **What do you need to rewrite if you want something to be different or are planning something in the future?** The script. Every movie, every drama has a script the actors read from. You are the director, producer, and actor of your own life and dreams. Write and rewrite the script.

## Chapter 37: Prophetic Prayer

1. **What helps with the "flow" during a prophetic prayer?** Knowledge of the Scriptures.
2. **How many words should a prophecy contain?** It could be one or a million and one. The length is not what is important. It is the message that is the strength, not the length.

## Chapter 38: Getting into the Anointing to Prophesy

1. **How do you prepare yourself to prophesy to others and enter into God's anointing?** Through music, singing praise and worship, prayer, quiet meditation, reading the Word of God, praying in tongues, standing to the music or prayer, running, jumping, waving your arms or a banner. There are many ways to enter in, but music is a sure way.

## Chapter 39: Handling a False Word

1. **Why would a person receive a false word?** They may be testing the prophet. Their intentions are not honorable. If they are false people, they might receive a false word. You only meet yourself in prophecy. If you think it to be false, it will be false. *"According to your faith, be it unto you," Matt. 9:29.* It is up to the receiver to receive.
2. **Why would a prophet give a false word?** Just being in the flesh will cause this. The enemy tries to discourage you from prophesying and so you might say something of the flesh. But do not worry. God is in control. He knows how to handle all this. You just keep doing what God has called you to do, and do not question it.

## Chapter 40: Handling Satan's Attacks

1. **Who gives you the bread of adversity and the water of affliction?** The Lord
2. **Who is your teacher?** The adversary
3. **How do you handle certain attacks?** With spiritual warfare – be established in the Word, know who God is and that He

is in control, know your spiritual rights; know the promises of God. Memorize Romans 8:28.

## Chapter 41: Hearing Jesus Speak

1. **How does Jesus usually speak to you?** Is it through signs, songs, pictures etc.?

## Chapter 42: Hearing the Father Speak

1. **Does the Father sound the same as the Son?** Yes and No. The words are the same but the sound does not have to be. They can be, but they don't have to be. I believe it is an individual thing, according to each person's relationship, and also according to what role God is playing at the moment: Is He being the Father, the Son, or the Holy Spirit?

## Chapter 43: Hearing the Holy Spirit Speak

1. **The Holy Spirit directs you with IMPRESSIONS or LEADINGS/FEELINGS.**
2. **Is it possible to hear the Holy Spirit and yourself talking at the same time?** No

## Chapter 44: Making the Bible Come Alive

1. **What are some ways of making the Bible come alive to you?** Pray to the Lord that He makes it come alive to you before your daily study. The Holy Spirit will help you read in such a way that it comes alive for you. The closer you draw yourself to God, the closer and more alive He will be to you. Getting deep into the Word causes it to come alive and you will begin to see the significance of even the small things.

## Chapter 45: My Visions of Heaven

1. **Who would write a book from a first draft produced in only two days?** Only a dreamer – someone like Joseph, someone like Matthew Robert Payne, maybe someone like you.

2. **Share any "out of this world" experiences or heavenly visions you have had.**

## Chapter 46: My Visions of Heaven, Part Two

1. **What two earth elements are not needed in heaven?** Time and space.
2. **Where is heaven?** Within you. Luke 17:21, *"…The kingdom of God is within you."*

## Chapter 47: Meeting Jesus on Earth in Visions

1. **Have you ever seen Jesus or anyone else who has already passed on to the "other side"?**

## Chapter 48: Meeting Angels on Earth in Visions

1. Angels bring us a **MESSAGE**; that is why they are called messengers. Even if the message is as simple as a smile to encourage you to let you know you are not alone in this world.

## Chapter 49: Having Visions and Talking to Jesus in Your Sleep

1. The future is **NOW**.
2. *Déjà vu* is really just **REMEMBERING** what you have already seen. The future is now. (or **SEEING** what you have already seen.)
3. **What do you need to do to talk with Jesus in your sleep?** Just ask Jesus to talk to you in your sleep.

## Chapter 50: Dreams and Interpretation

1. Dreams are God's way of getting a **MESSAGE** to us.
2. The language of dreams is **SYMBOLIC**.

## Chapter 51: Being a Friend of God

1. All true prophets are **FRIENDS** of God.

## Chapter 52: Developing Intimacy with God

1. **List some ways in which you can develop or expand your intimacy with God.**
   - Digging deep into His word and deep within yourself.
   - Praise and worship
   - Quiet time alone with Him
2. **What does it take most of all to develop anything?** Time and Effort

## Chapter 53: Humility

1. **What is there a lot of in a prophet's life?** Rejection and misunderstandings – which builds character and humility
2. **Who does the real power of God come to?** To those with an intimate relationship with God – the humble
3. **What is the key to the gifts?** Christ's Humility.
4. **What is the key to humility?** True servant-hood, self-denial, no complaining, resist taking credit, judge not

## Chapter 54: Obedience to God

1. **How complete was the surrender of Christ's will to his Father?** Totally
2. **How do you walk through the door to the Kingdom?** Through Obedience

www.ingramcontent.com/pod-product-compliance
Lightning Source LLC
Chambersburg PA
CBHW071857290426
44110CB00013B/1187